Microsoft Copilot in Azure

AI-powered cloud automation and optimization

David Rendón
Steve Miles

‹packt›

Microsoft Copilot in Azure

Portfolio Director: Kartikey Pandey
Relationship Lead: Preet Ahuja
Project Manager: Sonam Pandey
Content Engineer: Apramit Bhattacharya
Technical Editor: Simran Ali
Copy Editor: Safis Editing
Indexer: Tejal Soni
Proofreader: Apramit Bhattacharya
Production Designer: Shankar Kalbhor
Growth Lead: Shreyans Singh

First published: September 2025
Production reference: 1290825

Published by Packt Publishing Ltd.
Grosvenor House
11 St Paul's Square
Birmingham
B3 1RB, UK.

ISBN 978-1-83620-025-3

www.packtpub.com

I dedicate this book to my son, my wife, and my entire family, whose support and encouragement have been my steadfast foundation. I also owe deep gratitude to the hundreds of colleagues, mentors, and friends whose character and leadership have shaped and inspired me over the course of my career. By sharing this knowledge, I hope to give back to the community that has guided me, honoring all those who have contributed to this remarkable journey.

– David Rendón

This content creation is my contribution to the worldwide technical learning community, and I would like to thank all of you who are investing your valuable time in learning new skills and committing to reading this book.

– Steve Miles

Foreword

I have had the privilege of collaborating with Dave and Steve for several years already. Whether I saw them sharing knowledge about Azure in meeting rooms or on a larger conference stage, in public blog posts, or by supporting their writing efforts as a technical reviewer for several of their books, I always admired their passion and the expertise they bring to every project. Over the years, they have both become a leading voice in the Azure community, sharing their fascination with cloud-based solutions and AI technologies.

Imagine what this means for you, holding this book, bringing the passion, the fire for sharing knowledge, and the spark to enlighten your day-to-day job as a cloud admin, architect, or developer with AI, from both gentlemen together. You will be amazed!

In this book, Dave and Steve take you on a journey to learn about Copilot in Azure that begins with the fundamental concepts of artificial intelligence and then quickly deep dives into Copilot in Azure and more advanced topics to manage your infrastructure, data management, code generation, and troubleshooting your Azure environments.

Copilot in Azure integrates AI features into your development process. Through practical examples and step-by-step exercises, which you can immediately reapply to your own Azure cloud environments, Dave and Steve detail how to leverage Copilot in Azure capabilities.

The real brilliance of this book lies in its clear, approachable style. You will learn the technical details of Copilot in Azure and how to apply them in your daily work.

By the time you finish reading this book, you will have a more than solid understanding of how AI will significantly improve your daily workflows. More importantly, you will gain the knowledge to use Copilot in Azure to improve the way you work with your cloud environments in Azure, making your job easier, more compelling, more exciting, and more efficient.

I invite you to read through these pages and discover how Copilot in Azure empowers you to build smarter, faster, and more innovative applications than ever before.

Peter De Tender

Lead Microsoft Technical Trainer

Contributors

About the authors

David Rendón is a Microsoft Azure and AI **Most Valuable Professional (MVP)**, a **Microsoft Certified Trainer (MCT)**, and a highly respected authority on the Azure cloud platform. With over 15 years of IT experience, he has focused on Microsoft technologies, particularly Azure, since 2010.

David has delivered private technical training classes worldwide—covering EMEA, South America, and the United States—and regularly speaks at premier IT events such as Microsoft Ignite, Microsoft Build, and regional user group gatherings throughout the U.S., Europe, and Latin America. Stay connected with him on LinkedIn at /daverndn.

Steve Miles works in a senior technology enablement role with a focus on Azure, AI, and data for a European Microsoft Cloud Solutions Provider distributor. He is an Azure & AI Microsoft MVP, MCT, and an Alibaba Cloud MVP. He has 25+ years of technology experience in hosted datacenter services, hybrid and multi-cloud platforms, and a previous military career in engineering, signals, and communications. Steve is the author of many books on Microsoft technologies with a focus on Azure, AI, and data, as well as security. Steve is a petrolhead and can also be found tinkering with cars when he is not writing.

About the reviewers

Mario Rodríguez Hernández, from the Canary Islands, holds degrees in computer science and business administration. With over 20 years of IT experience, he has worked in nearly every role—from HelpDesk to CIO, in various corporate groups—and currently works as a cloud architect. A dedicated learner, he holds 40 Microsoft Azure certifications, is fully certified in Google Cloud, and has multiple credentials in AWS, Oracle Cloud, and many others. He uses technology as a means to support business goals, not as an end in itself.

I thank my parents, Gregorio and Bárbara, for giving me the education they never had, and my wife, Ana, and daughter, Lucía, for the time I borrow from them to keep learning.

Viachaslau Matsukevich is an esteemed professional with over a decade in DevOps and cloud solutions, and has led significant projects for Fortune 500 and Global 2000 companies. His expertise, certified by Microsoft, Google, and the Linux Foundation, extends to writing insightful articles on cloud-native technologies and Kubernetes. As a technical reviewer, Viachaslau ensures quality in technology publications. He's also recognized as an industry expert and judge at tech innovation events and hackathons. Passionate about education, he authors online courses and has founded a DevOps school. Viachaslau's commitment as a DevOps Institute Ambassador highlights his dedication to the DevOps community.

My heartfelt thanks to my family and parents for their enduring support and for instilling in me the values of resilience and learning. Special gratitude to my wife, whose patience and encouragement have been vital. I am deeply grateful for her belief in my goals, which has been a guiding force in both my life and career.

Table of Contents

Part 3: Ensuring Comprehensive Security and Compliance 175

Chapter 10: Integrating AI-Driven Insights for Cost-Management 177

Chapter 11: Implementing Security Measures with Microsoft Copilot in Azure   193

Chapter 12: Putting It All Together 207

Other Books You May Enjoy 223

Index 227

Preface

This book provides you with a clear and structured path to working with Copilot in Azure. Throughout its chapters, you will acquire the knowledge and skills to partner with Copilot in Azure effectively.

We will start with foundational concepts and build up to advanced topics to fully understand Copilot in Azure. This book empowers you to fully comprehend Copilot in Azure through practical examples and step-by-step instructions, ensuring a hands-on and immersive learning experience.

By the time you reach the final pages of this book, you will have acquired the knowledge and expertise needed to leverage Copilot in Azure and its integrations with other services.

Operating a cloud environment with the assistance of AI has become indispensable for organizations of all sizes, and Copilot in Azure is at the forefront of this revolution. You will discover techniques and best practices for utilizing Copilot in Azure to foster innovation and organizational success. Ultimately, this book will equip you with the tools and knowledge needed to leverage Copilot Azure in your daily workflow.

Who this book is for

This book is targeted toward Azure architects and developers who build cloud-based computing services or focus on deploying and managing applications and services in Microsoft Azure, responsible for various IT operations, including budgeting, business continuity, governance, identity, networking, security, and automation. It's for people with experience in operating systems, virtualization, cloud infrastructure, storage structures, and networking, who want to learn how to implement best practices in the Azure cloud using Copilot in Azure.

What this book covers

Chapter 1, Understanding Microsoft Copilot in Azure, provides a foundational understanding of Microsoft Copilot in Azure. It starts by covering the impact of AI and automation in cloud operations, emphasizing the importance of these technologies in modern IT environments

Chapter 2, Getting Started with Microsoft Copilot in Azure, explains how to start with Microsoft Copilot in the Azure portal. It provides a step-by-step walk-through on the initial setup and configuration settings for optimal use.

Chapter 3, Managing Access to Microsoft Copilot in Azure, explores the access management features of Microsoft Copilot in Azure and explains how to manage user permissions securely through role-based access control.

Chapter 4, Deploying and Managing Cloud Infrastructure – Part 1, guides you through the process of starting with Microsoft Copilot in Azure to deploy and manage infrastructure, including storage and virtual machines.

Chapter 5, Deploying and Managing Cloud Infrastructure – Part 2, guides you through the process of managing Azure Kubernetes and Azure App Service.

Chapter 6, Improving Development Efficiency, focuses on how Microsoft Copilot in Azure and AI Shell can help you enhance development workflows.

Chapter 7, Advanced Data Management with Microsoft Copilot in Azure, focuses on enhancing data management for Azure Database for MySQL and Azure SQL Database using Microsoft Copilot. Topics include data optimization, performance tuning with AI-driven insights, and practical data management examples.

Chapter 8, Exploring Real-Time Monitoring and Troubleshooting, explores the capabilities of Microsoft Copilot in Azure for real-time monitoring and diagnostics of Azure resources. It covers the utilization of AI-driven insights for proactive management and optimization of cloud infrastructure, detailing troubleshooting techniques and the use of Copilot for ensuring high availability and reliability.

Chapter 9, Scaling and Optimizing Cloud Operations, discusses strategies for scaling and optimizing cloud infrastructure to handle growing and fluctuating business demands using Microsoft Copilot. It provides insights into resource management techniques and the application of AI-driven recommendations from Copilot to make strategic decisions regarding scaling and optimization.

Chapter 10, Integrating AI-Driven Insights for Cost Management, focuses on leveraging Microsoft Copilot to manage and optimize cloud costs effectively. It covers topics such as interpreting cost metrics, forecasting and budgeting, and setting cost alerts using AI-driven insights.

Chapter 11, Implementing Security Measures with Microsoft Copilot in Azure, focuses on how to meet compliance and organizational standards using Copilot in Azure. This chapter will also provide practical examples of Copilot in Azure to improve your organization's security posture by getting recommendations on security policies.

Chapter 12, Putting It All Together, provides you with a summary of the previously revised chapters and encourages you to continue learning and experimenting with Copilot in Azure. We will also share additional reading materials, tools, and online resources to improve your learning experience.

To get the most out of this book

You will need to have an understanding of the basics of Azure and its main services, such as Azure App Service, Azure storage accounts, Azure Kubernetes, databases, and tools such as Azure PowerShell, Azure CLI, and the Azure portal.

Download the example code files

The code bundle for the book is hosted on GitHub at `https://github.com/PacktPublishing/Microsoft-Copilot-in-Azure`. We also have other code bundles from our rich catalog of books and videos available at `https://github.com/PacktPublishing`. Check them out!

Conventions used

There are a number of text conventions used throughout this book.

`CodeInText`: Indicates code words in text, database table names, folder names, filenames, file extensions, pathnames, dummy URLs, user input, and Twitter handles. For example: "Is my East US resource group running smoothly?"

Any command-line input or output is written as follows:

```
Invoke-Expression "& { $(Invoke-RestMethod 'https://aka.ms/installaishell.ps1') }"
```

Bold: Indicates a new term, an important word, or words that you see on the screen. For instance, words in menus or dialog boxes appear in the text like this. For example: "In the left-hand menu pane, select **Access control (IAM)**"

Warnings or important notes appear like this.

Get in touch

Feedback from our readers is always welcome.

General feedback: If you have questions about any aspect of this book or have any general feedback, please email us at customercare@packt.com and mention the book's title in the subject of your message.

Errata: Although we have taken every care to ensure the accuracy of our content, mistakes do happen. If you have found a mistake in this book, we would be grateful if you reported this to us. Please visit http://www.packt.com/submit-errata, click **Submit Errata**, and fill in the form.

Piracy: If you come across any illegal copies of our works in any form on the internet, we would be grateful if you would provide us with the location address or website name. Please contact us at copyright@packt.com with a link to the material.

If you are interested in becoming an author: If there is a topic that you have expertise in and you are interested in either writing or contributing to a book, please visit http://authors.packt.com/.

Your Book Comes with Exclusive Perks - Here's How to Unlock Them

Unlock this book's exclusive benefits now

UNLOCK NOW

Scan this QR code or go to `https://packtpub.com/unlock`, then search this book by name. Ensure it's the correct edition.

Note: *Keep your purchase invoice ready before you start.*

Enhanced reading experience with our Next-gen Reader:

Multi-device progress sync: Learn from any device with seamless progress sync.

Highlighting and notetaking: Turn your reading into lasting knowledge.

Bookmarking: Revisit your most important learnings anytime.

Dark mode: Focus with minimal eye strain by switching to dark or sepia mode.

Learn smarter using our AI assistant (Beta):

Summarize it: Summarize key sections or an entire chapter.

AI code explainers: In the next-gen Packt Reader, click the **Explain** button above each code block for AI-powered code explanations.

Note: The AI assistant is part of next-gen Packt Reader and is still in beta.

Learn anytime, anywhere:

Access your content offline with DRM-free PDF and ePub versions—compatible with your favorite e-readers.

Unlock Your Book's Exclusive Benefits

Your copy of this book comes with the following exclusive benefits:

Next-gen Packt Reader

AI assistant (beta)

DRM-free PDF/ePub downloads

Use the following guide to unlock them if you haven't already. The process takes just a few minutes and needs to be done only once.

How to unlock these benefits in three easy steps

Step 1

Keep your purchase invoice for this book ready, as you'll need it in *Step 3*. If you received a physical invoice, scan it on your phone and have it ready as either a PDF, JPG, or PNG.

For more help on finding your invoice, visit `https://www.packtpub.com/unlock-benefits/help`.

Note: Did you buy this book directly from Packt? You don't need an invoice. After completing Step 2, you can jump straight to your exclusive content.

Step 2

Scan this QR code or go to https://packtpub.com/unlock.

On the page that opens (which will look similar to Figure 0.1 if you're on desktop), search for this book by name. Make sure you select the correct edition.

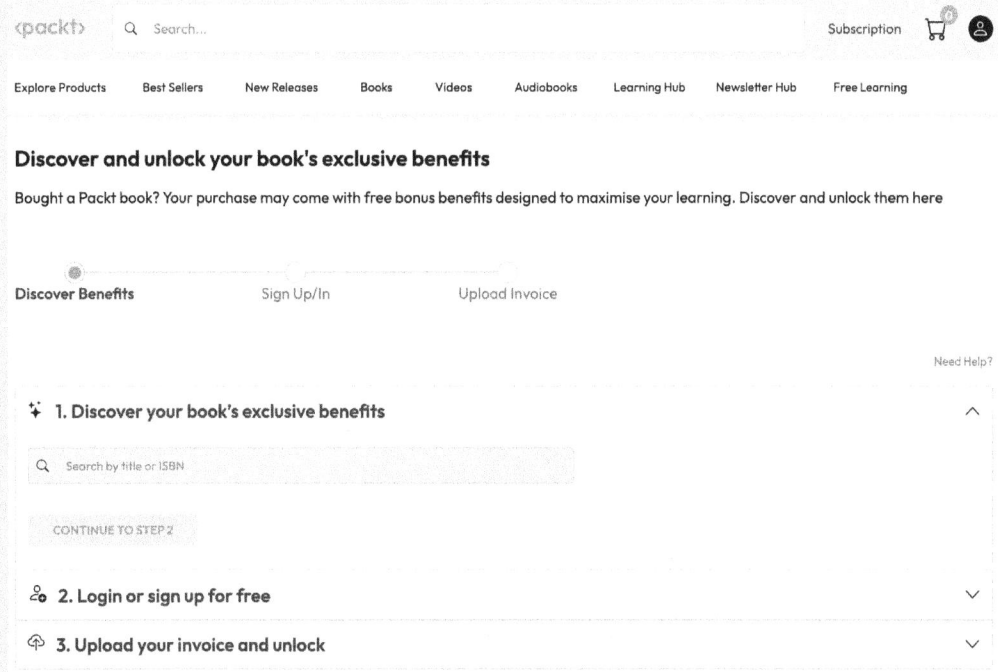

‹packt›   Q Search...   Subscription 🛒 👤

Explore Products   Best Sellers   New Releases   Books   Videos   Audiobooks   Learning Hub   Newsletter Hub   Free Learning

Discover and unlock your book's exclusive benefits

Bought a Packt book? Your purchase may come with free bonus benefits designed to maximise your learning. Discover and unlock them here

Discover Benefits   Sign Up/In   Upload Invoice

                                                                    Need Help?

✦ **1. Discover your book's exclusive benefits**   ⌃

    Q   Search by title or ISBN

    CONTINUE TO STEP 2

👥 **2. Login or sign up for free**   ⌄

☁ **3. Upload your invoice and unlock**   ⌄

Figure 0.1: Packt unlock landing page on desktop

Step 3

Sign in to your Packt account or create a new one for free. Once you're logged in, upload your invoice. It can be in PDF, PNG, or JPG format and must be no larger than 10 MB. Follow the rest of the instructions on the screen to complete the process.

Need help?

If you get stuck and need help, visit `https://www.packtpub.com/unlock-benefits/help` for a detailed FAQ on how to find your invoices and more. The following QR code will take you to the help page directly:

Note: If you are still facing issues, reach out to `customercare@packt.com`.

Share your thoughts

Once you've read *Microsoft Copilot in Azure*, we'd love to hear your thoughts! Scan the QR code below to go straight to the Amazon review page for this book and share your feedback.

`https://packt.link/r/1836200250`

Your review is important to us and the tech community and will help us make sure we're delivering excellent quality content.

Part 1

Foundations of Microsoft Copilot in Azure

The first part of this book lays the foundation for working with Microsoft Copilot in Azure by introducing its purpose, architecture, and core capabilities. You'll explore how AI and automation are reshaping cloud operations, gain an understanding of large language models (LLMs) that power Copilot, and learn how Copilot integrates with Azure services to simplify daily tasks. By the end of this section, you'll have the essential context and setup knowledge needed to confidently start using Copilot in Azure.

This part of the book includes the following chapters:

- *Chapter 1, Understanding Microsoft Copilot in Azure*
- *Chapter 2, Getting Started with Microsoft Copilot in Azure*
- *Chapter 3, Managing Access to Microsoft Copilot in Azure*

1

Understanding Microsoft Copilot in Azure

Welcome to *Microsoft Copilot in Azure*, a practical guide designed specifically for Azure architects, engineers, administrators, and consultants who want to elevate their cloud environments with AI-powered efficiency. In this book, you will discover how Copilot in Azure simplifies complex tasks, improves operational workflows, and helps you manage resources intelligently within your Azure ecosystem. With your foundational understanding of Azure services, you are ready to take the next step toward smarter, faster, and more secure cloud management.This chapter provides a foundational understanding of Copilot in Azure. It explains its architecture, integration, and features, helping you understand its role as a powerful **artificial intelligence (AI)** assistant. You will learn how its underlying **large language models (LLMs)** are utilized to streamline operational tasks in Azure environments. This chapter also acts as an introduction to the principles and foundations of AI and automation, while also explaining how Copilot functions within Azure. It is designed to provide you with valuable insights, help you explore various capabilities, and streamline your tasks.

In this chapter, you will learn about the following main topics:

- Embracing AI to evolve work and communication
- Understanding LLMs
- Introducing Copilot in Azure

In the first section, you'll learn about the impact that AI and automation have on cloud operations. It emphasizes the importance of these technologies in modern and rapidly evolving digital environments.

Embracing AI to evolve work and communication

In today's digital landscape, AI plays a crucial role in automating repetitive tasks, enhancing communication, and supporting human creativity. From autocorrect to complex decision support, AI's integration into daily workflows is now the norm.

In the following sections, you will understand how AI is reshaping collaboration and productivity, with a focus on practical integration through tools such as Copilot in Azure. You'll gain a working knowledge of LLM, including key concepts such as prompts, tokens, and completions, all of which are essential for leveraging context-aware AI effectively.

The impact of AI on work and collaboration

Before we dive into how Copilot fits into our workflows, it's worth taking a moment to think about how AI is already showing up in our daily lives, often in ways we barely notice. Whether it's finishing our sentences in emails or suggesting a better way to phrase a message, AI has quietly become a regular part of how we work and communicate. Understanding this everyday impact gives us a better starting point for exploring what it means to partner with AI, not just as a tool, but as a smart assistant that can help us solve problems and make better decisions.

Everyday AI in communication

Thinking about the last year of our lives, we have all been in a situation where we have had to work with a tool to send a message, receive a message, or simply communicate with another person through an electronic form, such as email or instant messaging solutions. We dedicate significant energy to communicating with each other through various channels, including email, which is only a fraction of our communication. In most cases, when using our phones, we notice the auto-corrector suggestions popping up while we type on our keyboards.

Every day, people exchange over 361 billion emails. In such high-volume, high-frequency interactions, tools with embedded AI—such as grammar assistants and predictive text—are no longer luxuries; they are essential components of our digital routines that have been widely adopted across the world through devices we use daily to the point that they are now a commodity.

These tools help reduce errors, adjust tone, and streamline communication, often functioning without much conscious user input. These tools are now so common that you might overlook their presence and underestimate their full potential.

The dual view of AI: Hope and apprehension

Today, despite its helpfulness, AI is still met with both excitement and caution. There's an ongoing debate about whether AI will replace existing jobs or simply transform the way we work. As professionals, the first step is to consider where AI excels and where its limitations remain. Understanding what AI can and cannot do well is essential for navigating this shift.

AI systems have become increasingly adept at recognizing speech, translating languages, identifying visual patterns, generating content—whether that be written text, code, or images—and summarizing large volumes of information. These advances position AI as a strong candidate for automating repetitive or structured tasks that rely on recognizing patterns rather than understanding nuance.

It is important to acknowledge that if a significant portion of a current job involves tasks that AI can perform efficiently, then that job is likely at risk of being automated. There are tasks that AI is unlikely to perform, particularly those involving soft skills such as empathy, judgment, and ethical reasoning, and collaboration will remain essential for all organizations.

While AI may assist professionals with certain tasks, it is improbable that it will replace their work and roles entirely. Similar to other emerging technologies in the market, AI has the potential to impact, eliminate, or alter current jobs. AI also has the potential to change industries and create new career opportunities. It is anticipated to alter job responsibilities and introduce new roles, rather than just reducing the amount of work available.

AI as a collaborator, not just an automator

AI has rapidly evolved and has been widely adopted. While traditionally, AI has been seen as a means to reduce manual labor, it has also emerged with a new perspective where AI is positioned as a potential collaborator through knowledge across various business sectors, particularly through generative AI tools.

Partnering with AI in the context of generative AI tools will significantly enhance human problem-solving and innovation by fostering the skill of asking more thoughtful and targeted questions. While AI's capabilities evolve, the ability to craft precise and meaningful prompts becomes crucial, enabling users to explore new dimensions of problems that were previously inaccessible.

As generative AI evolves, it doesn't just automate—it collaborates. It empowers users to explore angles and solutions that may have otherwise remained undiscovered, making it a vital resource for professionals working in complex environments such as cloud infrastructure.

Evolving with AI in the workplace

While AI may replace task-oriented roles, as we covered earlier in this chapter, it is unlikely to fully displace jobs requiring human judgment and empathy; instead, it offers collaboration—especially with generative tools—to empower professionals to ask better questions and solve problems more creatively.

With the increasing adoption of AI in cloud environments, tools such as Copilot in Azure are emerging not just as productivity enhancers but as partners in managing complexity. AI is more than just a productivity booster—it's reshaping how we collaborate and work. With increasing adoption in cloud environments, the need to partner with AI tools such as Copilot in Azure becomes essential. Understanding how to work alongside AI effectively will be a defining skill in any modern cloud professional's toolkit.

In the next section, we'll look at LLMs, the underlying technology powering Copilot in Azure. You will explore what LLMs are, what they can do, and concepts such as prompts, tokens, and completions.

Understanding LLMs

While there's no universally agreed-upon definition of AI across the technology industry, you can draw that AI, in general, involves a computer system that can learn from experience, discern patterns in data fed to it, and make decisions. Simply put, at its core, AI aims to mimic human-like reasoning and behavior.

An LLM is a specialized type of AI designed to understand and generate natural human language at scale. LLMs are fundamental to tools such as Copilot in Azure, powering their ability to respond to user queries, generate code, images, and written content, summarize information, and offer context-aware guidance.

These models are trained on massive datasets consisting of text from books, articles, websites, and other public sources. Among the most notable LLMs is the **Generative Pre-trained Transformer (GPT)**.

GPT is a type of LLM developed by **OpenAI** (a leading AI research and deployment company known for creating and pioneering advanced language models such as ChatGPT) that's designed to process and generate human-like text based on the input it receives.

It excels at a wide range of language tasks, such as answering questions, writing summaries, generating code, and engaging in natural dialogue.

GPT operates by predicting the next word in a sequence, allowing it to create coherent, contextually relevant responses. Microsoft integrates *GPT-based models* through **Azure OpenAI Service**, enabling enterprise-grade capabilities such as Copilot in Azure to deliver intelligent, secure, and scalable interactions grounded in natural language understanding.

To build on this foundational understanding, it is important to explore key LLM concepts such as prompts, tokens, and completions, which will help you interact with and harness the capabilities of Copilot in Azure effectively.

LLM concepts: Prompts, tokens, and completions

The concept of LLMs is relevant to our understanding since traditional **natural language processing (NLP)** needs *one model* per capability. A single LLM can be utilized for many NLP use cases, utilizing many terabytes of unlabeled data, and is optimized for specific use cases. As you will see later in this chapter, Copilot in Azure leverages several LLMs.

On the other hand, it is important to highlight the potential limits of LLMs. We could think of an LLM as a predictive engine capable of pulling patterns together based on pre-existing text to produce more text. However, LLMs are not intended to understand math or language.

While LLMs can generate text by predicting the next most probable token, it is important to note that they do not truly understand math, language, or context in the way humans do. They do not have explicit modes for accurate information retrieval or reasoning and may produce text that sounds plausible without factual grounding. Additionally, as mentioned earlier in this chapter, LLMs cannot replicate soft skills such as ethical judgment or empathy, which remain essential human strengths, even in AI-supported environments.

Despite these limitations, LLMs remain powerful tools for generating context-aware text and assisting with a variety of tasks in Azure environments. To use these models effectively, it is crucial to understand a few key concepts: prompts, tokens, and completions:

- **Prompts** guide the model's output
- **Tokens** are units of processed text
- **Completions** are generated outputs

Let's understand each of these further.

Prompts

This is a sentence or phrase that serves as a guide to the LLM on what you want it to do. The wording of the prompt will significantly influence the model's response and obtain multiple results based on the different phrasings. LLMs can be leveraged in multiple languages. A simple example of a prompt could be `Write a Python script that reads from a CSV file and outputs to an HTML table`.

The more context you can provide in your prompt, the more accurate and relevant the output will be.

Tokens

These are the fundamental units of text that an LLM can process. A token can be a single character, part of a word, or an entire word. Copilot in Azure uses OpenAI's LLMs to boost productivity in writing, coding, and data analysis. However, OpenAI models don't work directly with words or letters—they break down the text into intermediary tokens. This process allows the models to generate text that includes words not found in any dictionary.

Completions

When the LLM generates text, it does so one token at a time. At each step, the model provides a list of potential tokens, along with their probabilities, and one token is selected based on these insights. Then, this token is added to the prompt, and the process repeats until a certain limit is reached. Usually, each LLM has a specific limit on the number of tokens it can handle.

In summary, LLMs form the cognitive core of Copilot in Azure, enabling it to deliver intelligent, contextual assistance. Understanding prompts, tokens, and completions is key to making the most of its capabilities.

In this section, you learned that LLMs are highly effective for tasks that involve generating text, images, or even code. With this understanding of the core LLM concepts, we can now start looking at how Copilot in Azure works.

Introducing Copilot in Azure

In a nutshell, **Copilot in Azure** is a *conversational AI assistant* integrated with Azure. It helps design, operate, and optimize cloud environments by leveraging LLMs, Azure's access controls, and service plugins. Copilot in Azure brings together advanced LLM capabilities with Azure's data governance, Resource Manager access controls, and Azure Graph to help you manage your growing cloud environment more effectively and streamline your daily operations.

Copilot in Azure is your AI agent and can be accessed through the Azure portal, Azure mobile app, or **command-line interface (CLI)**, which simplifies the way you access and manage the knowledge embedded within your growing cloud environment. By leveraging the latest advancements in LLMs with Azure's data governance and access controls, Copilot in Azure allows you to easily interact with your entire cloud environment. It assists with designing, operating, optimizing, and troubleshooting applications, services, and infrastructure.

Microsoft developed Copilot in Azure to create experiences that enable you to gain deep insights into your environment and your operations, identify the most suitable functionality, and complete complex tasks more efficiently.

Before we uncover its architecture and components, let's explore the features and benefits of Copilot in Azure and understand *why* you would want to use Copilot in Azure, before we look at *what* Copilot in Azure is and *how* it can be used.

Key features of Copilot

As AI becomes integral to modern operations, every organization—businesses, governments, and nonprofits—is evolving into a technology-driven entity. In this landscape, ensuring that your teams can fully leverage Copilot in Azure is essential for maximizing its potential and maintaining a competitive edge.

To thrive in the AI age, companies must attract top-tier talent and be aware that, at its core, technology is a people-driven business. You need to ensure that the teams in your organization can fully leverage the potential of Copilot in Azure the right way.

Copilot in Azure represents a powerful solution designed to simplify and enhance the way you manage cloud operations. It acts as an intelligent assistant that integrates with Azure's vast ecosystem, providing users with the ability to interact with their resources through natural language queries.

Copilot in Azure focuses on three pillars:

- **Obtain tailored insights**: You can get personalized solutions for your workloads with the assistance of an AI solution that understands your environment.
- **Explore cloud capabilities**: You can use natural language to interact with Copilot in Azure and utilize the full functionality of Azure services.
- **Simplify complex tasks**: You can optimize processes, resources, and workloads through AI-driven orchestration and analysis.

Whether you're managing virtual machines, optimizing costs, or troubleshooting issues, Copilot in Azure's intuitive interface can simplify complex tasks significantly. One of the outstanding capabilities of Copilot in Azure is its ability to provide personalized insights tailored to your specific Azure environment.

When you ask a question or issue a command, Copilot in Azure doesn't just offer a generic response; it taps into the vast resources available in Azure, including your subscriptions, Azure Resource Graph, and Microsoft's extensive documentation to ensure that the information you receive is accurate and relevant to your current context, helping you make informed decisions quickly.

When you consider the tasks tackled daily in Azure, they generally fall into four main categories:

- **Design**: This involves designing and figuring out how to structure your entire infrastructure and architecture. It includes making decisions on which services to use and how to configure them to achieve specific goals, such as optimizing resiliency, performance, or cost-effectiveness.

- **Operate**: This category, as the name suggests, is helpful in operations. Consider the scenario where there's a user involved with a new production environment issue. If there's a potential production issue, the user can receive an alert about the problem, but they may not be sure where it originated. Asking Copilot in Azure to show all the machines with open ports can resolve this issue in minutes.

- **Optimize**: Organizations often need to fine-tune individual resources and entire systems working together. AI can analyze vast amounts of data from your services to suggest the best ways to optimize cost, performance, or resilience, helping you get the most out of your cloud environment.

- **Troubleshoot**: Problems will inevitably arise, whether in code or configuration, or due to external factors. Copilot in Azure can help you quickly identify and address these issues, saving valuable time and allowing you to focus on more critical tasks.

We will deep dive into each of these areas throughout *Parts 2* and *3* of this book.

As you can infer, Copilot in Azure is more than an assistant—it's an intelligent collaborator that helps you design, manage, optimize, and resolve issues in your cloud environment with precision and ease.

Having explored the key features and practical benefits of Copilot in Azure, it is now important to understand the architecture that powers these capabilities and enables seamless integration within your Azure environment.

Architectural overview of Copilot in Azure

As AI becomes a central part of modern cloud experiences, Copilot in Azure stands out by blending conversational intelligence with deep integration into the Azure platform. At its core, this architecture is designed to make complex tasks simpler, more intuitive, and highly contextual. To understand how it achieves this, let's explore its three foundational layers—each playing a distinct role in delivering intelligent, secure, and responsive interactions within the Azure ecosystem.

Let's take a closer look at these three key layers:

- **Frontend interface**: User interaction point (portal, CLI, mobile)
- **Orchestration layer**: Processes intent and queries services
- **AI infrastructure**: Built on Azure OpenAI models

The following figure shows these three layers:

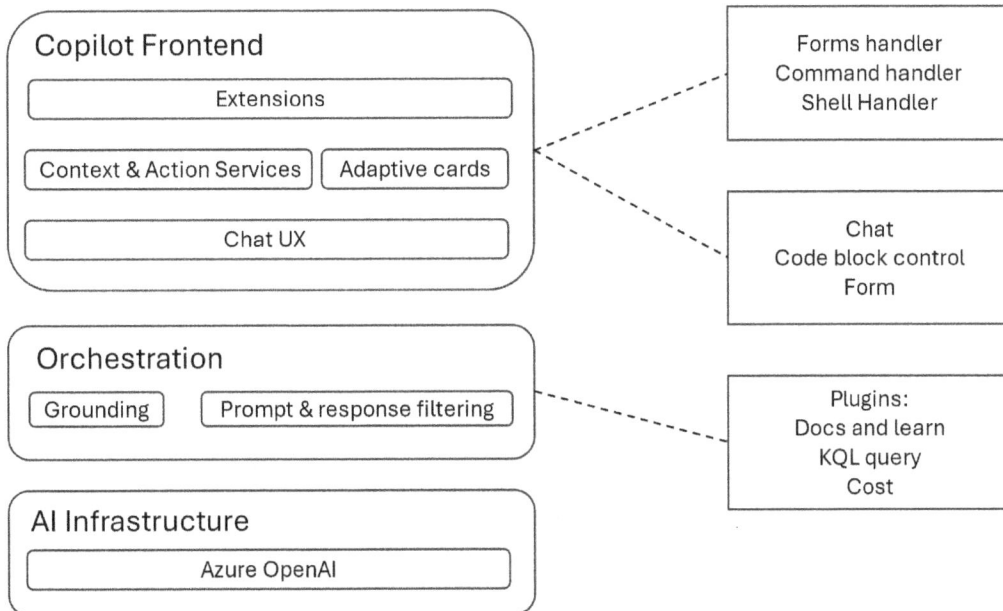

Figure 1.1 – Copilot in Azure architecture components

Let's delve deeper into them:

- **Frontend interface**: This is the first layer, at the very top, and can be accessed through the Azure portal, the Azure mobile app, or the CLI. The frontend layer offers a unified and consistent user interface. It features a conversation window, delivers responses in various formats, such as text, charts, and illustrations, and gathers user feedback.

  Simply put, the frontend layer is where the conversational user interface comes into play, allowing the system to gather additional context from your current location in the portal. It recognizes the current navigation context, allowing users to naturally ask questions about the resources displayed on the active portal page.

  For example, if you're on a virtual machine blade, Copilot in Azure can retrieve details such as the virtual machine's size and version to enhance your conversation. Then, this information, along with your query, is sent to the orchestration layer.

- **Orchestration layer**: This is the second main component in the Copilot in Azure architecture. This is the core of Copilot in Azure, and it is a powerful processing engine that ensures your interactions are grounded in the vast knowledge available within the Azure environment. This includes service telemetry, Azure Resource Manager, Azure Resource Graph, and Azure Documentation.

  Given the vast number of services in Azure, the orchestration layer leverages LLMs to deeply understand the user's question, analyze the relevant Azure resources and types, and direct the query to the appropriate domain-specific plugins.

  LLMs at this layer can call specific plugins to provide service-specific actions or insights. These plugins then leverage their specific service graphs or observability data to respond accurately. For example, a Kubernetes plugin might help with YAML editing, or a cost management plugin could provide detailed insights into your spending.

  The orchestration layer is also capable of handling complex, multi-step queries, such as `Show all virtual machines with less than 9% utilization that were deployed in the last three hours in North Europe`. In this case, Copilot in Azure will utilize the Azure Resource Graph plugin to query the data and provide results.

  The orchestration layer also handles other aspects, such as security, privacy, and responsible AI practices, ensuring that all responses adhere to these principles.

- **AI infrastructure:** The third component of the Copilot in Azure architecture is built on top of the Azure OpenAI platform, which is also available to any developer using Azure. This layer ensures that you can leverage the latest models and innovations, providing the foundational LLMs that power Copilot's natural language understanding and generation capabilities. It also enables secure, scalable access to advanced AI models while adhering to Azure's compliance and data privacy standards, ensuring that your interactions with Copilot in Azure are both powerful and enterprise-ready.

Copilot's multi-layered architecture enables it to interact contextually with Azure resources while respecting permissions and delivering accurate outputs through plugins and orchestration.

Now, let's better understand how these components interact with each other.

Data flow in Copilot in Azure

To truly understand how Copilot in Azure delivers intelligent, context-aware assistance, it's essential to explore how data moves through the system. This section breaks down the flow of information between components—starting from the user's interaction in the Azure portal, through the orchestration and plugin layers, and back to the user—all while maintaining strict adherence to security and privacy standards.

The moment you start a session in the Azure portal, even without initiating a conversation, Copilot in Azure can engage based on actions or notifications in the Azure portal. Copilot in Azure can collect context from your user and pass it to the orchestration layer, all while respecting your security settings. Copilot in Azure also has access to data that your user is authorized to view or manage. If you don't have permission for a particular action, Copilot in Azure won't be able to perform it, but it will inform you accordingly.

As mentioned previously, the orchestration layer can interact with hundreds of Azure services through the **Plugin Store**, which is composed of various plugins, each tailored to specific needs. The Plugin Store includes various plugins that can assist with your daily workflow. For instance, a **documentation plugin** can query extensive resources, while a **compute plugin** might pull data from Azure Resource Manager or service telemetry to provide relevant insights, including access to **Kusto Query Language (KQL)** and Resource Graph.

Responses to prompts are returned to the client, where they are displayed in the most useful format, including text, forms, or charts. The client can also call other endpoints, such as Azure Resource Manager, to gather additional information as needed.

At the time of writing, Microsoft does not use your data or conversations to train its models. Privacy, security, and responsible AI are built into every layer of this architecture, ensuring that your interactions with Copilot in Azure are safe and secure throughout the process. Feel free to check out Microsoft's privacy statement for more details: `https://www.microsoft.com/en-us/privacy/privacystatement`.

Now, let's take a closer look at how data flows and how security is maintained in the interactions with Copilot in Azure. The following diagram illustrates the interconnected architecture of Copilot in Azure, highlighting how the different components, such as the Azure portal, the frontend layer, the orchestration layer, and the Plugin Store, work together to deliver context-aware information and the best experience possible to the user.

When the user submits a query to the AI in the form of a question, the following data flow is executed to generate the response:

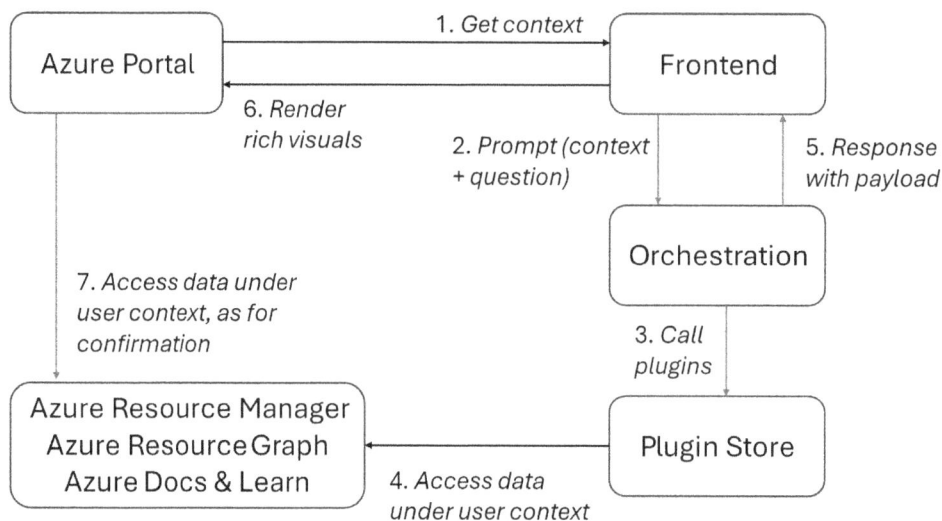

Figure 1.2 – Copilot in Azure data flow example

The AI infrastructure layer is not shown for clarity; it has no action in the data flow.

Let's take a closer look at the data flow in Copilot in Azure, as shown in *Figure 1.2*:

1. The process begins with a user in the Azure portal and Copilot in Azure collecting metadata about the current navigational context. For example, if you are on a Kubernetes deployment page, details such as the version, node pools, and node sizes are gathered. This metadata will be utilized to build a semantic understanding of your query and is added as grounding context to the prompt for Azure OpenAI.

It is possible to interact with Copilot in Azure based on the actions and even notifications you see in the Azure portal. At this point, Copilot in Azure has collected additional context from the user journey in that session, which is passed on to the orchestration layer. All this happens in the context of you as a user. Copilot in Azure will match your user **role-based access control (RBAC)** permissions; if you, as a user, don't have access to specific data, Copilot in Azure will not have access to that data. Similarly, if you don't have permission to execute an Azure Resource Manager operation or API call, Copilot in Azure will not be able to perform that operation and will show the relevant error or information.

2. Then, the frontend interface will call the orchestration layer with the fully grounded prompt and inject it into Azure OpenAI, which then reasons over the available domain-specific plugins to find the best match for your query. If the query is off-topic or malformed, a friendly message specifying the error or information will be returned.

3. After this, the orchestration layer selects the most appropriate plugin from the **Plugin Store** based on its semantic understanding of the query. It then calls this plugin to process the query. These plugins can have different implementations.

4. The selected plugin runs, fetching and combining data from various sources within your security context. For example, the **Docs and Learn** plugin can query documentation, while a **Compute** plugin can go ahead and call other endpoints, such as Azure Resource Manager or Azure Resource Graph, to bring in additional insights and specifications from your virtual machines.

5. Then, the response payload is sent back to the Azure portal for rendering.

6. The response is formatted with rich graphics or other relevant visual elements to ensure it is presented clearly.

7. If the user's query involves making changes to the environment, the Azure portal prompts the user for confirmation. Once confirmed, the requested changes are applied to Azure Resource Graph, completing the process.

In this section, we examined how data flows within Copilot in Azure, from the initial user interaction in the Azure portal to processing queries through the orchestration layer and the Plugin Store, and finally back to the user with a contextual response. It highlighted how Copilot gathers metadata, respects user permissions, and ensures that all interactions remain secure and privacy-compliant throughout the process.

Now that you have a better understanding of the data flow in Copilot in Azure, let's see how Copilot in Azure interacts with other Azure services and resources.

How Copilot in Azure connects with Azure services

At this point, you might be wondering how Copilot in Azure gets information about your Azure subscriptions and resources. Copilot in Azure is your AI assistant and knows how to talk to all the services in your Azure environment. It gathers the right information by using the orchestrator layer, which helps Copilot in Azure connect with other parts of Azure.

Copilot connects to services such as Azure Resource Manager, Azure Resource Graph, Cost Management, and Docs and Learn through plugins. It enhances user prompts with relevant resource data and generates solutions within your access context.

Think about what happens when you interact with Copilot in Azure. You start by opening the Azure portal, which acts as a control center where you manage all your cloud resources. While you're there, you might have a specific question or task to complete, such as finding out which of your virtual machines are the most expensive. When you ask Copilot in Azure this, it sends this question, along with basic details about what you are currently doing in the Azure portal, to the orchestration layer.

If Copilot in Azure were to use only a general language model, it would probably be limited, as it would need additional information about your Azure configuration. This is where the orchestration layer steps in. The orchestration layer helps Copilot in Azure reach out to different parts of Azure, such as Microsoft documentation, Azure Resource Manager, Azure Resource Graph, Cost Management, and Service Health, among other services. All these sources provide Copilot in Azure with the details and information it needs to provide a useful response.

Copilot in Azure gathers all this information and then uses this data to improve the prompt you initially gave. This process is called **retrieval-augmented generation** (**RAG**) and is where Copilot in Azure enhances your question with more context and details. Then, it creates a **meta prompt**, which is a more refined version of your request. Copilot in Azure uses this meta prompt to ask the LLM for the final response or solution. If needed, Copilot in Azure can create a plan that involves running specific tasks or queries to make sure it provides the most accurate response.

The LLM that powers Copilot in Azure will never directly access your Azure resources; it can only respond to the information that is given. If it needs more details, it has to ask the orchestrator to get that data from Azure. As you can see, this configuration ensures that everything stays safe and controlled, with no unwanted changes being made to your resources, and can help you keep all your data secure efficiently.

That said, Copilot in Azure works within the boundaries of your existing user permissions. For example, if you have certain roles and access controls set up in Azure, Copilot in Azure will only act within those limits. It's not a separate service with its own set of permissions; it operates entirely based on what your user is allowed to do.

Everything Copilot in Azure performs is on behalf of the current user, which means that it can only see and interact with resources that are accessible to the current user. If the current user cannot see a resource or doesn't have permission to modify it, neither can Copilot in Azure. Simply put, Copilot in Azure acts as an extension of your current user, following the same rules and restrictions applicable to the current user when interacting with Azure Resource Manager, which is the control management layer for all Azure operations.

Azure Resource Manager is crucial to this context as it enforces all the policies and permissions you've set up. Copilot in Azure cannot bypass these safeguards; it adheres to them.

Additionally, there's traceability when a user utilizes Copilot in Azure to perform a task. Just like any actions taken in the Azure portal, all operations are logged under the user's name. These logs can be found in the Azure activity logs, where each operation is linked to the specific user who performed it. This ensures you can see which user performed which task, providing a transparent record in the logs.

With this understanding of how Copilot in Azure integrates with Azure services and resources, it is important to highlight that, given the amount of AI adoption by organizations today, a tech company is only as strong as its next innovation. You must ensure that you set expectations and understand Copilot in Azure's key capabilities.

Through careful integration and RBAC alignment, Copilot operates as your personal Azure assistant, without bypassing security or policy restrictions.

Now that you have a better understanding of how Copilot in Azure works, let's see how we can adopt a strategy and governance before we start utilizing it.

Aligning Copilot in Azure with the Well-Architected Framework

As solution architects, we need to think about creating reliable, secure, and high-performing workloads that fully leverage the value of the organization's investment in the Azure infrastructure. We generally align our efforts with the foundational pillars of the Azure **Well-Architected Framework (WAF)**, drawing upon its guidance to construct a robust foundation for our workloads. This approach allows us to thoughtfully address the critical technical design areas.

It's essential to clearly understand how AI solutions such as Copilot in Azure align with the Azure WAF. Understanding this framework and how Copilot in Azure can fit will help us better partner with AI to improve our daily tasks in Azure.

The Azure WAF focuses on five pillars: **reliability**, **security**, **cost optimization**, **operational excellence**, and **performance efficiency**. Each pillar addresses specific workload concerns and includes a set of design principles to drive architectural excellence at the workload level.

Copilot in Azure can integrate and support each pillar, which allows us to become more productive and efficient in our daily tasks:

- **Reliability**: AI can assist us in automating how we deploy and monitor resources. It can provide recommendations on existing environments to minimize downtime and enhance availability.

- **Security**: Organizations can improve the security posture of their environment by using AI guidance to implement best practices such as proper identity management and data protection. Copilot in Azure can also provide steps to remediate potential vulnerabilities.

- **Cost optimization**: Insights into resource utilization can be provided by Copilot in Azure to help organizations reduce costs and optimize the utilization of existing resources.

- **Operational excellence**: AI-driven automation can simplify routine tasks and enable better management of our infrastructure. It can also provide insights to ensure we are aligned with best practices.

- **Performance efficiency**: Copilot in Azure can analyze existing workloads in our environment and suggest resource allocation and performance improvements.

By aligning Copilot in Azure with the Azure WAF, you can ensure that your AI adoption enhances, rather than disrupts, your existing cloud practices. Copilot in Azure is not just a tool for convenience; it is a strategic asset that can help you build reliable, secure, cost-optimized, high-performing, and operationally excellent workloads. As you continue through this book, you will gain practical insights into applying Copilot in Azure to real-world scenarios, empowering you to harness AI as a collaborative partner in designing, managing, and optimizing your Azure environment with confidence.

In *Parts 2* and *3* of this book, you will review how Copilot in Azure can be utilized across a range of scenarios. For now, it is important to understand that partnering with AI through Copilot in Azure requires careful consideration of its impact on our Azure environments. Hence, understanding fundamental concepts regarding AI, such as LLMs, is necessary.

Summary

This chapter reviewed how Copilot in Azure represents a significant advantage in how you design, operate, optimize, and troubleshoot cloud environments. You learned about the impact of AI and automation in today's organizations' cloud operations. You also learned about the architectural components of Copilot in Azure, examined how Copilot in Azure integrates with other Azure services and resources, and got a comprehensive overview of its key features.

The next chapter will help you learn how to get started with Copilot in Azure. It will provide a step-by-step approach to accessing Copilot in Azure and explain how to perform the initial setup and configuration, while also providing basic use cases and scenarios that will help you become familiar with it.

2

Getting Started with Microsoft Copilot in Azure

This chapter will provide you with the essentials of getting started with Copilot in Azure using the Azure portal. It is focused on guiding the initial access to Copilot in Azure in your tenant. You will learn about the fundamentals of using Copilot in Azure and how you can access it using the Azure portal. You will also review the main scenarios for Copilot in Azure use cases, and we will touch upon how to start interacting with it.

These fundamental concepts will be crucial to fully understand Copilot in Azure and lay the groundwork for the more advanced topics covered later in the book, ensuring you have a solid understanding of how you can interact with it.

In this chapter, you will cover the following main topics:

- Initial considerations for Copilot in Azure
- Getting started using the Azure portal
- Scenarios for Copilot in Azure

Technical requirements

You will require access to an active Azure subscription to follow the examples that will be provided in this chapter.

It is recommended to first complete *Chapter 1, Understanding Microsoft Copilot in Azure,* to set a baseline knowledge of some concepts for working with Microsoft Copilot in Azure.

Initial considerations for Copilot in Azure

Microsoft has made Copilot in Azure simple to access through the Azure portal to ensure you are set up to fully utilize its capabilities.

One of the most useful aspects of Copilot in Azure is its ability to access specific Azure services or data sources that you frequently work with. For example, if your role involves managing cost and billing, you can leverage Copilot in Azure to gather information and insights related to these areas.

When prompting, the guidance is to be very specific with the phrases and words used to articulate the desired output. The more specific and concise you can be in the prompt, the better results you will get in the response. As of the time of publishing, Copilot in Azure has a *500-character limit* per prompt; therefore, you need to be thoughtful about how you write your prompts to maximize value and achieve the desired output.

The first step to getting started with tasks you need to perform for your role is to review your user permissions. Remember that Copilot in Azure operates within the security context of your user account, meaning it only has access to those resources and actions you are authorized to view and manage. Therefore, verifying that your account has the appropriate permissions in the context of **role-based access control** (**RBAC**) is important, especially if you plan to make changes to Azure resources. Additionally, some services must be explicitly enabled/configured to provide data or surface relevant insights to Copilot.

> You will still always need to manually review the code generated by AI and potentially modify the output to be able to complete the task or operation on the resource type. Outputs or code generated by AI may not be fully accurate or functional.

Setting up access control

Copilot in Azure runs under the user's security context, and its functionality depends on the roles and permissions assigned to the user via Azure RBAC. When access control is set up appropriately for your needs, you can start using Copilot in Azure, which you will discover in the next section of this chapter, *Getting started using the Azure portal*.

In the following subsections, you will look at the role requirements, any additional data access requirements, and how to verify your assigned roles, as well as how to assign roles that you may need.

Firstly, you will look at the role requirements.

Role requirements

To use Copilot in Azure, users need *one* of the following Azure RBAC roles, based on the intended level of access:

- **Contributor (recommended)**: Grants full functionality, including the ability to read and modify Azure resources
- **Reader**: Allows viewing data and generating insights, but does not permit changes to resources

Additional data access requirements

For certain services, additional permissions may be required even if the user has an appropriate RBAC role. Examples include the following:

- **Azure Data Explorer (Kusto)**: Requires read access to specific databases or tables
- **Azure Resource Graph**: Requires permission to query resource metadata

Ensure users are granted the necessary access to any services they intend to use with Copilot in Azure.

The next step is to review your user permissions. As mentioned previously, Copilot in Azure operates within the security context of your account. This means it can only access the resources and perform the actions that your Azure RBAC roles allow. Verifying that your account has the appropriate role—such as *Contributor* or *Reader*—is essential, especially if you intend to create or modify resources.

Next, you will look at how to verify your assigned Azure RBAC roles.

How to verify your RBAC role in the Azure portal

To verify your role, follow these steps:

1. Sign in to the Azure portal at `https://portal.azure.com`.

2. Navigate to the resource, resource group, or subscription where you intend to use Copilot.

3. In the left-hand menu pane, select **Access control (IAM)**.

4. Go to the **Check Access** tab, and then click on **View my access**. This displays your current role assignments for the selected scope.

5. Confirm that you have either of the following roles:

    1. **Contributor**, for full functionality

    2. **Reader**, for view-only access

If you do not see the appropriate role, follow the steps in the next section to assign roles as needed.

How to assign a role

You must have *Owner* or *User Access Administrator* privileges to assign roles. Follow these steps:

1. In the Azure portal **Access control (IAM)** panel, select the **+ Add** > **Add role assignment** option.

2. Choose the role (e.g., **Contributor** or **Reader**).

3. From the **Members** tab, leave **Assign access to** > **User, group, or service principal** at default; then, select the appropriate members.

4. Click **Review + assign** to confirm the changes.

Now that access has been verified and remediated as needed, let us start by familiarizing ourselves with accessing Copilot in Azure and navigating its interface. Microsoft has made access to Copilot in Azure fairly simple to ensure you are set up to fully utilize its capabilities. This next section focuses on using Copilot in Azure through the Azure portal.

Getting started using the Azure portal

As you reviewed in *Chapter 1*, Copilot in Azure is your AI assistant that enhances your interaction with Azure services and resources. Copilot in Azure can be accessed through the Azure portal, and it is possible to use the Azure mobile application available for iOS or Android.

You will access Copilot in Azure using the Azure portal, which serves as the **graphical user interface (GUI)** to access all Azure services and resources.

The steps to getting started with Copilot in Azure are as follows:

1. Log in to the Azure portal and access Copilot in Azure from the top-right corner, as shown in *Figure 2.1*:

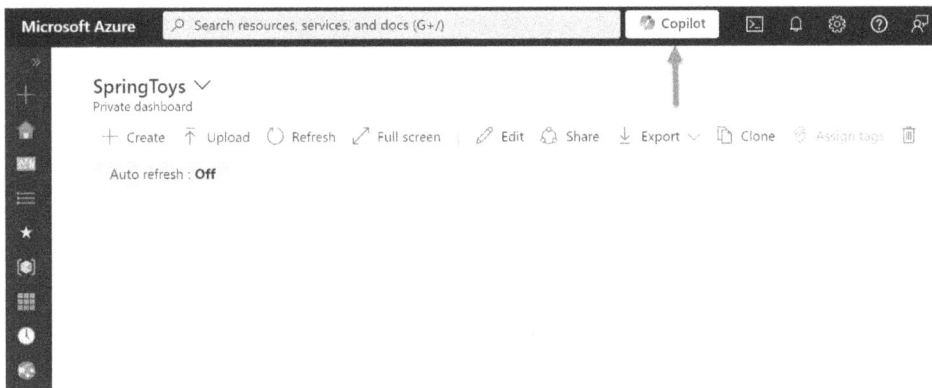

Figure 2.1 – Copilot in Azure in the Azure portal

2. When you click on **Copilot** in the Azure portal, if this is the first time you access it, a quick start guide will be displayed.

3. After this, you can start using Copilot in Azure, and a blade will open on the right side of the Azure portal, displaying an interface that allows you to interact with Copilot in Azure using natural language, as shown in *Figure 2.2*:

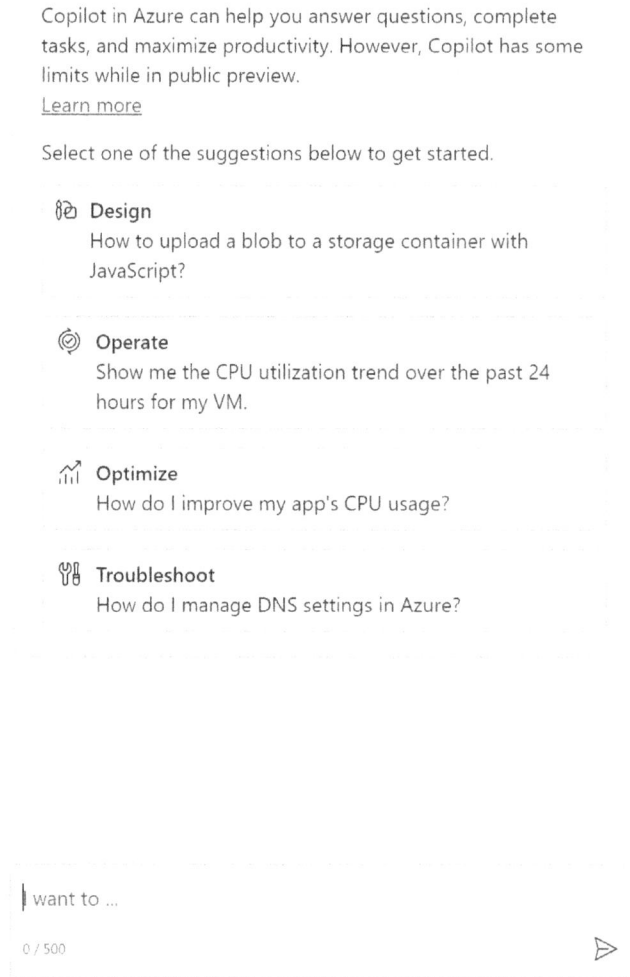

Copilot in Azure can help you answer questions, complete tasks, and maximize productivity. However, Copilot has some limits while in public preview.
Learn more

Select one of the suggestions below to get started.

🎛 **Design**
    How to upload a blob to a storage container with JavaScript?

◎ **Operate**
    Show me the CPU utilization trend over the past 24 hours for my VM.

📈 **Optimize**
    How do I improve my app's CPU usage?

🛠 **Troubleshoot**
    How do I manage DNS settings in Azure?

I want to ...

0 / 500   ▷

Figure 2.2 – The Copilot in Azure interface in the Azure portal

The interface shown in *Figure 2.2* integrates with the frontend layer of Copilot in Azure, as discussed in *Chapter 1*. This is the place where you will be able to write your prompts and interact with Copilot in Azure in natural language.

One of the main benefits of using Copilot in Azure is its ability to provide contextual assistance based on your current view of the portal. Whether you are managing virtual machines, databases, or Kubernetes clusters, Copilot in Azure will gather relevant information from the context you are working in and provide tailored guidance.

Consider that you are in the Azure portal looking at a virtual machine; if you open Copilot in Azure, it will help you understand performance metrics, suggest optimizations, or even guide you through making configuration changes—all from the same interface.

Remember that Copilot in Azure supports multimodal responses, which means it does not just provide text answers but can also present information in various formats, including charts, tables, or interactive elements, depending on what best suits the data being presented in the response. This flexibility to make complex data more understandable is especially useful in scenarios where visual data, such as performance trends or cost analysis, needs to be more comprehensible and actionable.

It is important to spend time exploring the Copilot in Azure interface to make the most of it and experiment with different types of queries. The more you familiarize yourself with it, the more you will realize its capabilities and understand how it can help you manage your Azure environment more effectively.

That said, let's explore some common scenarios where you can leverage Copilot in Azure.

Scenarios for Copilot in Azure

As organizations increasingly adopt cloud platforms such as Microsoft Azure, the complexity of managing, optimizing, and troubleshooting environments can grow quickly. Copilot in Azure emerges as a collaborative assistant, streamlining operations through intelligent, conversational interactions.

While it is helpful to explore Copilot in Azure's capabilities in isolation—such as designing resources or troubleshooting issues—real-world workflows are rarely siloed. In practice, users move fluidly between design, operations, optimization, and troubleshooting. In this section, we'll explore a continuous scenario that illustrates how Copilot supports the entire lifecycle of a cloud workload.

Let us consider the journey of an Azure project team tasked with deploying and maintaining a new web application in Azure. This walk-through demonstrates how Copilot assists across four core areas:

- Design
- Operations
- Optimization
- Troubleshooting

Now, let us look at each of these.

Designing a new application environment

Our team begins with a requirement: deploy a secure and scalable environment for a customer-facing web application. Instead of manually researching best practices or default configurations, they ask the following:

```
Design an environment for a .NET web app with SQL storage and blob storage, following
security best practices.
```

Copilot in Azure interprets the request and recommends a solution architecture using Azure App Service, Azure SQL Database, and Azure Blob Storage. It also includes recommendations for RBAC, networking via a private endpoint, encryption, and backup configurations.

By understanding both the user's intent and contextual access, Copilot quickly assembles a tailored solution, saving hours of manual effort.

With the architecture in place, attention shifts to *operating and managing* the environment effectively—an area where Copilot continues to deliver value.

Operating and scaling the deployment

Once the environment is provisioned, the project moves to day-to-day operations. Rather than navigating through various Azure service interfaces, the team simply asks Copilot the following:

```
Is my East US resource group running smoothly?
```

```
Scale the app service to handle 1,000 concurrent users.
```

Copilot responds with a health summary of all resources in the selected scope and proposes scaling options for App Service. After confirming the scale-up operation, the team moves on, confident that the environment is robust enough for the needs and demands of the business.

Once stable operations are in place, the next step is to *optimize the environment*, ensuring it runs efficiently and cost-effectively.

Optimizing for cost and efficiency

A few weeks later, a routine optimization review is performed; the following query is asked in Copilot:

```
Show me underutilized resources in this subscription.
```

```
Recommend cost-saving changes.
```

Copilot identifies a virtual machine running at 10% CPU usage and suggests resizing to a lower SKU, along with projected monthly savings. It also flags unused managed disks and unattached public IPs that can be decommissioned. These insights translate directly into cost savings and operational efficiency.

However, even in well-optimized environments, issues can arise. When performance problems surface, Copilot is ready to assist with *troubleshooting and diagnostics*.

Troubleshooting a performance issue

During a peak seasonal event, reports come in about slow response times from the application. The team quickly acts by asking the following in Copilot:

```
Why is the web app running slowly?
```

```
What's the current response time from the SQL database?
```

Copilot correlates logs and metrics, identifying that a spike in database latency is the probable cause. It recommends enabling query performance insights and scaling the SQL tier. After implementing the suggestion, application responsiveness improves.

In closing, this scenario illustrates how Copilot in Azure isn't just a tool for isolated tasks; it's a continuous partner throughout the cloud service operations lifecycle. From setting up the first resource to resolving high-impact incidents, Copilot empowers users to work more intuitively and effectively.

Now that you have a better idea of scenarios where Copilot in Azure can be adopted, let's see how you can get started with simple examples and understand how Copilot in Azure processes our queries and provides a response.

Getting started with basic scenarios with Copilot in Azure

Let's consider one of the basic scenarios, which involves the use of Copilot in Azure to get a quick overview of your Azure resources. For instance, you can ask Copilot in Azure to list all virtual machines in a specific region or summarize the current state of your deployed applications. This query helps you maintain an understanding of your environment without having to navigate through multiple sections of the Azure portal.

Copilot in Azure will first gather the current user context, and the frontend layer will forward this along with the query to the orchestration layer. The current context plus the query is called the **prompt**.

Copilot in Azure builds the prompt by combining the user's current context with their natural language query.

The context includes things such as the following:

- Your user identity and RBAC roles
- The active subscription or resource scope
- Any filters or selections in the Azure portal

For example, if you ask, `List all virtual machines in the EastUS region`, Copilot uses both your query and your access context to return results you are authorized to see, filtered to the `eastus` region if that scope is active.

This combined prompt is sent to the backend to generate a secure, personalized response.

This response is seen in the active chat session in Copilot in Azure, as shown in *Figure 2.3*:

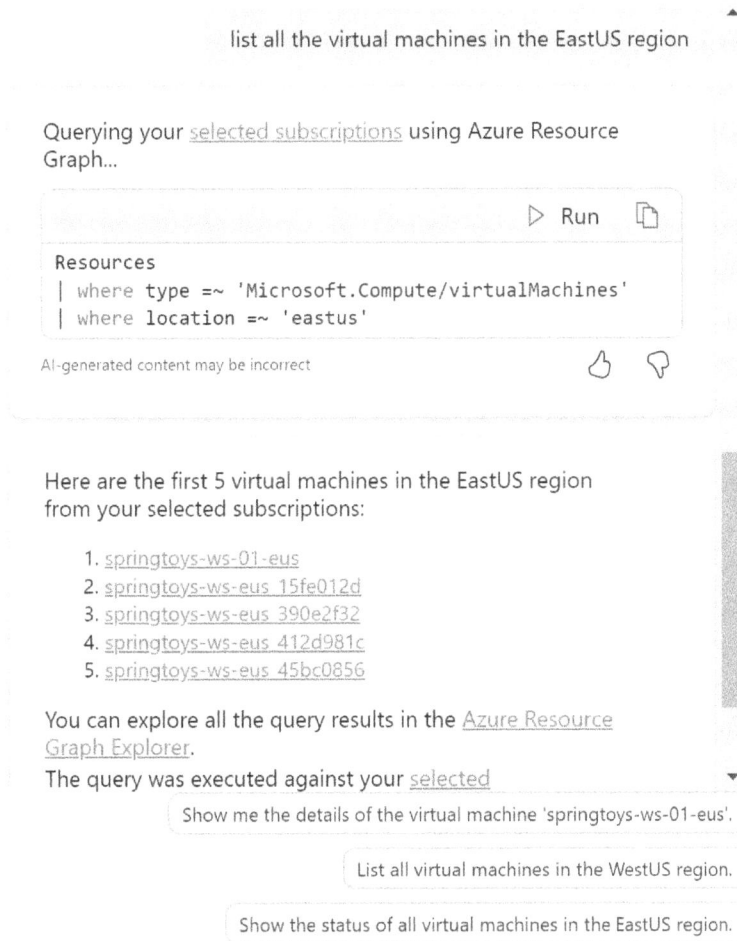

list all the virtual machines in the EastUS region

Querying your selected subscriptions using Azure Resource Graph...

```
                                                    ▷ Run    ▢

Resources
| where type =~ 'Microsoft.Compute/virtualMachines'
| where location =~ 'eastus'
```

AI-generated content may be incorrect   👍 🖒

Here are the first 5 virtual machines in the EastUS region from your selected subscriptions:

1. springtoys-ws-01-eus
2. springtoys-ws-eus_15fe012d
3. springtoys-ws-eus_390e2f32
4. springtoys-ws-eus_412d981c
5. springtoys-ws-eus_45bc0856

You can explore all the query results in the Azure Resource Graph Explorer.
The query was executed against your selected ▼

Show me the details of the virtual machine 'springtoys-ws-01-eus'.

List all virtual machines in the WestUS region.

Show the status of all virtual machines in the EastUS region.

Figure 2.3 – Copilot in Azure query results

As seen in *Figure 2.3*, Copilot in Azure accesses different sources, such as Azure Resource Graph, to gather information from the current environment and retrieve relevant information related to the query.

Note that Copilot in Azure displays the **Kusto Query Language** (**KQL**) query with a concise list of the virtual machines in the selected region. It also offers suggestions for further actions to complete configurations or gain additional insights.

Another common use case is related to troubleshooting. Copilot in Azure can assist you by identifying issues, suggesting potential fixes, and guiding you through the resolution process. For example, let's consider the case where a virtual machine is underperforming; you can ask Copilot in Azure for insights into what might be causing the problem, such as CPU usage spikes. Copilot in Azure can draw from Azure's rich telemetry data to help you solve issues quickly.

Consider the scenario where you have a virtual machine and want to validate misconfigurations in its networking settings. You can ask Copilot in Azure to check whether your virtual machine is publicly accessible. For example, you can use the following query:

```
Check whether this virtual machine springtoys-ws-eus_15fe012d is accessible through
the internet
```

The query gives the output as shown in *Figure 2.4*:

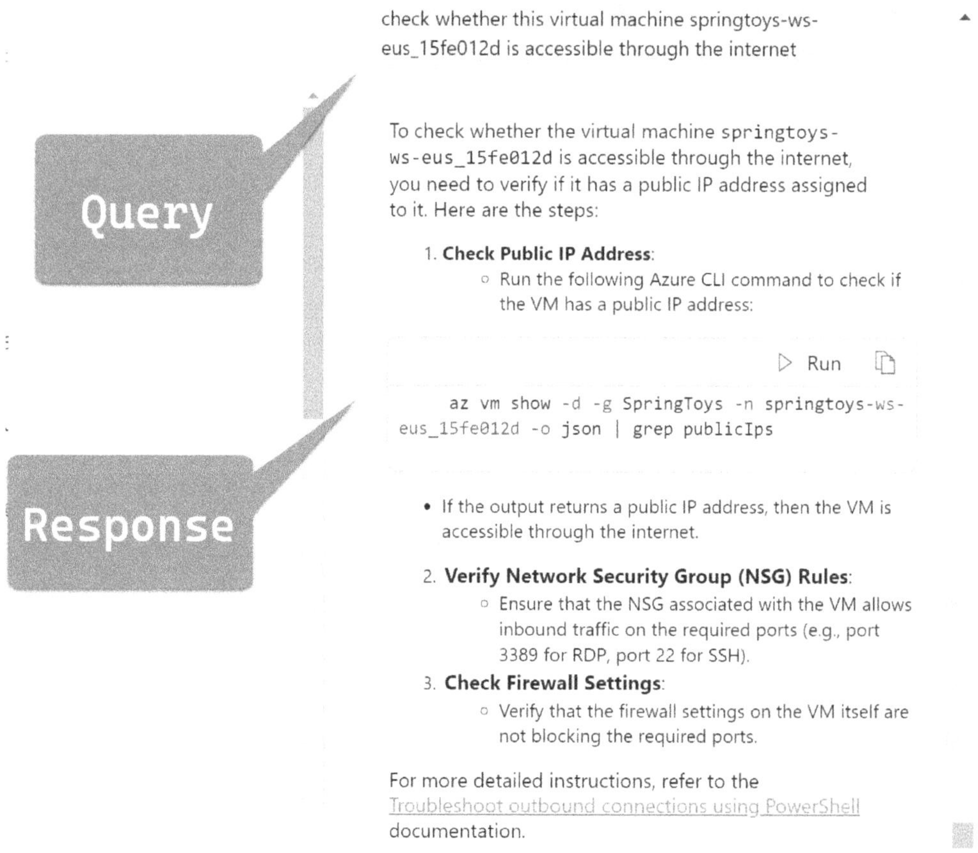

Figure 2.4 – Copilot in Azure — Response payload

In this case, Copilot in Azure presents the response payload using various formats, including an Azure CLI command, to determine whether the virtual machine has a public IP address. It also suggests verifying network security group rules and checking the virtual machine's firewall settings.

Performance optimization is another area where Copilot in Azure excels. It can be utilized to analyze usage patterns and suggest changes that could improve efficiency or reduce costs. For example, if you notice high storage costs, Copilot in Azure can recommend actions such as resizing your storage tiers, cleaning up unused resources, or switching to a more cost-effective option.

Since Copilot in Azure fully integrates with Azure Resource Manager and Azure Resource Graph, Copilot in Azure is also valuable when you need to perform management tasks such as scaling a service, rebooting a virtual machine, or applying tags to resources for better organization.

In the following scenario, you ask Copilot in Azure to reboot the virtual machine in context using the following query:

```
Reboot this virtual machine
```

Through natural language, you can simplify the execution of these actions quickly without having to remember specific commands or navigate through different settings. This significantly simplifies routine management and helps you stay focused on higher-value tasks.

Once Copilot in Azure sends the prompt to the orchestration layer, it will call the plugin store to access the necessary plugins and data under the user context. Then, it will display the response payload and ask for additional confirmations to act on behalf of the user, as shown in *Figure 2.5*:

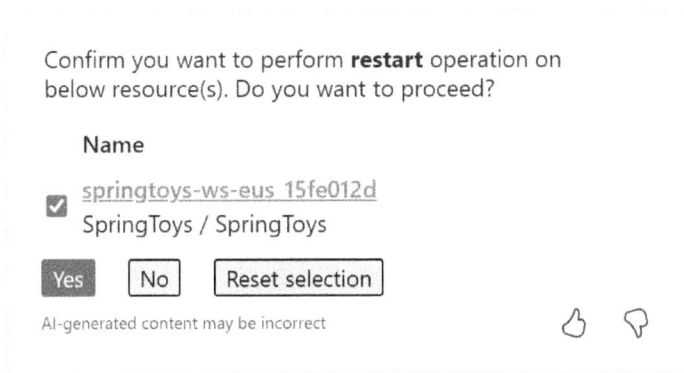

Figure 2.5 – Copilot in Azure confirmation

Once you confirm the action, Copilot in Azure will use this context and act on behalf of the current user, as shown in *Figure 2.6*:

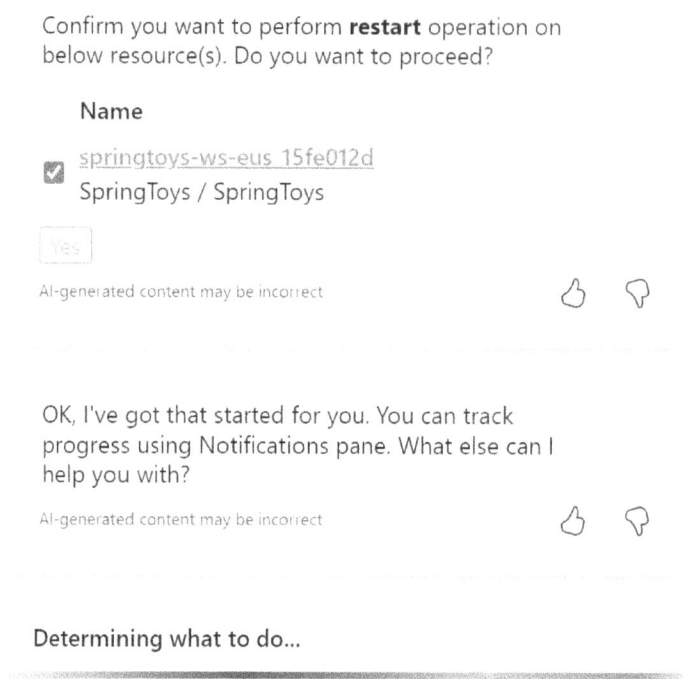

Confirm you want to perform **restart** operation on below resource(s). Do you want to proceed?

Name

☑ springtoys-ws-eus_15fe012d
SpringToys / SpringToys

Yes

AI-generated content may be incorrect

OK, I've got that started for you. You can track progress using Notifications pane. What else can I help you with?

AI-generated content may be incorrect

Determining what to do...

Figure 2.6 – Copilot in Azure action confirmation

Now, you can check the progress and status using the **Notifications** pane in the Azure portal, as shown in *Figure 2.7*:

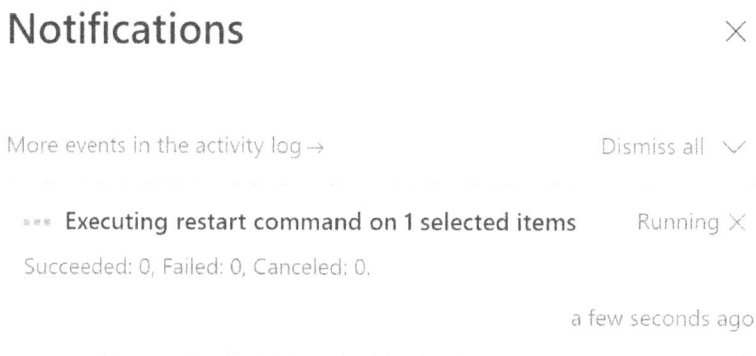

Notifications   ✕

More events in the activity log →   Dismiss all ∨

▪▪▪ **Executing restart command on 1 selected items**   Running ✕

Succeeded: 0, Failed: 0, Canceled: 0.

a few seconds ago

Figure 2.7 – Azure portal Notifications pane

As previously mentioned, one of the plugins available in the plugin store is the Microsoft documentation. Exploring documentation and learning resources is another practical use case. Copilot in Azure can point you to relevant Azure documentation, tutorials, or best practices directly related to the context of your question. This is particularly useful if you are trying to implement a best practice you are unfamiliar with, and it shortens the learning curve. You can read more about Copilot in Azure architecture, which covers the plugin store, in this article: `https://techcommunity.microsoft.com/blog/azureinfrastructureblog/copilot-in-azure-technical-deep-dive/4146546`.

In the following chapters of the book, you will dive deep into specific use cases that demonstrate how Copilot in Azure can significantly impact the way you work, enhance your understanding of your Azure environment, and help you resolve issues faster.

Summary

This chapter guided you through getting started with Microsoft Copilot in Azure via the Azure portal. You discovered the key considerations for beginning with Copilot in Azure and explored basic scenarios to help you effectively utilize its features.

In the next chapter, you will explore the access management features of Microsoft Copilot in Azure in more detail, focusing on how to manage user permissions securely through RBAC.

3

Managing Access to Microsoft Copilot in Azure

To use Copilot in Azure effectively, you must understand its operational scope, security controls, and how it interacts with user roles and data.

In this chapter, you'll learn how to manage access to Copilot in Azure using built-in tools such as **role-based access control** (**RBAC**) and Copilot in Azure admin center. You'll explore how permissions are enforced through Microsoft Entra ID, how to enable or restrict access for specific users or groups, and how Conditional Access policies can enhance security.

Through practical walk-throughs and examples, you'll also see how Copilot performs actions within the scope of each user's assigned roles, demonstrating how AI assistance can remain compliant with organizational access policies. In this chapter, we're going to cover the following main topics:

- Overview of Access Management capabilities
- Configuring Azure RBAC
- Performing tasks in the user's context

Let's start by exploring the Access Management features available in Copilot in Azure and how we can leverage some controls to ensure that only authorized users can interact with the data and perform actions.

Technical requirements

It is recommended to have access to an active Azure subscription to follow the examples that will be provided in this chapter. It is also suggested that a user with Global Admin permission be utilized in the Azure subscription.

Your organization must also allow WebSocket connections to:

`https://directline.botframework.com.`

It is recommended to have first completed *Chapter 1, Understanding Microsoft Copilot in Azure*, to set a baseline knowledge of some concepts for working with Microsoft Copilot in Azure, as well as completing *Chapter 2, Getting Started with Microsoft Copilot in Azure*, so that you are aware of how to use the Azure portal to access Microsoft Copilot in Azure.

When prompting, the guidance is to be very specific with the phrases and words used to articulate the desired output. The more specific and concise you can be in the prompt, the better results you will get in the response. As of the time of publishing, Copilot in Azure has a *500-character limit* per prompt; therefore, you need to be thoughtful about how you write your prompts to maximize value and achieve the desired output.

The first step to getting started with tasks you need to perform for your role is to review your user permissions. Remember that Copilot in Azure operates within the security context of your user account, meaning it only has access to those resources and actions you are authorized to view and manage. Therefore, verifying that your account has the appropriate permissions in the context of RBAC is important, especially if you plan to make changes to Azure resources. Additionally, some services must be explicitly enabled/configured to provide data or surface relevant insights to Copilot.

> You will still always need to manually review the code generated by AI and potentially modify the output to be able to complete the task or operation on the resource type.
>
> Outputs or code generated by AI may not be fully accurate or functional.

To start, let's look at how access to Copilot in Azure is managed and secured.

Overview of Access Management capabilities

Let's first understand how you can better safeguard your Azure resources and maximize the operational capabilities of Copilot in Azure.

Copilot in Azure includes a component named **Access Management**. Access Management in Copilot in Azure leverages Azure's established security principles, ensuring that only the right users have access at the right time with the right level of access. This component is tightly integrated with the Microsoft cloud-based identity and access management service, **Microsoft Entra ID**.

The integration of Copilot in Azure with Microsoft Entra ID allows administrators to better manage control as Entra ID provides a centralized way to manage users, groups, and their access to resources to simplify the assignment of permissions based on user roles.

Access Management in Copilot in Azure also provides the ability to integrate multi-factor authentication to require users to verify their identity with an additional factor, such as a security token or a mobile application. This reduces the risk of unauthorized access, especially in environments where sensitive data is involved.

Another benefit of integrating Copilot in Azure with Microsoft Entra ID is the ability to leverage Microsoft Entra ID Conditional Access. **Conditional Access (CA)** provides a smart policy engine that helps organizations have greater control over how users access protected resources.

Think of CA as an engine that works by establishing **policies**. These policies are conditions you can configure in the form of **if-then** statements. For example, **if** a user wants to access Microsoft 365, **then**, they must complete **multi-factor authentication (MFA)** for access.

You can leverage CA policies to define specific conditions to **grant** or **deny** access. For example, you can require users to be on an organization's network, or you can block access from specific geographical locations. Through this level of granularity, organizations can enforce security policies to align with their risk management strategies.

When you access the Azure portal, you will notice that Copilot in Azure is available for you, but also for all users within the tenant. However, only those users with the *Global Administrator* role assigned can manage and control access for their organization and grant permissions to specific users or groups.

For example, if there's a user in the organization who doesn't have access to Copilot in Azure, they will see the Copilot in Azure button in the Azure portal, but they'll notice an unauthorized message if they click on it.

In some instances, the tenant might not have access to Copilot in Azure by default. Global Administrators can enable it in those cases and grant access as needed.

Bear in mind that Copilot in Azure will only access the resources the user has permission to use. It can only perform actions the user is authorized to do and always asks for confirmation before making any changes.

Copilot in Azure adheres to all existing management rules and protection controls such as RBAC, Privileged Identity Management, Azure Policy, and resource locks.

When a user interacts with Copilot in Azure, all their operations will occur within the scope of their assigned permissions and are logged in the Audit logs and activity reports.

These logs will detail who accessed Copilot in Azure, when they accessed it, and the specific actions taken. Administrators can leverage these logs to monitor suspicious behavior, conduct security audits, and ensure policy compliance.

Now that we better understand the features integrated into Access Management, let's explore how to leverage Access Management in the Azure portal.

Copilot in Azure admin center is the place where you will be able to see the Access Management control; let us look at that in the following steps:

1. In the Azure portal, you can navigate to Copilot in Azure admin center. You can look for it in the top search bar of the Azure portal, as shown in the following figure:

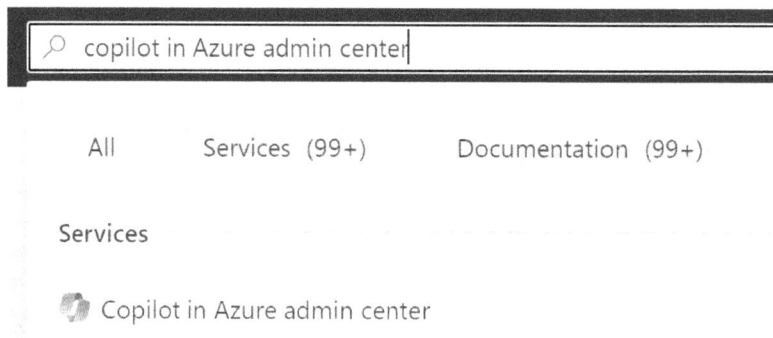

Figure 3.1 – Azure portal search bar — Copilot in Azure admin center

2. Once you click **Copilot** in Azure admin center, you will see the **Access Management** option, as shown in the following screenshot:

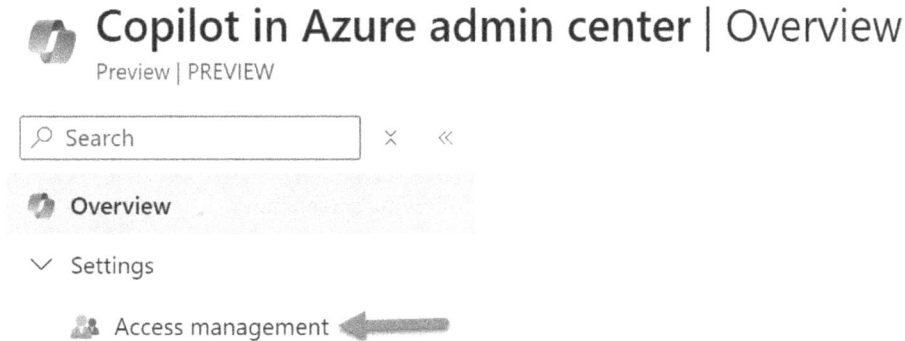

Figure 3.2 – Copilot in Azure admin center

3. Once in **Access Management**, you will see a control that you can toggle on to make Copilot in Azure available to all users in the tenant, as shown in the following screenshot:

Figure 3.3 – Copilot in Azure admin center — Access Management

4. RBAC can also be configured for more granular control. There might be cases where you want to provide access to Copilot to Azure to only a few users in your organization. To set up RBAC, we would need to switch off the option shown in *Figure 3.3* and proceed to configure Copilot in Azure for Azure RBAC.

Now let's review how role-based access control can be configured for Copilot in Azure.

Configuring Azure RBAC

Copilot in Azure can be made accessible only to certain users or groups in the tenant by using RBAC. To restrict this access to specific users or groups using RBAC, follow these steps to configure the necessary settings in Copilot in Azure admin center:

1. On the **Access Management** page, you can *toggle off* the option called **Available to all users**. This action will allow you to configure Copilot for RBAC. A *new button* will appear below, **Manage access**, as shown in the following screenshot:

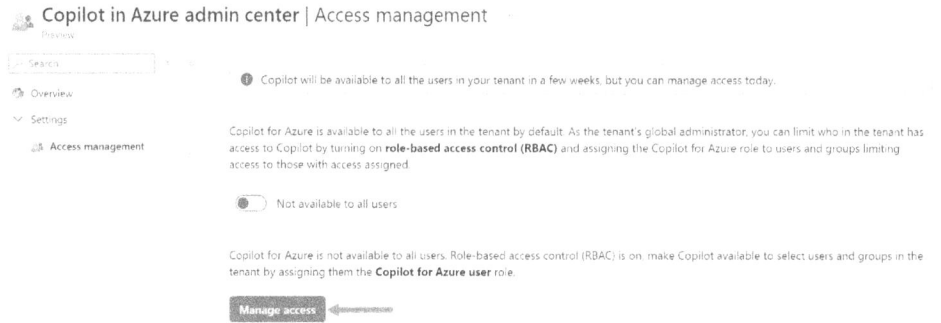

Figure 3.4 – Copilot in Azure admin center — Access Management, configure RBAC

2. Once you select the **Manage access** option, you will be redirected to the **Access Control** page, where you will be able to validate and add role assignments, as shown in *Figure 3.5*:

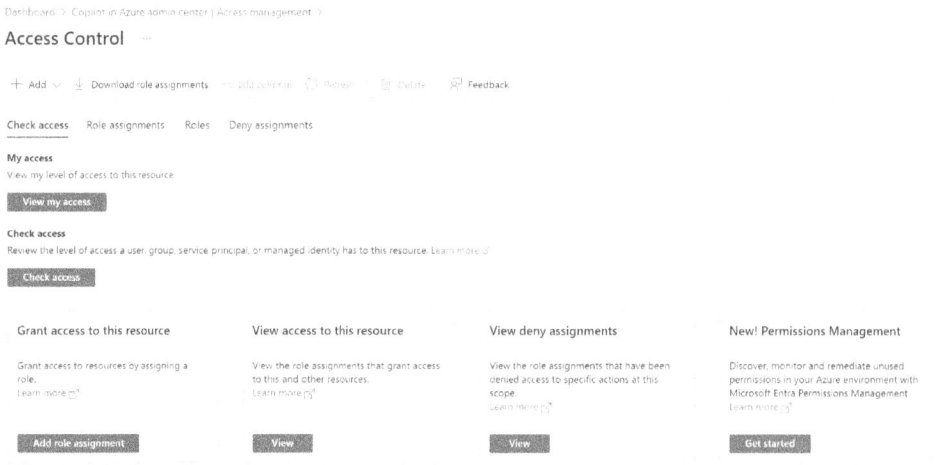

Figure 3.5 – Copilot for RBAC

3. To add a new role assignment for a user who needs access to Copilot in Azure in the SpringToys tenant, navigate to the **Access Control** page, select the **+ Add** option, and add a role assignment as shown in the following screenshot:

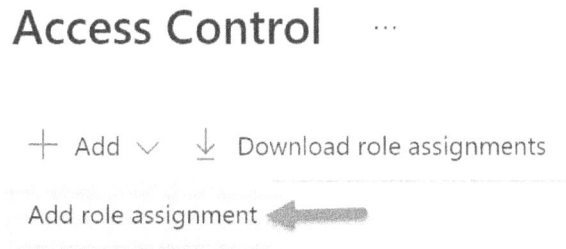

Access Control   ⋯

$+$ Add ⌄ $\downarrow$ Download role assignments

Add role assignment ◀━━

Figure 3.6 – Copilot for RBAC — Add role assignment

4. Once the **Add role assignment** option is selected, this action will take you to the page shown in the following figure:

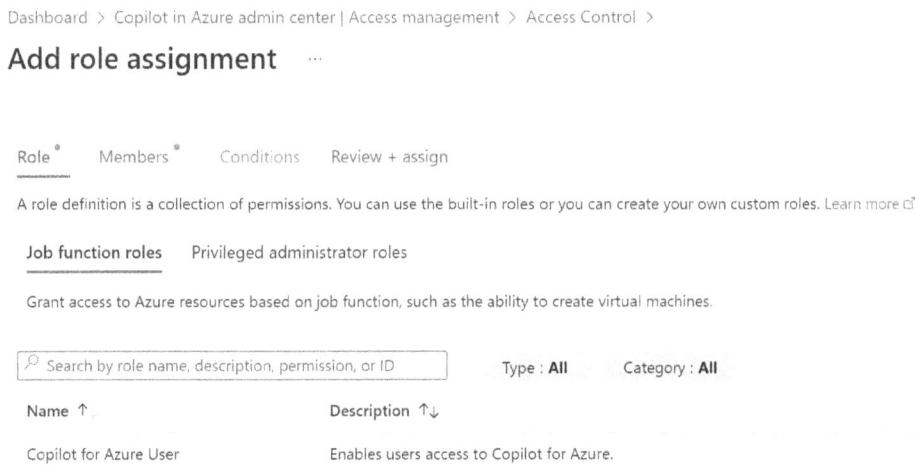

Dashboard > Copilot in Azure admin center | Access management > Access Control >

Add role assignment   ⋯

Role °   Members °   Conditions   Review + assign

A role definition is a collection of permissions. You can use the built-in roles or you can create your own custom roles. Learn more ⌐

Job function roles   Privileged administrator roles

Grant access to Azure resources based on job function, such as the ability to create virtual machines.

🔍 Search by role name, description, permission, or ID   Type : **All**   Category : **All**

Name ↑   Description ↑↓

Copilot for Azure User   Enables users access to Copilot for Azure.

Figure 3.7 – Add role assignment page

5. Copilot in Azure for RBAC includes a built-in role called **Copilot for Azure User**, which can be assigned to *users* or *groups*. You also have the option to create and apply custom roles if needed. This built-in role includes two key permissions from the Microsoft. Authorization provider configured by default:

- Microsoft.Authorization/roleAssignments/read: Allows users to view information about role assignments
- Microsoft.Authorization/roleDefinitions/read: Enables viewing of role definitions

In addition to these permissions, it's important to note that the role includes a **DataActions** entry: `Microsoft.PortalServices/copilotSettings/conversations/action`

This **DataAction** grants the ability to interact with Copilot settings, specifically to perform actions related to Copilot conversations in the Azure portal. It reflects the functional scope needed for users to access and engage with Copilot features. The role is also assigned at a specific **assignableScope**, which defines where in the Azure hierarchy (*such as a subscription or resource group*) the role can be used.

6. You can select **Copilot for Azure User** and then click **Next**, as shown in *Figure 3.8*:

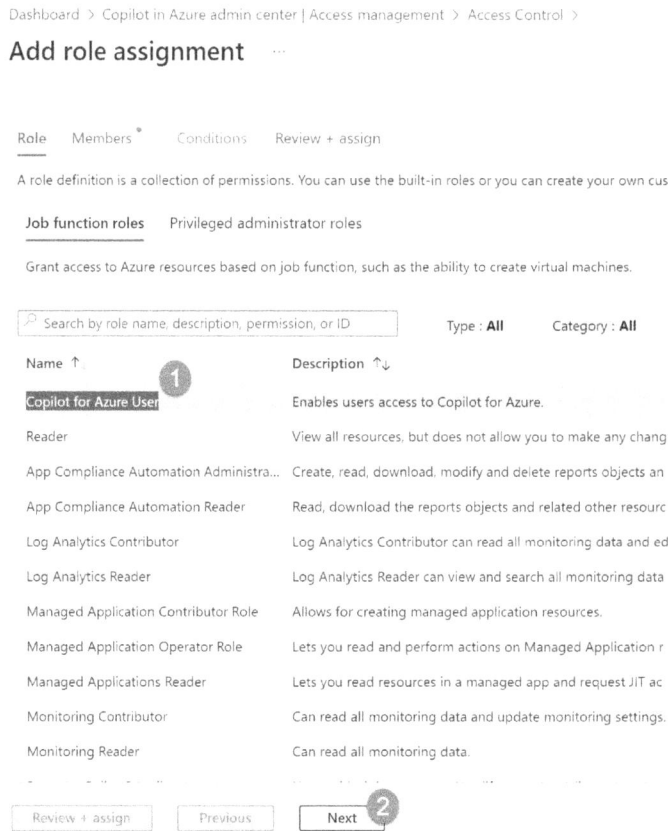

Figure 3.8 – Copilot for Azure user built-in role

7. Then, in the **Members** tab, we will select the *user or group*, *service principal*, or *managed identity* to assign access to. Select the **User, group, or service principal** option and then click on **Members** as shown:

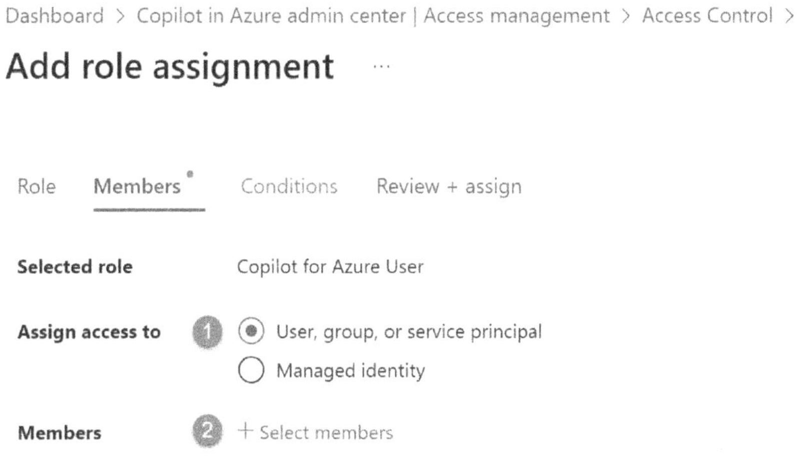

Dashboard > Copilot in Azure admin center | Access management > Access Control >

Add role assignment ···

Role   Members   Conditions   Review + assign

Selected role   Copilot for Azure User

Assign access to   ① ⦿ User, group, or service principal

                           ◯ Managed identity

Members   ② + Select members

Figure 3.9 – Add role assignment

8. Then, in this example, we will select a *user* in the tenant named **John**.

9. Then, in the **Review + assign** tab, confirm that the user selected is the correct one, and click the **Review + assign** button:

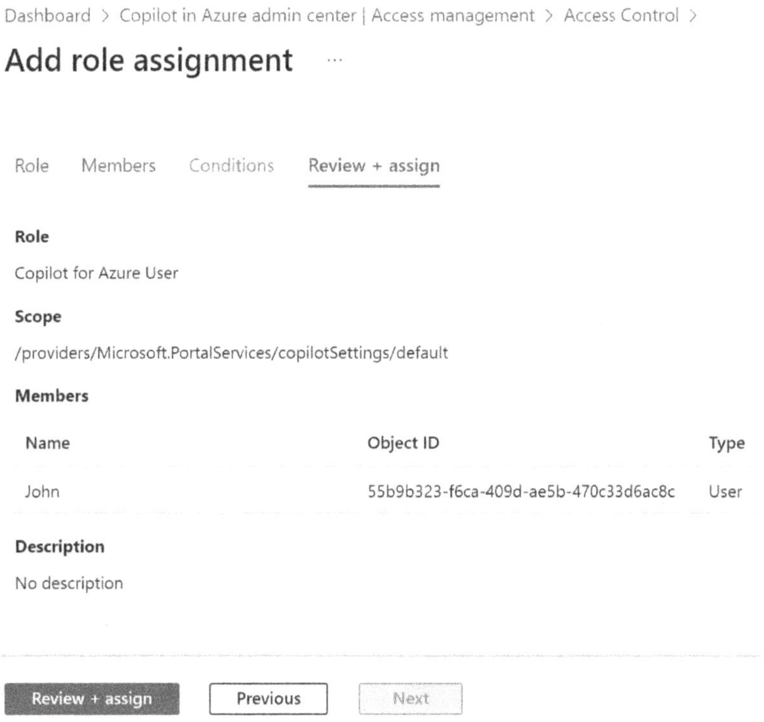

Dashboard > Copilot in Azure admin center | Access management > Access Control >

Add role assignment ···

Role   Members   Conditions   Review + assign

Role

Copilot for Azure User

Scope

/providers/Microsoft.PortalServices/copilotSettings/default

Members

Name	Object ID	Type
John	55b9b323-f6ca-409d-ae5b-470c33d6ac8c	User

Description

No description

Review + assign	Previous	Next

Figure 3.10 – Review + assign

10. After a few seconds, a notification will appear in the Azure portal with the confirmation of the added role assignment:

> ✅ **Added Role assignment**   ✕
>
> John was added as Copilot for Azure User for default.

Figure 3.11 – Added Role assignment

11. Once the role assignment process is complete, you should be able to see the list of users that have been granted access to Copilot in Azure on the **Access Control** page, as shown in the following screenshot:

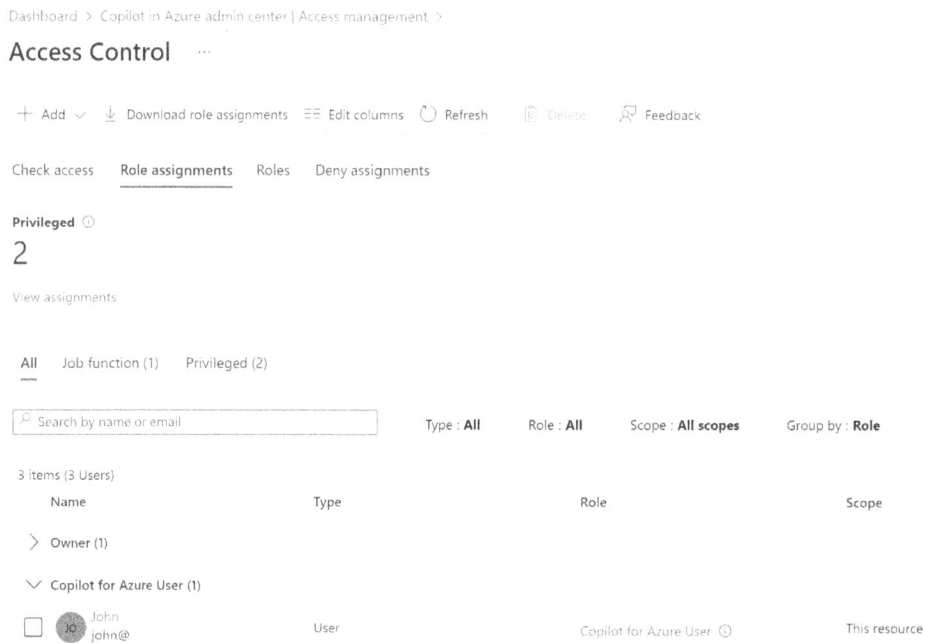

Dashboard > Copilot in Azure admin center | Access management >

Access Control   …

+ Add ⌄   ⌄ Download role assignments   ☰ Edit columns   ⟳ Refresh   🗑 Delete   🗨 Feedback

Check access   **Role assignments**   Roles   Deny assignments

Privileged ⓘ

2

View assignments

All   Job function (1)   Privileged (2)

| 🔍 Search by name or email | | Type : **All** | Role : **All** | Scope : **All scopes** | Group by : **Role** |

3 items (3 Users)

Name	Type	Role	Scope
⟩ Owner (1)			
⌄ Copilot for Azure User (1)			
☐ 🟣 John john@	User	Copilot for Azure User ⓘ	This resource

Figure 3.12 – Role assignments

12. Next, to validate the role assignment of Copilot for RBAC, you could go to a new private browser session and access the Azure portal with the user credentials – in this case, John's credentials – and click the **Copilot** button, as shown in the following screenshot:

| 🔵 Copilot | ◀ | >_ | 🔔 | ⚙ | ⓘ | 🗨 | john@cloudtraineeoutl… AZINSIDER (CLOUDTRAINEEOUT… | 👤 |

Figure 3.13 – Access Copilot in Azure with RBAC configuration

13. If the role assignment was correctly added, the Copilot in Azure quickstart guide should be visible, as shown in the following screenshot:

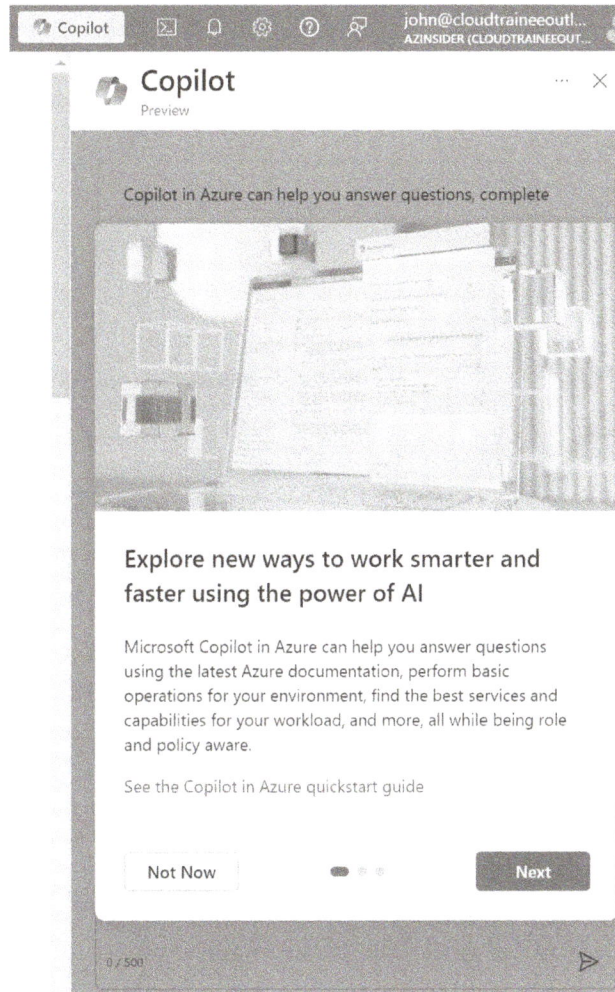

Figure 3.14 – Copilot in Azure – Quickstart guide

It must be noted that WebSocket connections should be allowed for the site (`https://directline.botframework.com`) so that Copilot in Azure can work properly.

14. Now, if this user, John, tries to access Copilot in Azure admin center, a page will be shown displaying the *"You don't have permissions to manage access"* message, as shown here, since this is a user with no Global Administrator role assigned:

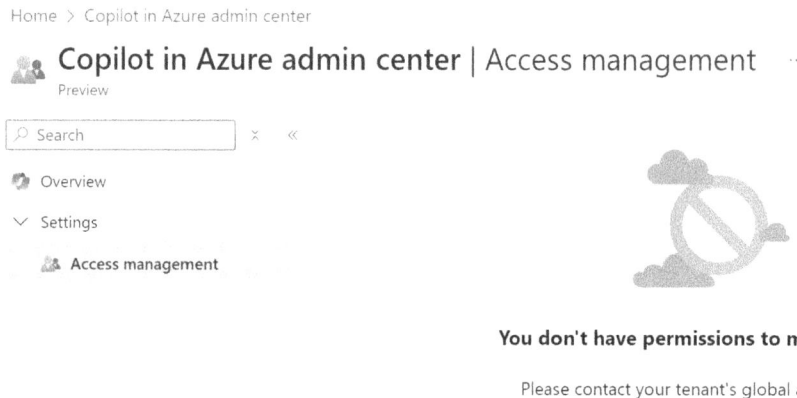

Figure 3.15 – Copilot in Azure admin center

Remember that Copilot in Azure works within the boundaries of the user's existing permissions. In this case, John can only work on resources he has access to and perform actions that this user is already authorized to execute.

If John requests to perform a change or update a resource, Copilot in Azure will always ask for confirmation before making any changes to the environment. This ensures it complies with all your current access control methods in RBAC, Privileged Identity Management, and Azure Policy.

With Copilot for Azure access successfully configured using RBAC, the next logical step is to understand how those permissions function in practice. The following scenarios walk through how Copilot operates within the user's assigned roles, illustrating how it respects security boundaries while enabling productivity through contextual assistance.

Performing tasks in the user's context

In the following scenarios, you will come to understand how Copilot in Azure operates within the boundaries of a user's assigned roles and permissions. These examples will show Copilot assisting with common administrative tasks—first with virtual machines, and then with storage, while always respecting RBAC policies and prompting for confirmation before acting.

Virtual machine task scenario

Let's take an example where John will try to perform actions in an environment that includes a resource group that contains five virtual machines, and for the simplicity of the scenario, no other services exist within the resource group.

In this scenario, John has been assigned two roles: the **Azure Virtual Machine Contributor** role and the **Copilot for Azure user** role:

1. John accesses the Azure portal and then uses Copilot in Azure to request to start the virtual machines using the following prompt:

    ```
    Start all virtual machines on this resource group
    ```

2. Copilot in Azure will retrieve the context of the resource group, and in this scenario, it will select all the virtual machines and perform the start operation.

    Note that in a scenario where there are more than five virtual machines, the default number of resources that Copilot in Azure would select by default is 5, that is, if you had 15 virtual machines, it would only start 5 by default if you do not explicitly state the number to start; in which case, you would modify the prompt to `"Start all 15 virtual machines on this resource group"`. This prompt response behavior is by design; this reinforces how you should always strive to improve prompts and/or carefully review the query results.

3. Copilot in Azure understands the context and will ask for confirmation before taking any action, as shown in the following screenshot:

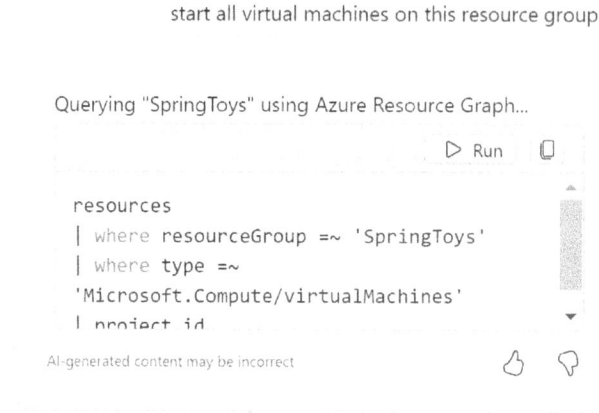

start all virtual machines on this resource group

Querying "SpringToys" using Azure Resource Graph...

▷ Run

```
resources
| where resourceGroup =~ 'SpringToys'
| where type =~
'Microsoft.Compute/virtualMachines'
| project id
```

AI-generated content may be incorrect

Confirm you want to perform **Start** operation on below resource(s). Do you want to proceed?

Name

☑ springtoys-ws-01-eus
SpringToys / SpringToys

☑ springtoys-ws-eus_15fe012d
SpringToys / SpringToys

☑ springtoys-ws-eus_390e2f32
SpringToys / SpringToys

☑ springtoys-ws-eus_412d981c
SpringToys / SpringToys

☑ springtoys-ws-eus_45bc0856
SpringToys / SpringToys

Yes   No   Reset selection

AI-generated content may be incorrect

Figure 3.16 – Copilot in Azure confirmation

4. As seen in the image, Copilot in Azure sent a payload response and asked for confirmation to start the virtual machines.

5. John could now confirm the action. Let's select the **Yes** option. This will trigger the start operation on the selected virtual machines, as shown in the following screenshot:

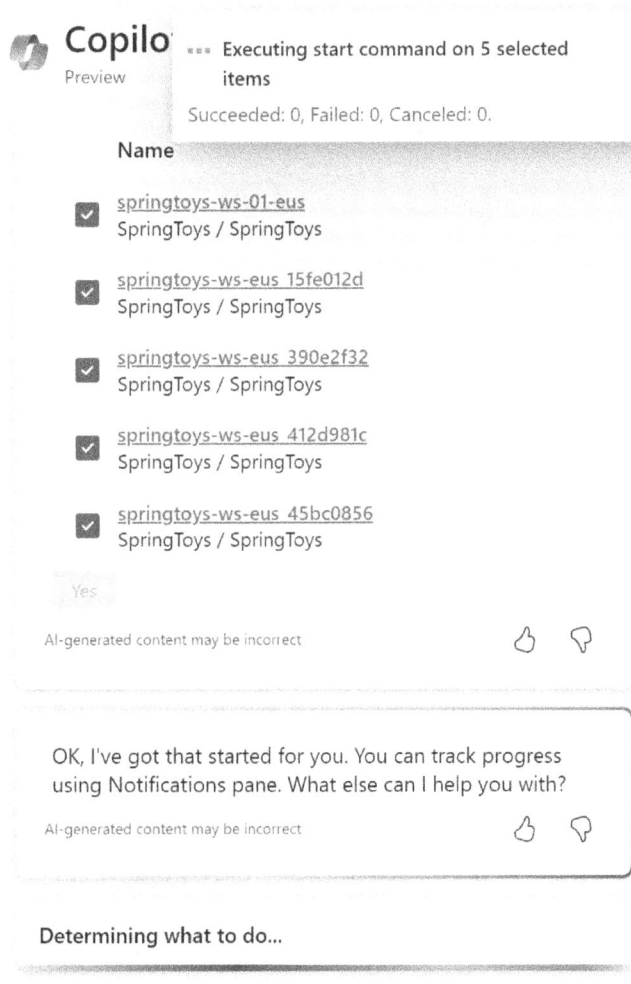

Copilo ••• Executing start command on 5 selected
Preview   items

Succeeded: 0, Failed: 0, Canceled: 0.

Name

✓ springtoys-ws-01-eus
  SpringToys / SpringToys

✓ springtoys-ws-eus_15fe012d
  SpringToys / SpringToys

✓ springtoys-ws-eus_390e2f32
  SpringToys / SpringToys

✓ springtoys-ws-eus_412d981c
  SpringToys / SpringToys

✓ springtoys-ws-eus_45bc0856
  SpringToys / SpringToys

Yes

AI-generated content may be incorrect

OK, I've got that started for you. You can track progress using Notifications pane. What else can I help you with?

AI-generated content may be incorrect

Determining what to do...

Figure 3.17 – Copilot in Azure operation

6. As seen in the screenshot, Copilot in Azure performs the operation to start all five virtual machines simultaneously.

7. Then, after a few seconds, you should see the notification that the start command execution is complete, as shown in the following screenshot:

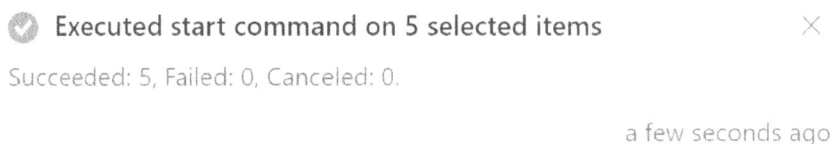

> ✅ **Executed start command on 5 selected items**   ✕
>
> Succeeded: 5, Failed: 0, Canceled: 0.
>
> a few seconds ago

Figure 3.18 – Azure portal notification

In this section, you learned how Copilot in Azure executes tasks within the scope of a user's assigned permissions, using practical examples. Through the virtual machine scenario, it became clear that Copilot defaults to a limited selection of resources unless prompted otherwise, emphasizing the importance of refining prompts and reviewing Copilot's responses before confirming actions.

Now, let's take a final short example. Consider that John is trying to get a feeling for the total storage allocated for the 11 virtual machines.

Storage task scenario

Building on the previous virtual machine example, this next scenario continues with John working in the same environment. Here, instead of performing an action, he uses Copilot in Azure to retrieve information about the storage associated with the virtual machines, demonstrating Copilot's ability to support query-based tasks while still operating within the scope of user permissions. Let's get started.

1. To get an overview of the total storage used by the virtual machines, we could use a basic prompt such as the following:

   ```
   What is the total storage capacity of all the disks combined?
   ```

2. Copilot in Azure will receive the requests and, based on the current context, will display the information requested by John.

3. After a few seconds, Copilot in Azure sends back the response payload that includes a Resource Graph query and the total size of all virtual machine disks, as shown in the following screenshot:

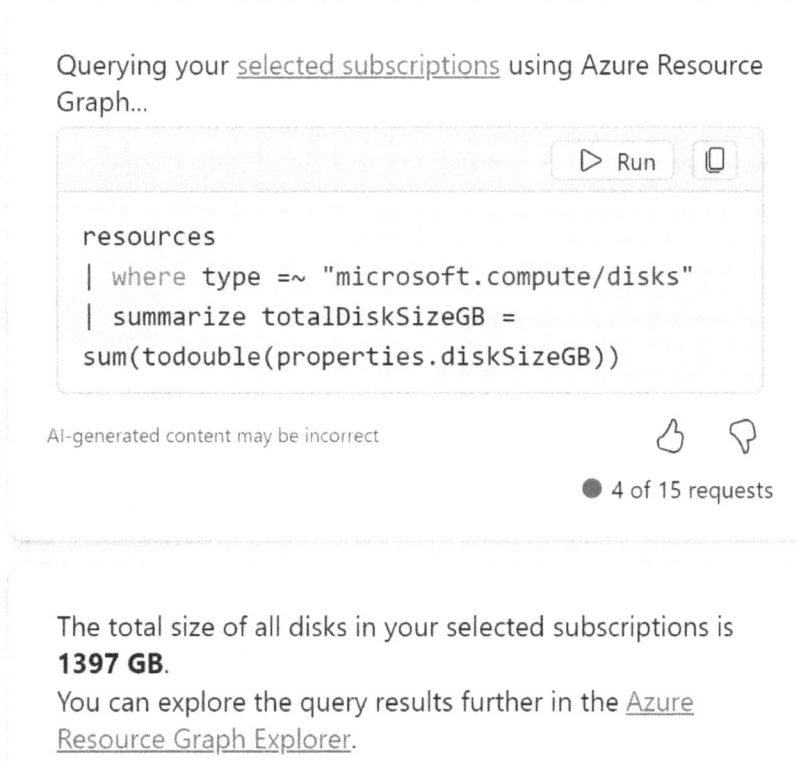

Querying your selected subscriptions using Azure Resource Graph...

> Run

```
resources
| where type =~ "microsoft.compute/disks"
| summarize totalDiskSizeGB =
sum(todouble(properties.diskSizeGB))
```

AI-generated content may be incorrect

● 4 of 15 requests

The total size of all disks in your selected subscriptions is **1397 GB**.
You can explore the query results further in the Azure Resource Graph Explorer.

Figure 3.19 – Copilot in Azure response payload

4. As seen in the screenshot, Copilot in Azure includes a Resource Graph query that can be leveraged to get the result displayed at the end of the response. This comes from the plugin store, which the orchestration layer accesses in the backend and then sends back to the frontend layer.

The storage example further illustrates how Copilot can retrieve insights, such as total disk capacity, using user context and backend services such as Resource Graph. Together, both scenarios highlight how Copilot enhances productivity while respecting Azure RBAC and requiring user confirmation for changes.

Summary

In this chapter, we reviewed how you can leverage the controls available in Copilot in Azure admin center to configure and grant access to users in the organization. We reviewed how you can access Copilot in Azure admin center and the different options for making Copilot in Azure available to all the users in the tenant or taking a more refined and granular approach through RBAC to grant access to specific users in the organization.

In the next chapter, we will guide you through the process of using Copilot in Azure to deploy and manage infrastructure efficiently. We will also take a look at how you can simplify complex deployment tasks.

Unlock this book's exclusive benefits now

UNLOCK NOW

Scan this QR code or go to `https://packtpub.com/unlock`, then search for this book by name.

Note: Keep your purchase invoice ready before you start.

Part 2

Practical Application and Effective Cloud Resource Management

This part moves from foundational understanding to hands-on application, showing you how to put Microsoft Copilot in Azure to work across real-world scenarios. You'll learn how to deploy and configure infrastructure and streamline development workflows—all through natural language prompts. From scaling environments and securing storage to troubleshooting and performance tuning, this section equips you with practical skills to use Copilot as an everyday partner in managing and optimizing your Azure environment.

This part of the book includes the following chapters:

- *Chapter 4, Deploying and Managing Cloud Infrastructure — Part 1*
- *Chapter 5, Deploying and Managing Cloud Infrastructure — Part 2*
- *Chapter 6, Improving Development Efficiency*
- *Chapter 7, Advanced Data Management with Microsoft Copilot in Azure*
- *Chapter 8, Exploring Real-Time Monitoring and Troubleshooting*
- *Chapter 9, Scaling and Optimizing Cloud Operations*

4

Deploying and Managing Cloud Infrastructure — Part 1

Having gained a deeper understanding of the concepts and architecture of **Copilot in Azure**, as well as its interaction through the Azure portal, you will look at practical applications. These include utilizing Copilot in Azure for the deployment and management of infrastructure-based solutions such as **virtual machines** and **Azure Kubernetes Service**.

In today's cloud-enabled world, infrastructure is more than just the foundation; it is the operational backbone that enables businesses to build, scale, and innovate, but infrastructure also brings complexity. Resource planning, deployment, scaling, and ongoing management all demand a deep understanding.

Enter **Copilot in Azure**, a *conversational AI assistant* that empowers you to define and manage infrastructure with *natural language prompts*. This chapter explores how Copilot transforms traditional infrastructure workflows, making them more accessible and efficient without compromising control or security.

In this chapter, you will cover the following topics:

- Deploying and managing Azure infrastructure resources
- Deploying and managing Azure Kubernetes Service

Technical requirements

It is recommended to have access to an active Azure subscription to follow the examples that will be provided in this chapter. It is also suggested that a user with Global Admin permission be utilized in the Azure subscription.

It is recommended to have first completed *Chapter 1, Understanding Microsoft Copilot in Azure*, to set a baseline knowledge of some concepts for working with Microsoft Copilot in Azure, as well as completing *Chapter 2, Getting Started with Microsoft Copilot in Azure*, and *Chapter 3, Managing Access to Microsoft Copilot in Azure*, so that you are aware of how to use the Azure portal to access Microsoft Copilot in Azure as well as understanding access management.

When prompting, the guidance is to be very specific with the phrases and words used to articulate the desired output. The more specific and concise you can be in the prompt, the better results you will get in the response. As of the time of publishing, Copilot in Azure has a *500-character limit* per prompt; therefore, you need to be thoughtful about how you write your prompts to maximize value and achieve the desired output.

The first step to getting started with tasks you need to perform for your role is to review your user permissions. Remember that Copilot in Azure operates within the security context of your user account, meaning it only has access to those resources and actions you are authorized to view and manage. Therefore, verifying that your account has the appropriate permissions in the context of role-based access control is important, especially if you plan to make changes to Azure resources. Additionally, some services must be explicitly enabled/configured to provide data or surface relevant insights to Copilot.

> You will still always need to manually review the code generated by AI and potentially modify the output to be able to complete the task or operation on the resource type.
>
> Outputs or code generated by AI may not be fully accurate or functional.

To start, let us look at how to deploy and manage infrastructure resources in Azure.

Deploying and managing Azure infrastructure resources

In the cloud and AI era, deploying infrastructure is still a core part of how modern applications, technology innovations, and business initiatives come to life. But what exactly is *infrastructure*, and why does deploying and managing it matter so much?

At its core, *infrastructure* is what gives your ideas a place to run. Whether you are spinning up virtual machines to host an internal tool, deploying Kubernetes clusters to manage microservices, deploying an AI model, or preparing scalable environments for a product launch, infrastructure is the engine that powers your applications and innovations. It is what transforms code from something theoretical into something real, live, accessible, usable, and of benefit.

But *infrastructure is not just a technical necessity*; it is a *strategic decision*. Choosing the right infrastructure impacts performance, cost, reliability, control, and security. Those decisions are not static. They evolve across environments (*development, staging, production*), workloads (*monolithic versus containerized*), and business goals (*innovation, scaling, global reach, compliance*).

The *when* is equally critical: infrastructure is needed any time an application or service must be tested, deployed, or scaled to meet user demand. Managing it properly ensures that what you have built continues to run efficiently and securely over time.

That is where **Copilot in Azure** can change the game.

This chapter explores how AI-driven tools such as Copilot can help cloud practitioners simplify and accelerate the deployment and management of essential infrastructure. Instead of navigating dozens of CLI commands or portal screens, you can now describe your goals in plain language and let Copilot guide you through the process, generating, validating, and even executing resource deployments with your oversight.

You will focus on two foundational pillars of cloud infrastructure:

- **Virtual Machines (VMs)**: You will learn how to deploy Windows and Linux VMs, configure disks and networking, expose ports, and validate connectivity, all using Copilot-generated scripts.
- **Azure Kubernetes Service (AKS)**: You will then move on to container orchestration, where you will see how to use Copilot to deploy AKS clusters, configure autoscaling, integrate with Azure Container Registry, and set up secure authentication and authorization using Microsoft Entra ID.

Rather than just showing *how* to run scripts, this chapter is more directed toward the *art of the possible* than a *prescriptive* cookbook approach, which will help you understand *why* each step matters, *when* to apply it, and *how* to interpret the responses Copilot provides. By the end, you will be better equipped to think strategically about infrastructure while working tactically through Copilot to deliver results.

Deploying and managing virtual machines using Copilot in Azure

Before you jump into deploying virtual machines with the help of Copilot in Azure, let us take a quick step back and talk about VMs themselves, what they are, why they matter, and how they fit into modern cloud infrastructure.

Imagine you are tasked with setting up a new server for a project. In traditional, non-public cloud environments, this meant dealing with physical hardware at some point, buying the server, finding space in a suitable location and with sufficient power and cooling, installing the host operating system onto the bare metal, and maintaining it all yourself. It was inefficient and inflexible.

Virtual machines changed that. A VM is essentially a software-based guest computer that runs on a physical host machine but behaves like a separate, independent system. You can run multiple VMs on a single physical host server, each with its own operating system and configuration; this utilizes a virtualization layer, with a hypervisor such as Microsoft Hyper-V. This makes it easy to scale as needed, test different setups, and keep environments isolated from one another.

Now, on a public-cloud platform such as Azure, spinning up a VM is as simple as clicking a few buttons, or even better, just telling Copilot in Azure what you want using simple natural language.

That is what you will dive into in this section. You will see how you can start with a simple prompt to deploy Windows and Linux virtual machines in your Azure environment. From there, you will build on those prompts and explore how to manage your VMs, such as configuring settings, installing software, or automating tasks, all through natural language with Copilot.

Let us start by looking at how you can utilize Copilot in Azure to simplify the deployment of a Windows VM.

Deploying a Windows VM using Copilot in Azure

Let us get started with deploying a Windows VM. This is a common first step for many development and testing environments, where teams need a consistent and reliable Windows-based setup without the overhead of managing physical infrastructure. Whether you are hosting an application, running automated tests, or creating a shared dev box, Windows VMs remain a flexible and familiar choice.

Copilot in Azure makes this process remarkably simple. With a single prompt, you can generate all the necessary configuration to provision your VM – no need to click through the Azure portal or manually piece together CLI commands.

It is highly recommended to review any scripts that are generated by Copilot in Azure before performing any action in your environment. Copilot in Azure will ask you to confirm the operation of executing a script.

Scenario:

A cost-effective Windows VM is required for development and testing purposes, as it allows developers to efficiently create, test, and deploy applications in a consistent environment without the need for expensive physical hardware. This setup helps in streamlining workflows, enhancing collaboration among team members, and reducing overall costs associated with software development and testing. Additionally, a VM provides the flexibility to easily scale resources according to project needs and enables quick recovery from any system failures or issues.

Example Copilot prompt:

```
Create a Windows VM of size 'Standard_B2ms' named 'mylowcostvm' in the EastUS. Use
Windows Server 2022 Datacenter as the OS. Configure with 2 data disks. Create a
VNet called "springtoys-vnet-eus" virtual network with a subnet called "frontend"
and connect to this. Use an availability zone for infrastructure redundancy. Add an
"environment" tag with "dev" as the value and do not assign a Public IP to the VM.
```

Make sure to make the prompts discussed in this chapter your own by using actual values from your environment, or experiment and tailor the prompts in a way that meet your needs.

Outputs or code generated by AI may not be fully accurate or functional. It may require review, testing, and adjustments to meet your specific needs and expectations.

Expected Copilot response:

An Azure CLI script to create a Windows VM named `mylowcostvm` with the specified configurations, which include the following:

- Creating the VM
- Attaching data disks
- Creating tags
- Securing exposure on the network

Practical impact:

This ensures a complete, repeatable, consistent, and cost-effective setup suitable for dev environments, all done through a single prompt with automated script generation.

Now that you have seen how to use Copilot in Azure to deploy and manage virtual machines, the next step is making sure those VMs are configured the way you expect.

Validating VM configuration

You have now deployed a VM in Azure, but how do you make sure it is set up the way you intended? Is it using a cost-efficient instance type? Are you paying for more power than you need? Is it accessible for remote management, and is it secure?

These are the kinds of questions you will face when managing VMs at scale. Even small misconfigurations can lead to unnecessary costs or prevent you from accessing your VMs when needed. Fortunately, with Copilot in Azure, you can ask these questions directly, without needing to sift through multiple dashboards or memorize CLI commands.

Scenario:

You need Copilot to validate the configuration of an existing VM to ensure it is aligned with cost-efficiency and operational best practices. You will ask Copilot to verify the VM's instance size, SKU, and storage setup. You will also check for public IP address assignment. Finally, you will also see how Copilot can generate a **Kusto Query Language** (**KQL**) query that can be used to extract the data you need.

Example Copilot prompt:

```
Please validate the configuration of the virtual machine named 'mylowcostvm'.
Ensure it is optimized for low cost by checking the instance type, VM SKU, and
storage configuration. Additionally, check that it does not have a public ip address
assigned. Finally, please provide a KQL query to get those details.
```

Expected Copilot response:

A KQL query you can run in Azure Resource Graph Explorer to review the following:

- Instance type
- VM SKU
- Storage profile
- Public IP address assignment

If you select the **Run** option to execute the query, Copilot in Azure will trigger the query in Azure Resource Graph Explorer. The query will provide the necessary details. You can optionally save this query for further reference and use the editor to modify the query as needed.

Practical impact:

You validate that the VM is not only running but also appropriately configured for secure network exposure and budget alignment.

With validation complete, it's time to explore how Copilot can help you deploy a Linux-based VM just as efficiently.

Deploying a Linux VM using Copilot in Azure

Linux virtual machines are a popular choice for development environments, thanks to their speed, flexibility, and open source ecosystem. Whether you are building web applications, running automation scripts, or hosting APIs, Linux VMs offer a lightweight and cost-effective platform.

In this example, you will use Copilot in Azure to deploy a Linux VM tailored for development. Instead of navigating through manual steps or writing out complex configuration files, you will provide a natural language prompt, and Copilot will generate a ready-to-use script for you. This drastically reduces setup time and helps ensure consistency across environments.

Scenario:

You need to set up a budget-friendly Linux VM for development within the "SpringToys" resource group in East US. The VM should run Ubuntu Server 24.04 LTS and be named myLinuxVm. It must include two data disks, connect to the existing springtoys-vnet-eus virtual network (specifically the frontend subnet), and have port 80 open for web access. You will also enable boot diagnostics using a new storage account named springtoysvmlogs5, assign a public IP, and tag the VM for the dev environment. To complete the setup securely, you'll ask Copilot to suggest strong credentials.

Example Copilot prompt:

```
Create a low-cost Linux VM named 'myLinuxVm' in the "SpringToys" resource group
in EastUS. Use Ubuntu Server 24.04 LTS as the OS. Configure 2 data disks and
connect them to the "springtoys-vnet-eus" virtual network in the frontend subnet.
Expose port 80 and enable boot diagnostics in a new storage account named
"springtoysvmlogs5." Add an "environment" tag with "dev" as the value and assign
a Public IP to the VM. Suggest secure credentials.
```

Expected Copilot response:

Similarly to the Windows VM deployment, in this case, Copilot in Azure will help you create a CLI script to complete the deployment of the Linux VM. The prompt provides an Azure CLI script to create a low-cost Linux VM named `myLinuxVm` in the "SpringToys" resource group in EastUS with the specified configurations and with secure credential suggestions.

Validating the Linux VM configuration

After deploying your Linux VM, it's important to confirm that it was provisioned according to your intended settings. In this scenario, you'll ask Copilot to help verify the VM's configuration, including the instance size, storage setup, and whether port 80 is correctly open for web traffic.

Scenario:

You need a query that will help you verify the VM's configuration and network settings, ensuring that port 80 is accessible.

Example Copilot prompt:

```
Provide a query that validates the configuration of the virtual machine named
'myLinuxVm' by checking the VM SKU, and storage configuration. Also, verify that
port 80 is accessible.
```

Expected Copilot response:

A KQL script that can be used as an Azure Resource Graph query that validates the configuration of the virtual machine named `myLinuxVm` by checking the VM SKU, storage configuration, and ensuring that port 80 is accessible.

Practical impact:

This streamlines the provisioning of Linux app server environments for test or development, with consideration for web traffic access and secure credentials.

With virtual machines covered, let us now shift focus to containers. If your workload needs to scale dynamically or follow a microservices model, AKS offers a powerful, managed solution for deploying and managing containers at scale.

Deploying and managing Azure Kubernetes Service

While virtual machines are great for running full operating systems and traditional workloads, they can be heavyweight when you are looking to deploy lightweight, fast-moving applications, especially those built with a *microservices* approach. That is where **containers** come in.

Containers package an application and its dependencies into a single, portable unit that can run consistently across environments. They are faster to start, easier to scale, and more efficient in terms of resource usage than VMs. However, managing lots of containers across multiple servers can get complex, this is where **Azure Kubernetes Service (AKS)** steps in.

AKS is a *managed container orchestration service* that simplifies the deployment, scaling, and management of containerized applications. It abstracts away the complexity of managing the Kubernetes control plane, allowing developers to focus on building and deploying apps rather than managing infrastructure.

With AKS, developers can independently scale and update microservices, automatically adjust to demand, and integrate seamlessly with tools such as Azure DevOps and Azure Container Registry for streamlined CI/CD workflows and secure image pulling.

Deploying AKS using Copilot in Azure

Now that you understand the value of AKS, let us look at how easy it is to deploy an AKS cluster using Copilot in Azure. With just a single prompt, you can spin up a fully configured Kubernetes environment tailored to your development needs, with no manual setup or YAML files required.

Scenario:

You need to create a development Kubernetes cluster using AKS in the SpringToys resource group located in the East US region. The cluster, named SpringToys-Dev-Aks-Cluster, should include a single node pool with two nodes using the Standard_DS2_v2 VM size. It also needs to be connected to the Azure container registry named stoys so it can pull container images. Finally, you want the script to ensure SSH keys are generated if they do not already exist.

Example Copilot prompt:

Generate a CLI script to create a development AKS cluster named 'SpringToys-Dev-Aks-Cluster' in the 'eastus' region within the resource group 'SpringToys'. The cluster should have a single node pool with 2 nodes of size 'Standard_DS2_v2'. Connect this cluster to the Azure Container Registry named 'stoys' to pull images. Create SSH keys if they don't already exist.

Expected Copilot response:

An Azure CLI script to create an AKS cluster with the specified configurations, which includes creating SpringToys-Dev-Aks-Cluster in eastus within the SpringToys resource group. This script sets up a single node pool with 2 'Standard_DS2_v2' nodes and connects the cluster to the stoys Azure container registry.

Practical impact:

This quickly deploys a production-ready container platform with minimal manual setup.

With your AKS cluster up and running, the next step is to make it responsive to workload demands. Let's look at how to enable and configure cluster autoscaling using Copilot in Azure.

Configuring cluster autoscaler in AKS using Copilot in Azure

In a production environment, workloads often fluctuate, sometimes spiking unexpectedly. To handle this, AKS includes a built-in **cluster autoscaler** that can automatically adjust the number of nodes in your cluster based on resource needs.

When Pods cannot be scheduled due to insufficient resources, the autoscaler adds more nodes to the node pool. Conversely, if nodes are underutilized, it removes them to help reduce costs. Copilot in Azure makes it easy to enable and configure this behavior using a simple prompt.

Scenario:

You need to configure `SpringToys-Dev-Aks-Cluster` in the `SpringToys` resource group to automatically scale based on workload demands. By enabling the cluster autoscaler, the number of nodes in the cluster can adjust dynamically, scaling down to one node during low usage and up to five nodes when demand increases.

Example Copilot prompt:

Enable the cluster autoscaler in the Azure Kubernetes Service named 'SpringToys-Dev-Aks-Cluster' in the 'SpringToys' resource group. Set a Minimum Node Count of 1 and a Maximum Node Count of 5.

Expected Copilot response:

An Azure CLI command to enable cluster autoscaler with the specified configurations, which includes the following:

- Setting a minimum node count of 1
- Setting a maximum node count of 5

Practical impact:

This ensures the cluster automatically adjusts to workload demands, improving cost-efficiency and availability.

Now that your AKS cluster is scaling intelligently, it's equally important to control who can access it and what they can do. Let's explore how to configure authentication and authorization in AKS using Copilot in Azure.

Configuring authorization and authentication in AKS using Copilot in Azure

When deploying applications to AKS, setting up authentication and authorization properly is just as important as provisioning the cluster itself. By default, AKS uses RBAC with local user accounts, which can work for smaller or short-lived environments. However, for enterprise-grade security, centralized identity management, and tighter integration with Azure governance, enabling **Microsoft Entra ID** (*formerly Azure Active Directory*) is the way to go.

Microsoft Entra ID allows you to manage user access at scale while using **Azure RBAC** to enforce policies across your Kubernetes workloads. This approach provides a secure, seamless way to authenticate users and control their access to the cluster, without the complexity of managing local identities.

In this example, you will use Copilot in Azure to update your cluster's settings and enable Microsoft Entra ID integration using your tenant ID.

Scenario:

In our deployment, the default configuration is to use local accounts with Kubernetes RBAC for authorization and authentication. You need to update the authentication and authorization settings for `SpringToys-Dev-Aks-Cluster` in the `SpringToys` resource group. The goal is to enable Microsoft Entra ID (formerly Azure AD) integration for secure user authentication and apply Azure RBAC for access control. You will provide your tenant ID to configure this properly through the Azure CLI.

Example Copilot prompt:

```
Here is my tenant ID: 'Your-tenant-ID-here'. Generate a CLI script to update the
Authentication and Authorization settings of the 'SpringToys-Dev-Aks-Cluster' Azure
Kubernetes Service (AKS) cluster, located in the 'SpringToys' resource group, to
enable Microsoft Entra ID for authentication with Azure RBAC.
```

Expected Copilot response:

An Azure CLI command to configure the AKS cluster to use Azure Active Directory for authentication and set up the necessary permissions; this includes the following:

- Setting the `enable-aad` flag to enable Microsoft Entra ID (formerly Azure AD) authentication
- Setting the `enable-azure-rbac` flag to activate Azure RBAC for authorization

Practical impact:

This provides secure, centralized identity and access management for your AKS workloads.

With authentication and authorization now securely configured using Microsoft Entra ID and Azure RBAC, you've seen how Copilot in Azure can guide you through every major step of provisioning and managing cloud infrastructure, from deploying virtual machines to setting up and scaling containerized workloads with AKS.

Each scenario demonstrated how natural language prompts can streamline complex tasks, reduce manual effort, and help ensure best practices are followed. Whether you are optimizing a VM, enabling autoscaling, or securing access to a Kubernetes cluster, Copilot acts as a powerful assistant to accelerate your workflow.

Let us take a moment to recap in the following *Summary* section what you have accomplished and highlight the key takeaways from these examples.

Summary

In this chapter, you explored how **Copilot in Azure** can simplify and accelerate common infrastructure tasks using natural language prompts. Starting with virtual machines, you learned how to deploy cost-effective Windows and Linux VMs, validate their configurations for security and budget alignment, and manage access settings, all without diving into complex scripting or portal navigation.

You then shifted to **AKS**, where you saw how to provision a development cluster, enable autoscaling, and configure secure authentication with **Microsoft Entra ID** and **Azure RBAC**. Each scenario showed how Copilot can help reduce manual setup, enforce best practices, and keep your cloud resources aligned with organizational goals.

By using Copilot, you are not just automating tasks; you are enhancing consistency, saving time, and improving confidence in the infrastructure you deploy. As you continue to explore Azure's capabilities, Copilot can serve as a trusted tool and collaborative partner in making cloud management more intuitive, efficient, and secure.

The next chapter will explore how you can utilize Copilot in Azure to effectively manage your cloud platform services, such as app services, functions, and storage accounts.

Unlock this book's exclusive benefits now

UNLOCK NOW

Scan this QR code or go to https://packtpub.com/unlock, then search for this book by name.

Note: Keep your purchase invoice ready before you start.

5

Deploying and Managing Cloud Infrastructure — Part 2

With a solid understanding of how **Copilot in Azure** can assist in deploying core infrastructure, we now shift our focus to more **platform-based infrastructure services**.

This chapter demonstrates how Copilot in Azure can streamline tasks, helping you deploy, configure, and secure key platform-based infrastructure services such as **Azure App Service**, **Azure Functions**, and **Azure storage accounts** through intuitive *natural language prompts*.

By working through these real-world scenarios, you will gain hands-on experience with AI-assisted cloud management. You will learn how Copilot in Azure simplifies the creation of web apps and serverless functions, enforces storage security best practices, and eliminates the manual overhead associated with traditional scripting or portal navigation.

Mastering these workflows is essential not just for improving day-to-day productivity but for building a sustainable, AI-integrated approach to cloud operations.

In this chapter, you are going to cover the following main topics:

- Using Copilot in Azure for managing Azure App Service
- Using Copilot in Azure to manage Azure Functions
- Using Copilot in Azure to secure storage accounts

Technical requirements

It is recommended to have access to an active Azure subscription to follow the examples that will be provided in this chapter. It is also suggested that a user with Global Admin permission be used in the Azure subscription.

It is recommended to have first completed *Chapter 1, Understanding Microsoft Copilot in Azure*, to set a baseline knowledge of some concepts for working with Microsoft Copilot in Azure, as well as completing *Chapter 2, Getting Started with Microsoft Copilot in Azure*, and *Chapter 3, Managing Access to Microsoft Copilot in Azure*, so that you are aware of how to use the Azure portal to access Microsoft Copilot in Azure as well as understanding access management.

When prompting, the guidance is to be very specific with the phrases and words used to articulate the desired output. The more specific and concise you can be in the prompt, the better results you will get in the response. As of the time of publishing, Copilot in Azure has a *500-character limit* per prompt; therefore, you need to be thoughtful about how you write your prompts to maximize value and achieve the desired output.

The first step to getting started with tasks you need to perform for your role is to review your user permissions. Remember that Copilot in Azure operates within the security context of your user account, meaning it only has access to those resources and actions you are authorized to view and manage. Therefore, verifying that your account has the appropriate permissions in the context of role-based access control is important, especially if you plan to make changes to Azure resources. Additionally, some services must be explicitly enabled/configured to provide data or surface relevant insights to Copilot.

> You will still always need to manually review the code generated by AI and potentially modify the output to be able to complete the task or operation on the resource type.
>
> Outputs or code generated by AI may not be fully accurate or functional.

In this chapter's first section, you will explore how Copilot in Azure can streamline the deployment and configuration of Azure App Service, helping you move from code to a running app with fewer manual steps and greater confidence.

Using Copilot in Azure for managing Azure App Service

Azure App Service is a fully managed platform for building, deploying, and scaling web apps and APIs. It allows developers to run their code in the cloud without worrying about managing infrastructure. To host an app in Azure App Service, you first need an **App Service Plan**, which is referred to as the *infrastructure* that the app will be hosted on. The infrastructure within the service plan chosen to host your app defines the *region, operating system, performance tier*, and *pricing* for your app. The *web app* itself is then deployed into that *plan*. This separation allows you to host multiple apps under a single plan and scale them independently or together.

Azure App Service can benefit developers as it provides support for various languages, including *.NET, Java, Node.js, Python*, and *PHP*. This way, you can focus on the application code, and Azure takes care of the infrastructure hosting the code, security patches, and scaling needs.

In the following sections, you will explore how to use Copilot in Azure, *a natural language assistant*, to deploy and manage a full web application lifecycle, from provisioning to code deployment and enabling application monitoring and insights entirely through natural language prompts.

Provisioning a web app and App Service plan

Creating a new web application is often preferable to modifying an existing one. This approach ensures isolation between environments, allows for different configurations, supports independent testing and scaling, introduces new functionality beyond current services, and meets varying security, compliance, or performance needs.

> It is highly recommended to review any scripts that are generated by Copilot in Azure before performing any action in your environment. Copilot in Azure will ask you to confirm the operation of executing a script.

Scenario:

You are starting a new project that requires deploying a *Node.js application* to Azure. To prepare for this, you need to create an App Service plan, which is the provisioned infrastructure resources to host the application, and deploy a web app configured with the appropriate runtime stack. Your goal is to ensure that everything is deployed in the correct Azure region and resource group, with standardized naming and resource tiers for consistency and scalability.

Example Copilot prompt:

```
Create a CLI script to deploy a new web app named SpringToysWeb in the SpringToys
resource group within the EastUS region. Use Code as the publish method with
'node:20LTS', and allocate the web app to the SpringToysPlanEUS plan. Then, deploy
a new Windows App Service plan named SpringToysPlanEUS in the Standard S1 tier
within the same resource group and region.
```

> *Make sure to make the prompts discussed in this chapter your own by using actual values from your environment, or experiment and tailor these prompts in a way that meet your needs.*

Expected Copilot response:

Copilot in Azure generates a CLI script that does the following:

- Creates a Standard S1 App Service Plan (SpringToysPlanEUS) in the EastUS region
- Deploys a new web app named SpringToysWeb
- Sets the runtime stack to Node.js 20 LTS
- Links the app to the new service plan within the SpringToys resource group

> Outputs or code generated by AI may not be fully accurate or functional. It may require review, testing, and adjustments to meet your specific needs and expectations.

Practical impact:

Provisioning platform-based infrastructure services using *natural language* saves considerable time and reduces the chance of misconfiguration. You do not need deep knowledge of CLI syntax to correctly specify runtime environments, pricing tiers, or geographic locations. It enables development teams to focus on application logic rather than setup overhead.

With the infrastructure now in place and your App Service environment provisioned, the focus shifts from setup to functionality. The next step is to connect your application's code base and establish a deployment pipeline that brings your web app online.

Configuring application source code and deployment

With your App Service infrastructure ready, the next step is to deploy your application's source code. A common and efficient approach is to connect App Service directly to a version-controlled repository, such as **GitHub**.

GitHub is a widely used web-based platform that facilitates version control and collaborative software development. It is built on top of **Git**, a distributed version control system that allows developers to track changes in their code over time, collaborate on code bases without conflicts, and maintain a full history of edits and contributions. GitHub enhances this functionality by providing a user-friendly interface, tools for code review, issue tracking, and powerful integrations with **Continuous Integration/Continuous Deployment** *(CI/CD)* services. This makes it an ideal choice for managing the source code of modern applications, particularly in team-based or cloud-native development environments.

By integrating your GitHub repository with Azure App Service, you can automate the process of deploying new versions of your application whenever changes are pushed to the repository. This setup not only streamlines deployment but also supports continuous delivery practices, ensuring your application stays up to date with minimal manual effort. Additionally, with Azure Copilot, you can configure this integration using natural language commands, reducing complexity and aligning your deployment process with modern DevOps methodologies.

Scenario:

With the App Service plan infrastructure now in place, your next objective is to deploy the application's source code. This includes connecting App Service to a public GitHub repository that contains the application code. You want to automate this process so that the app is deployed directly from the source control system and updates can be managed through version control. The app should pull code from the main branch of a specified repository, allowing you to manage deployments with minimal manual overhead.

Example prompt:

```
Generate a CLI script to configure the App Service named SpringToysWeb in the
SpringToys resource group and hosted in the SpringToysPlanEUS App plan to use the
custom domain name springtoys.io.
```

Expected Copilot response:

Copilot in Azure responds with an Azure CLI command that does the following:

- Configures the web app's deployment source to a public GitHub repository: `https://github.com/Azure-Samples/nodejs-docs-hello-world`
- Uses the main branch of the repo as the source
- Sets up the deployment pipeline in Azure Deployment Center with External Git

This command will associate the custom domain `springtoys.io` with your App Service instance. Make sure that the domain is properly configured in your DNS settings to point to Azure App Service.

The result is a live deployment of the Node.js application. Navigating to the app's URL shows the default "Hello World!" page from the GitHub repository, verifying the success of the deployment.

Practical impact:

Automated deployment from source control allows you to establish continuous delivery pipelines with almost no manual intervention. It enforces version control practices and removes manual upload steps. This ensures faster rollouts, easier rollbacks, and better traceability of changes, vital for teams practicing DevOps or agile delivery.

In the next section, we'll use Copilot in Azure to enable monitoring for the `SpringToysWeb` application so that your team can detect issues early and optimize the app's performance over time.

Enabling application monitoring with Application Insights

With the application now deployed and live, your focus can shift from *delivery* to *operational visibility*. It is not enough to simply deploy an app; you also need to understand how it behaves in production. This includes monitoring performance, tracking errors, and gaining insights into user behavior. Azure provides a powerful built-in tool called **Application Insights** for this purpose.

Azure Application Insights is a feature of **Azure Monitor** that helps you track the *performance*, *availability*, and *usage* of your web applications in real time. It collects *telemetry data*, such as response times, error rates, and user activity, and presents it in dashboards that make it easy to detect issues and analyze how your app is performing. With built-in alerts and powerful analytics, Application Insights enables you to proactively monitor your app and quickly resolve problems before they impact users.

Scenario:

Now that your web app is deployed and accessible, the next step is to ensure it can be effectively monitored in production. You need a way to track performance, detect failures, and gain insights into how users interact with the app. To achieve this, you will enable Application Insights for the `SpringToysWeb` app to collect real-time telemetry and support proactive maintenance.

Example Copilot prompt:

```
Generate a CLI script to enable Application Insights in the resource group named
SpringToys to monitor the App Service named SpringToysWeb hosted in the App Service
Plan SpringToysPlanEUS.
```

Expected Copilot response:

Copilot in Azure provides a script that does the following:

- Creates an Application Insights resource named `SpringToysWebInsights` in the `EastUS` region
- Links the Application Insights instance to the web app via the instrumentation key
- Sets the necessary app settings so that telemetry starts flowing immediately

Once this is completed, you can view real-time data in the Azure portal, including request rates, failures, performance metrics, and logs.

Practical impact:

Application Insights gives your team deep visibility into application behavior without requiring extra instrumentation in the code. It supports proactive monitoring, alerts, and diagnostics, essential for minimizing downtime and enhancing user experience. Especially in production environments, it helps teams respond quickly to issues and continuously improve performance.

With your application now monitored and running in a stable environment, the next area of focus is adding event-driven capabilities using Azure Functions. Whether you need to process background jobs, respond to webhooks, or automate backend workflows, serverless functions offer a lightweight and scalable solution. In the following section, you will use Copilot in Azure to create and manage these functions with the same natural language approach you've applied throughout the project.

Using Copilot in Azure to manage Azure Functions

As your application evolves, it is common to need background processing, file-based automation, or integration with external services. Rather than provisioning full virtual machines or constantly running services, **Azure Functions** allows you to run small bits of code in response to specific triggers, without managing infrastructure. These serverless functions scale automatically, execute on demand, and integrate easily with other Azure services, making them ideal for extending your application architecture with minimal overhead.

In this section, you will use Copilot in Azure to create and manage functions using natural language prompts. These prompts will help you automate common tasks that complement the `SpringToys` web application you have looked at throughout this chapter.

Automatically resize uploaded images with a function triggered by Blob Storage

User-generated content is a core feature of many modern applications, but handling and optimizing media uploads can quickly become complex. To ensure a consistent experience across devices and improve performance, it is common practice to resize images automatically after they are uploaded.

With Azure Functions, you can automate this workflow using a *Blob Storage trigger*, and with Azure Copilot, setting it up becomes much simpler. In the SpringToys app, you can use Copilot to configure a function that listens for new image uploads and generates appropriately resized thumbnails in real time.

Scenario:

Your web app now stores user-uploaded images in a container of the springtoysassets storage account. You want to automatically resize these images after upload for performance and consistency across devices. Using Azure Functions, you want to set up a Blob Storage trigger that fires each time a new image is added.

Example Copilot prompt:

Create an Azure Function in the SpringToys resource group that triggers when a new blob is added to the 'images' container in the 'springtoysassets' storage account. The function should resize the image and store it in a 'thumbnails' container.

Expected Copilot response:

Copilot in Azure generates a CLI script to do the following:

- Create a Blob-triggered function in the specified resource group
- Bind it to the container for incoming blobs
- Configure the output binding to another container for the thumbnails
- Scaffold the basic function code (*e.g., in JavaScript or C#)* for resizing logic

This task offloads compute-intensive image processing from your main application and automates it in real time. Using Copilot to configure the function reduces setup time and helps enforce best practices such as separating responsibilities and maintaining scalability.

With image processing now automated on the storage side, let us shift focus to enhancing the user experience. A common next step after user registration is to deliver immediate, personalized communication. In the next scenario, you will use Azure Functions to send a welcome email whenever a new user signs up.

Sending a welcome email for a new user

In many modern applications, delivering a smooth onboarding experience is key to user retention. A simple yet effective way to do this is by sending a personalized welcome email immediately after a new user registers. With Azure Functions, this task can be automated easily, ensuring fast, scalable, and cost-effective execution.

Let us explore how you can use Azure Copilot to help implement this functionality within your SpringToys app, starting with an *HTTP-triggered* function that sends a welcome email upon user registration.

Scenario:

As part of your SpringToys app, you have implemented user registration. Now, you want to send a personalized welcome email when a new user signs up. This can be achieved using an *HTTP-triggered* function that is called from your app's backend.

Example Copilot prompt:

Create an Azure Function in the SpringToys resource group that is triggered by an HTTP POST request and sends a welcome email to the new user using SendGrid.

Expected Copilot response:

Copilot in Azure responds with a CLI command to do the following:

- Provision an HTTP-triggered function
- Set up the required SendGrid binding or environment variables
- Scaffold code that reads the request payload and sends an email

Practical impact:

This approach helps decouple user communication logic from your main application while improving responsiveness. It also allows you to evolve or reuse the function independently. Using Copilot for setup accelerates the integration with external APIs such as SendGrid and avoids manual setup errors.

While user-triggered functions enhance engagement, many operational tasks benefit from automation as well. One such task is routine cleanup to manage storage costs and maintain system hygiene. In the next scenario, you will use a scheduled function to automatically remove outdated data from your storage account.

Cleaning up old data with a scheduled timer trigger

Over time, applications accumulate temporary or outdated data, such as logs, cache files, or media that's no longer in use. If unmanaged, this data can increase storage costs and impact performance. Automating cleanup tasks ensures your system remains efficient without requiring manual intervention. In this example, you will use a function triggered on a daily schedule to automatically delete blobs older than a set number of days.

Scenario:

To manage storage costs and maintain performance, you need to regularly clean up unused or outdated blobs (e.g., old logs, expired media). This is a perfect use case for a **timer-triggered function** that runs on a schedule.

Example Copilot prompt:

Create a timer-triggered Azure Function in the SpringToys resource group that runs once per day and deletes blobs older than 30 days from the 'logs' container in the 'springtoysassets' storage account.

Expected Copilot response:

Copilot in Azure generates a timer-based function app and does the following:

- Sets it to run daily (e.g., using a CRON expression)
- Connects it to the springtoysassets storage account
- Provides a basic function body to identify and delete old blobs

Practical impact:

Scheduled cleanup is critical for managing resource costs and maintaining a tidy environment. Timer-triggered functions allow you to automate routine maintenance tasks with zero manual effort. Copilot makes it simple to deploy these jobs without needing to script schedules or write full maintenance tools.

Now that you have extended your application with serverless automation using Azure Functions, it is time to focus on how and where your application stores data. Reliable, secure, and well-structured storage is essential for handling everything from user uploads to configuration files. In the next section, you will use Copilot in Azure to provision and manage Azure storage accounts, ensuring your app has the storage foundation it needs to operate efficiently and securely. By using natural language prompts, we can automate repetitive tasks such as provisioning storage and securing access policies with minimal manual intervention.

Using Copilot in Azure to secure storage accounts

One of the most common resources utilized in the cloud is storage. Azure storage accounts provide a scalable and secure storage solution for various scenarios. They support multiple types of storage services, including blob, file, queue, and table storage.

You could store unstructured data for your web and mobile applications using blob storage to store large amounts of unstructured data such as images, video, or audio. Moreover, storage accounts can help organizations securely store their backups and ensure redundancy. For example, financial institutions might need to back up transactional data and customer records to comply with regulatory requirements and ensure data integrity.

On the other hand, Azure files can provide managed file shares that can be accessed via **Server Message Block (SMB)** and **Network File System (NFS)** protocols to allow integration with on-premises applications. For example, universities can offer shared drives for faculties and students to enable collaboration and access to resources from any location.

Creating a new storage account for web application assets

When deploying application resources, it is important to set up reliable and secure cloud storage. Azure storage accounts provide scalable storage solutions for web apps, enabling you to store assets such as media files, configuration data, or backups. In this section, you will use Copilot in Azure to generate a CLI command that creates a new storage account using your preferred settings, helping you streamline provisioning while retaining manual oversight.

Scenario:

You are preparing to deploy a web application that will store static content such as images, documents, or configuration files. To support this, you need a dedicated Azure storage account. Rather than creating it manually through the Azure portal, you want to generate a CLI command that you can review, test, and run yourself. This approach allows you to maintain control over the deployment process while still benefiting from the speed and accuracy of Copilot in Azure.

Example Copilot prompt:

```
I need to use a new storage account for a web application. This new storage account
should be provisioned in the 'SpringToys' resource group. The name of the storage
account must be 'springtoysassets' and use local redundant storage. Create an
Azure CLI command to run to create the storage account.
```

Expected Copilot response:

Copilot in Azure responds by generating an Azure CLI command tailored to your request. The command includes the following:

- The `SpringToys` resource group

- The storage account name is `springtoysassets`

- The redundancy type is set to **Local Redundant Storage** (**LRS**)

- Placement in the appropriate Azure region (inferred or asked interactively if not specified)

Copilot does not immediately execute the command but instead provides it for review. You can copy, validate, or modify the command before manually running it, giving you full control over the provisioning process while benefiting from automation.

Practical impact:

Using natural language to provision cloud storage eliminates the need to memorize CLI syntax or search for configuration options. It streamlines setup, reduces onboarding time for new users, and enforces consistent naming and replication policies across teams.

With the storage account successfully created, the next step is to organize the data it will hold by defining logical containers for different types of content.

Creating blob containers for organizing application data

After provisioning your Azure storage account, the next logical step is to structure the data it will hold. Azure Blob Storage uses containers to organize files, making it easier to manage permissions, lifecycle policies, and access patterns. By separating different asset types, such as images and video, into their own containers, you establish a clean, scalable foundation for your application's storage layer. In this step, you will use Copilot in Azure to define and create those containers through a simple prompt.

Scenario:

Once your storage account is in place, you need to organize its contents by creating separate containers for different types of assets, such as images and videos. This helps you keep data structured and access policies more manageable. You'll use Copilot to automate this step as well.

Example Copilot prompt:

```
Create two containers in the storage account named springtoysassets. One container
named 'images' and another container named 'videos'.
```

Expected Copilot response:

Copilot in Azure generates Azure CLI commands to do the following:

- Create a blob container named images
- Create a blob container named videos

Practical impact:

Automating container creation ensures consistent naming conventions and eliminates manual steps. It allows you to quickly prepare storage for application data while reducing the chances of human error during setup.

Securing blob containers by restricting public access

Once your blob containers are created and populated, it's critical to review their access settings to ensure data security. By default, some containers may allow public access, which can expose your application's assets to unintended users. To prevent data leaks or unauthorized downloads, it's important to validate and lock down access as needed. In this step, you will use Copilot in Azure to check the current access levels of your containers and apply restrictions that limit access to trusted private endpoints only.

Scenario:

By default, blob containers may be configured for public read access, which can introduce security risks. As a best practice, you want to validate whether your containers are publicly accessible and, if so, restrict access to private endpoints only. Copilot in Azure can help assess the current state and guide you through securing access.

Example Copilot prompt:

```
Validate if these blob storage containers are publicly accessible and update the
access to allow access only from private endpoints.
```

Expected Copilot response:

Copilot performs a two-step process:

1. Audits the current access level for each container (e.g., public or private)

2. Generates the appropriate CLI commands to update access control, disabling public access, and enforcing private endpoint access only

Practical impact:

Enforcing private access to storage containers helps protect sensitive assets from unauthorized access. Copilot enables even non-experts to quickly assess and harden storage security, an essential task in production and compliance-focused environments.

With core infrastructure, application deployment, and storage security in place, you have now seen how Copilot in Azure can assist across a range of operational tasks, from provisioning to hardening. Let us now take a step back and summarize the key takeaways from this chapter.

Summary

In this chapter, you explored how Copilot in Azure enables you to manage key platform-based infrastructure services using natural language prompts, reducing the need to write or memorize complex command-line syntax. Building on foundational knowledge from previous chapters, this chapter focused on practical, real-world tasks to help you deploy and manage services such as Azure App Service, Azure Functions, and Azure storage accounts.

You began by using Copilot to provision an Azure App Service plan and deploy a Node.js web application, then configured deployment from GitHub and enabled telemetry using Application Insights. This full lifecycle workflow, from infrastructure to code deployment to monitoring, demonstrated how Copilot simplifies traditionally multi-step processes.

Next, you extended your application capabilities using Azure Functions, adding event-driven serverless components that are ideal for lightweight background processing, automation, or integration tasks. Through Copilot, you generated scripts to create and configure these functions quickly, with minimal overhead.

You also explored storage provisioning using Azure storage accounts, creating storage resources with local redundancy, adding blob containers, and applying access restrictions to ensure security and compliance. These steps showed how Copilot in Azure can help you build storage solutions that are both scalable and secure.

This chapter demonstrated how Copilot is not just a tool for simplifying tasks—it's a key enabler for modern, AI-powered cloud operations. In the next chapter, you will go even deeper by learning how to use Copilot in Azure for code suggestions and debugging, bringing AI-assisted development into your application lifecycle.

Unlock this book's exclusive benefits now

UNLOCK NOW

Scan this QR code or go to `https://packtpub.com/unlock`, then search for this book by name.

Note: Keep your purchase invoice ready before you start.

6

Improving Development Efficiency

Copilot in Azure can assist you in operating and managing your Azure resources effectively. In this context, tools such as Azure PowerShell and the Azure CLI are involved in the process of creating, updating, and deleting Azure resources. AI Shell and Copilot in Azure have been designed to improve your Azure CLI and Azure PowerShell experience by integrating AI assistance directly into your workflow. In this chapter, you will explore how these two tools can reduce the complexity of working with CLI commands.

You will also review how you can use AI Shell and Copilot in Azure so that you have a personal AI assistant integrated into your **command-line interface (CLI)** to reduce potential errors. You will also go through guided suggestions to simplify the management of your resources in Azure. This chapter will also review code suggestions and debugging features provided by Copilot in Azure and offer practical examples to reduce development time.

The chapter will help you get the most out of AI-driven tools such as AI Shell and Copilot in Azure and simplify the integration of these tools into your daily workflows. You will gain the knowledge needed to get started with AI assistance and seamlessly integrate Azure PowerShell and the Azure CLI to operate and manage your Azure resources more efficiently. This will help you simplify the creation, updating, and deletion of resources, but also enhance your development process through intelligent code suggestions.

Ultimately, the goal of this chapter is to equip you with the tools you need to improve code quality and boost your productivity.

In this chapter, you are going to cover the following main topics:

- Utilizing AI Shell and Copilot in Azure for code suggestions
- Improving code quality and development efficiency

Technical requirements

It is recommended to have access to an active Azure subscription to follow the examples that will be provided in this chapter. It is also suggested that a user with *Global Admin* permission be used in the Azure subscription.

It is recommended to have first completed *Chapter 1, Understanding Microsoft Copilot in Azure*, to set a baseline knowledge of some concepts for working with Microsoft Copilot in Azure, as well as completing *Chapter 2, Getting Started with Microsoft Copilot in Azure*, and *Chapter 3, Managing Access to Microsoft Copilot in Azure*, so that you are aware of how to use the Azure portal to access Microsoft Copilot in Azure as well as understand access management.

When prompting, the guidance is to be very specific with the phrases and words used to articulate the desired output. The more specific and concise you can be in the prompt, the better results you will get in the response. As of the time of publishing, Copilot in Azure has a *500-character limit* per prompt; therefore, you need to be thoughtful about how you write your prompts to maximize value and achieve the desired output.

> You will still always need to manually review the code generated by AI and potentially modify the output to be able to complete the task or operation on the resource type.
>
> Outputs or code generated by AI may not be fully accurate or functional.

Utilizing Copilot in Azure and AI Shell for code suggestions

AI Shell is a command-line tool that directly connects you with different AI assistants in your console to accelerate your workflow when using the Azure CLI, Azure PowerShell, or any commands you might need help with. AI Shell can connect you with AI assistants to help you generate the commands you need to achieve specific tasks. It understands the context of your code and can provide intelligent suggestions, from a single line of code to entire blocks.

For example, when you start by typing a function or a code block, Copilot will analyze the context and predict what you intend to implement. When you write a comment such as `//commands to create a Linux VM`, Copilot will suggest the entire implementation. These types of suggestions are helpful for routine coding tasks and will allow you to focus on more complex aspects of the project. You can also get suggestions on how to adhere to coding standards and style guidelines. More importantly, the immediate benefit of this integration is that you will have a second pair of eyes catching potential syntax errors or mistakes before they become issues.

That said, let us go ahead and install AI Shell in the next subsection.

Installing AI Shell

To get started, you need to install AI Shell, which can be integrated with Windows Terminal and iTerm2 on macOS. You will utilize Windows Terminal for the following examples.

You can install AI Shell by following these instructions:

1. Open PowerShell (*7.4.6 or higher*).
2. Run the following script:

```
Invoke-Expression "& { $(Invoke-RestMethod 'https://aka.ms/install-aishell.ps1') }"
```

Instructions on how to install manually, and further reference information and system requirements can be found at `https://learn.microsoft.com/en-us/powershell/utility-modules/aishell/install-aishell`.

> To be clear on terminology, this document will refer to an *agent* as an AI assistant, and vice versa. Version one of the AI Shell release can be integrated with two agents: Azure OpenAI with GPT-4o and the Copilot in Azure agent.

Once you have successfully installed AI Shell, you should see a welcome message, as shown in *Figure 6.1*:

```
AI Shell
1.0.0-preview.1

Welcome to AI Shell! We're excited to have you explore our Public Preview. Documentation is available at
aka.ms/AIShell-Docs, and we'd love to hear your thoughts — share your feedback with us at aka.ms/AIShell-Feedback.

Please select an AI agent to use:
(You can switch to another agent later by typing @<agent name>)

> openai-gpt
  azure
```

Figure 6.1 – AI Shell welcome message

🔍 **Quick tip**: Need to see a high-resolution version of this image? Open this book in the next-gen Packt Reader or view it in the PDF/ePub copy.

📕 **The next-gen Packt Reader** is included for free with the purchase of this book. Scan the QR code OR go to `packtpub.com/unlock`, then use the search bar to find this book by name. Double-check the edition shown to make sure you get the right one.

When you start AI Shell, you will see that there are two agents you can work with:

- Azure OpenAI with GPT-4o
- Copilot in Azure

Once you close your Windows Terminal session, the next time you open it, you can run the `Start-AIShell` command to work with AI Shell, which will trigger the AI Shell console, as shown in *Figure 6.2*:

Figure 6.2 – AI Shell console

Once you start your AI Shell console and select the Azure agent, the authentication and authorization process for Copilot in Azure will automatically start.

You will see the welcome message to Copilot in Azure a few seconds later, as shown in *Figure 6.3*:

```
AI Shell
1.0.0-preview.1

Using the agent azure:
This AI assistant connects you to the Copilot
in Azure and can generate Azure CLI and Azure
PowerShell commands for managing Azure
resources and answer questions about Azure.

Try one of these sample queries:

  "How do I create a resource group?"
  "Help me create a storage account"

Terms | Privacy | FAQ | Transparency

Run /help for more instructions.

Welcome to Microsoft Azure Copilot. Here are a
few things you should know before getting start
ed.
Any action taken on more than 10 resources must
 be performed outside of Copilot. While in limi
ted public preview you can only make 15 request
s during any given chat and you only have 10 ch
ats in a 8 hour period. This is chat #2.

AI Generated content may be incorrect.

@azure> |
```

Figure 6.3 – AI Shell with Copilot in Azure

Now, you can start using AI Shell with Copilot in Azure. You will begin by looking at how you can get code suggestions to create an Azure **virtual machine** (**VM**) using natural language.

Getting code suggestions to create an Azure Windows VM

When utilizing natural language in AI Shell with Copilot in Azure to create an Azure VM, our main goal is to see how you can get code suggestions right in the CLI. You can use the following prompt in AI Shell with Copilot in Azure to generate the code that creates the Azure VM:

Suggest the code for a Bicep file that creates a low-cost Windows VM named 'mylowcostvm' in the "SpringToys" resource group in EastUS. Use Windows Server 2022 Datacenter as the OS. Configure it with 2 data disks and connect them to the "springtoys-vnet-eus" virtual network in the frontend subnet. Use availability zones for HA, expose port 80, and enable boot diagnostics in a new storage account named "springtoysvmlogs4." Add an "environment" tag with "dev" as the value and assign a Public IP to the VM.

After a few seconds, you should see in the output that AI Shell with Copilot in Azure provides the Bicep file with the code to create the Azure VM, as shown in *Figure 6.4*:

```
@azure> Suggest the code for a Bicep file that creates a
low-cost Windows VM named 'mylowcostvm' in the "SpringToy
s" resource group in EastUS. Use Windows Server 2022 Data
center as the OS. Configure it with 2 data disks and conn
ect them to the "springtoys-vnet-eus" virtual network in
the frontend subnet. Use availability zones for HA, expos
e port 80, and enable boot diagnostics in a new storage a
ccount named "springtoysvmlogs4." Add an "environment" ta
g with "dev" as the value and assign a Public IP to the V
M.

    param adminUsername string
    param adminPassword string

    resource storageAccount 'Microsoft.Storage/storageAcc
ounts@2021-04-01' = {
        name: 'springtoysvmlogs4'
        location: 'East US'
        sku: {
          name: 'Standard_LRS'
        }
        kind: 'StorageV2'
    }

    resource virtualNetwork 'Microsoft.Network/virtualNet
works@2020-06-01' existing = {
        name: 'springtoys-vnet-eus'
        location: 'East US'
    }

    resource frontendSubnet 'Microsoft.Network/virtualNet
works/subnets@2020-06-01' existing = {
        parent: virtualNetwork
        name: 'frontend'
    }

    resource publicIP 'Microsoft.Network/publicIPAddresse
s@2020-06-01' = {
        name: 'myPublicIP'
        location: 'East US'
        properties: {
          publicIPAllocationMethod: 'Dynamic'
        }
    }

    resource networkInterface 'Microsoft.Network/networkI
nterfaces@2020-06-01' = {
        name: 'myNIC'
        location: 'East US'
        properties: {
          ipConfigurations: [
            {
              name: 'myIPConfig'
              properties: {
                subnet: {
                  id: frontendSubnet.id
                }
                publicIPAddress: {
                  id: publicIP.id
                }
              }
            }
          ]
        }
    }
```

Figure 6.4 – AI Shell with Copilot in Azure output

The complete Bicep file that creates the Azure VM that AI Shell generated with Copilot in Azure can be found in the GitHub repository at https://github.com/PacktPublishing/Microsoft-Copilot-in-Azure/blob/main/Chapter6-AIShell-generatedcodeexample-createAzurevirtualmachine.txt.

The code suggestion from AI Shell with Copilot in Azure is particularly helpful in speeding up the workflow and management of your Azure resources using natural language.

You can also utilize AI Shell with Copilot in Azure to ensure you have the correct syntax for Azure CLI or Azure PowerShell.

Using AI Shell with Copilot in Azure to create a Linux VM

AI Shell is also helpful in simplifying the process of using the Azure CLI or Azure PowerShell to create, update, or delete resources. For example, you can use the following prompt to create a Linux VM:

Suggest the CLI commands to create a low-cost Linux VM named 'myLinuxVm' in the "SpringToys" resource group in EastUS. Use Ubuntu Server 24.04 LTS as the OS. Configure 2 data disks and connect the VM to the "springtoys-vnet-eus" virtual network in the frontend subnet. Use availability zones for HA, expose port 80, and enable boot diagnostics in a new storage account named "springtoysvmlogs5." Add an "environment" tag with "dev" as the value and assign a Public IP to the VM. Suggest secure credentials.

This prompt should output the correct CLI commands and reduce potential manual errors when creating an Azure Linux VM. This will output the CLI command set to create the Azure Linux VM. This is the code generated by AI Shell with Copilot in Azure:

```
# Create a new storage account for boot diagnostics
    az storage account create --name springtoysvmlogs5 --resource-group
SpringToys --location EastUS --sku Standard_LRS


    # Create a public IP address
    az network public-ip create --resource-group SpringToys --name
myPublicIP --location EastUS


    # Create a network interface
    az network nic create --resource-group SpringToys --name myNIC --vnet-
name springtoys-vnet-eus --subnet frontend --public-ip-address myPublicIP
--location EastUS


    # Create a network security group and a rule to allow port 80
    az network nsg create --resource-group SpringToys --name myNSG
```

```
--location EastUS
    az network nsg rule create --resource-group SpringToys --nsg-name
myNSG --name Allow-HTTP --protocol tcp --priority 1000 --destination-port-
range 80 --access allow

    # Associate the network security group with the network interface
    az network nic update --resource-group SpringToys --name myNIC
--network-security-group myNSG

    # Create the VM with 2 data disks, availability zone, and boot
diagnostics enabled
    az vm create --resource-group SpringToys --name myLinuxVm --image
UbuntuLTS --size Standard_B1s --admin-username <adminUsername>
--admin-password <adminPassword> --nics myNIC --zone 1 --os-disk-name
myLinuxVmOSDisk --data-disk-sizes-gb 1024 1024 --boot-diagnostics-storage
springtoysvmlogs5 --tags environment=dev

    # Open port 80 to allow web traffic
    az vm open-port --port 80 --resource-group SpringToys --name myLinuxVm

  Replace the placeholders with your specific values:
  •   <adminUsername> : Admin username for the VM
  •   <adminPassword> : Admin password for the VM

  Run  /replace to get assistance in placeholder replacement.
```

AI Shell will also provide placeholders, such as adminUsername and adminPassword, that you might need to tailor based on the current scenario.

AI Shell has its own commands to help you simplify the way you interact with the agent. You can find the list of current commands at https://learn.microsoft.com/en-us/powershell/utility-modules/aishell/how-to/aishell-reference.

You have reviewed how you can utilize AI Shell with Copilot in Azure to get code suggestions, and now it is time to explore additional capabilities, including how you can improve code quality and development efficiency.

> 💡 **Quick tip**: Enhance your coding experience with the **AI Code Explainer** and **Quick Copy** features. Open this book in the next-gen Packt Reader. Click the **Copy** button
>
> **(1)** to quickly copy code into your coding environment, or click the **Explain** button
>
> **(2)** to get the AI assistant to explain a block of code to you.

```
                                                    Copy      Explain
function calculate(a, b) {                           1          2
    return {sum: a + b};
};
```

🔖 **The next-gen Packt Reader** is included for free with the purchase of this book. Scan the QR code OR visit packtpub.com/unlock, then use the search bar to find this book by name. Double-check the edition shown to make sure you get the right one.

Improving code quality and development efficiency

Consider the scenario where you need to create a new application that will run on top of a VM, and you will utilize Azure Key Vault to store secrets. You will deploy these resources in a new resource group. This means that you need to create a new resource group, a key vault, and a VM with specific configurations.

Typically, you could use various tools such as the Azure portal to create these resources, or the Azure CLI, Azure PowerShell, ARM templates, or Bicep files. Most of the time, when you use the Azure CLI or Azure PowerShell, you have to switch to multiple browser tabs to recall the correct CLI syntax or the latest recommended parameters. You can leverage AI Shell with Copilot in Azure to improve code quality and be more efficient when developing solutions for Azure. Let us explore how AI Shell with Copilot in Azure can help us develop our solutions in Azure more efficiently.

In our scenario, you can start AI Shell:

1. The first step is to ask how you can create a resource group in the Azure CLI. You can use the following prompt:

    ```
    How do I create a new resource group in Azure CLI?
    ```

    AI Shell will send this request to the Copilot in Azure agent and return a relevant CLI command, as shown in *Figure 6.5*:

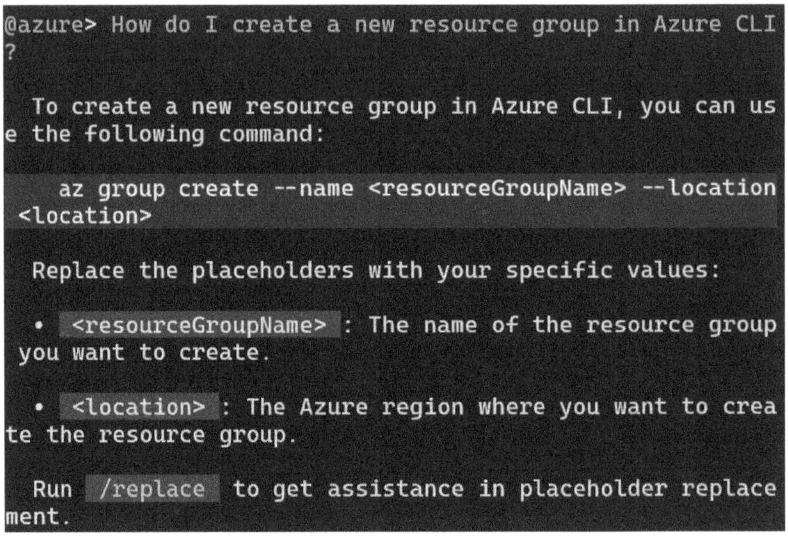

Figure 6.5 – AI Shell with Copilot in Azure prompt to create a resource group

2. Now, you can just use the /replace option to get assistance and fill in the parameters interactively.

3. Next, you need to create a new key vault in the resource group you just created.

    Instead of memorizing the command to create the Key Vault instance, you can ask AI Shell with Copilot in Azure using the following prompt:

    ```
    How do I create an Azure Key Vault in the 'SpringToys' resource group and enable soft delete?
    ```

    Figure 6.6 shows the response of AI Shell with Copilot in Azure, which provides the CLI commands to create the key vault:

```
@azure> How do I create an Azure Key Vault in the 'Spring
Toys' resource group and enable soft delete?

 To create an Azure Key Vault in the 'SpringToys' resour
ce group and enable soft delete, you can use the followin
g command:

    az keyvault create --name <keyVaultName> --resource-g
roup SpringToys --enable-soft-delete --retention-days 90

 Replace the placeholders with your specific values:

 •  <keyVaultName> : The name of the Key Vault you want
to create.

 Run  /replace  to get assistance in placeholder replace
ment.
```

Figure 6.6 – Creating a key vault using AI Shell with Copilot in Azure

Now, you have created the resource group and the Key Vault instance.

4. The next step is to create the VM. More often than not, the creation of VMs is prone to errors due to syntax. In this scenario, you can just write a comment in AI Shell as follows:

I want to create a Linux VM with Ubuntu 24.10, and I need a public IP. How do I do that with az vm create?

Copilot in Azure will respond with a detailed suggestion, as shown in *Figure 6.7*:

```
@azure> I want to create a Linux VM with Ubuntu 24.10, an
d I need a public IP. How do I do that with az vm create?

 To create a Linux VM with Ubuntu 24.10 and a public IP
using  az vm create , you can use the following command:

    az vm create --resource-group <resourceGroupName> --n
ame <vmName> --image Ubuntu:24.10 --admin-username <admin
Username> --generate-ssh-keys --size <vmSize> --public-ip
-address <publicIpName>

 Replace the placeholders with your specific values:

 •  <resourceGroupName> : The name of the resource group
 where the VM will be created.

 •  <vmName> : The name of the virtual machine.

 •  <adminUsername> : The admin username for the VM.

 •  <vmSize> : The size of the virtual machine.

 •  <publicIpName> : The name of the public IP address t
o be assigned to the VM.

 Run  /replace  to get assistance in placeholder replace
ment.
```

Figure 6.7 – AI Shell with Copilot in Azure response

The response includes the CLI command to create the VM and recommended parameters to create this resource type.

5. Similarly to the previous prompts, you can interactively use the /replace option to get assistance and fill in the parameters.

As demonstrated in the previous example, AI Shell with Copilot in Azure can make your workflow more consistent and rely less on trial-and-error or external documentation lookups.

Summary

In this chapter, you explored how AI Shell integration with the Copilot in Azure agent can significantly enhance your development process, helping you write code in less time and leading to a more efficient and reliable manner of deploying your solution in Azure.

You reviewed in detail how you could utilize these tools to get code suggestions, including infrastructure such as code with the Bicep language, and an example of getting suggestions for an Azure CLI deployment.

You also saw how you can leverage AI Shell with Copilot in Azure to improve code quality and become more efficient when developing your solution in Azure.

In the next chapter, you will look at how you can utilize Copilot in Azure for advanced data management.

7

Advanced Data Management with Microsoft Copilot in Azure

In this chapter, we will explore the use cases of **Microsoft Copilot in Azure** to enhance data management for **Azure Database for MySQL** and **Azure SQL Database**. This chapter will guide you on how Microsoft Copilot in Azure can offer insights for optimizing data performance.

Regarding the Azure **Well-Architected Framework (WAF)**, this chapter maps to the **security**, **operational excellence**, and **performance efficiency** pillars.

By mastering these skills, you will gain the ability to make database management more efficient, smarter, and proactive. By integrating Microsoft Copilot in Azure into your workflow, you can automate and optimize the most essential and crucial tasks, decreasing manual effort and allowing you to focus on strategic initiatives.

Through practical, prompt examples, you will learn how to apply AI-driven insight to speed up database performance, resulting in faster, more responsive applications and services. This chapter aims to impart technical and strategic competence in using AI to enable data performance, the basis of data management in a dynamic world.

In this chapter, we will cover the following main topics:

- Unlocking the benefits of Azure Database for MySQL and Azure SQL Database
- Data optimization and performance tuning with AI-driven insights
- Practical examples of data management and optimization

Technical requirements

It is recommended to have access to an active Azure subscription to follow the examples provided in this chapter.

It is recommended to have first completed *Chapter 1, Understanding Microsoft Copilot in Azure,* to set a baseline knowledge of some concepts for working with Microsoft Copilot in Azure, as well as completing *Chapter 2, Getting Started with Microsoft Copilot in Azure*, so that you are aware of how to use the Azure portal to access Microsoft Copilot in Azure.

When prompting, the guidance is to be very specific with the phrases and words used to articulate the desired output. The more specific and concise you can be in the prompt, the better results you will get in the response. As of the time of publishing, Copilot in Azure has a *500-character limit* per prompt; therefore, you need to be thoughtful about how you write your prompts to maximize value and achieve the desired output.

Ensure you have the appropriate *Azure role assignments* for any resources you are investigating, as Copilot can only operate within the scope of your existing permissions and cannot grant access to data or services you are not already authorized to use. Additionally, some services must be explicitly enabled to provide data or surface relevant insights to Copilot. For example, for the use of **Azure Monitor Investigator** by Copilot, this does not need to be *enabled manually*; it is built into Azure Monitor and becomes available automatically when your resources are sending telemetry data, such as logs and metrics. However, Azure Monitor monitored resources must have diagnostic settings configured to send telemetry (such as logs and metrics) to a **Log Analytics workspace** for Investigator to surface relevant insights.

> You will still always need to manually review the code generated by AI and potentially modify the output to be able to complete the task or operation on the resource type. Outputs or code generated by AI may not be fully accurate or functional.

Unlocking the benefits of Azure Database for MySQL and Azure SQL Database

Data is central to business functions today in the modern digital world. Managing your database solutions is essential, as this is where we store and manage our most critical data and paths to retrieve it for customer interactions and real-time analytics.

However, managing Azure Database for MySQL and Azure SQL Database can be quite complex and consumes lots of human resource time, so people must constantly watch and handhold these cloud-based data services to achieve the best operational efficiency, performance, security, and cost optimization.

This is where Microsoft Copilot in Azure comes into play as an *intelligent assistant* to help **database administrators (DBAs)** streamline their activities and processes. Leveraging the Microsoft cloud services platform to empower user experience using **artificial intelligence (AI)** assistance is the essence of Microsoft Copilot in Azure.

Microsoft Copilot in Azure uses sophisticated AI capabilities to accelerate the capabilities to manage resources more efficiently and optimize cloud operations. Integrating smoothly into the Azure ecosystem, Microsoft Copilot in Azure provides context-aware suggestions, automates repetitive tasks, and improves data professionals' overall productivity and efficiency.

Moreover, Copilot's capabilities extend beyond simple task automation. The tool harnesses advanced analytics to deliver deeper insights into usage patterns, resource allocation, and performance metrics, empowering organizations to make informed decisions that enhance efficiency and scalability. This is particularly crucial in dynamic business environments, where adaptability and speed are essential for maintaining a competitive edge.

The monitoring and remediation of database health is one of the big benefits of Copilot's AI capabilities. The insights and proactive recommendation actions, which include things such as potential resource bottlenecks as well as security vulnerabilities, are provided in real time by Copilot. For example, if you have a MySQL or SQL instance under the weight of heavy CPU usage or slowing queries, Copilot will offer specific steps to mitigate those issues.

In addition to improving operational efficiency, organizations must protect the database from external digital threats and optimize its performance. Microsoft Copilot in Azure can also be utilized in this security area; it aids in ensuring compliance and security within Azure environments.

By facilitating automated reporting, organizations are better equipped to adhere to regulatory requirements and best practices, reducing the risk of data breaches and ensuring data integrity. It also offers AI-generated security recommendations, such as finding potential database configuration weaknesses or vulnerabilities that need patching.

As you continue to explore the transformative capabilities of Copilot, it becomes evident that this integration is not just about optimizing existing workflows but redefining the entire data management paradigm. Organizations can now harness the power of AI to drive smarter, faster decision-making while fostering an environment that promotes innovation and growth in the cloud.

With Microsoft Copilot in Azure, **AI-powered automation** is at the forefront of database management, freeing administrators from repetitive tasks.

As with self-driving cars, Microsoft Copilot for Azure will take some of the mundane tasks away from the driver's control; this can mean Copilot can be asked to perform many common database management tasks, such as the following:

- **Backup and restore processes**: Microsoft **Copilot in Azure** can suggest the best timing and configuration to ensure your data is secure and up to date during optimal Windows.

- **Data archiving and retention:** Aside from managing active data, **Microsoft Copilot in Azure** can also help manage the data lifecycle by automatically detecting data eligible for data archival (based on age, usage frequency, etc.). In cases where data access patterns indicate infrequent use, Copilot can analyze and propose retention policies for infrequently accessed data that result in cost-optimized storage costs, reducing database load while not compromising data deliverability for compliance or auditing purposes.

- **Scaling operations: Microsoft Copilot in Azure** can assist where resources such as Azure Database for MySQL and Azure SQL Databases instances are dynamically scaled up or down, not over-provisioned, or result in performance degradation, to make sure that your resources are always the right size for the work that's required.

- **Routine updates and patch management**: Keeping databases secure means being on top of updates and patches. Microsoft Copilot in Azure keeps databases secure and up to date with as little disruption as possible by recommending the best maintenance window. This provides DBAs with routine updates and patch management through reliable, robust, and controlled mechanisms, ensuring the database's protection against the latest vulnerabilities without interrupting ongoing operations.

All these examples dramatically cut down on manual intervention and minimize human error, freeing teams up to focus on more strategic work.

In this section, you looked at how Microsoft Copilot in Azure changes how data is managed and optimized for Azure Database for MySQL and Azure SQL Database through AI-provided insights. Adopting Microsoft Copilot for Azure for your database management strategy allows you to unlock new efficiency, safety, and performance levels with your cloud databases and deliver more value. The future of cloud-based data management is bright, and with tools such as Microsoft Copilot, organizations can confidently navigate this new frontier.

In the following section, you'll discover how Microsoft Copilot in Azure can extend data optimization and performance tuning for Azure Database for MySQL and Azure SQL Database. Using AI-powered insights, Copilot helps identify and make recommendations for improving database efficiency, decreasing query response times, and optimizing resource utilization.

Data optimization and performance tuning with AI-driven insights

Database performance is critical to business success in today's fast-paced digital world. The speed and efficiency of the underlying database that powers it can be impacted every time a customer completes a transaction, a student studies online learning materials, or an enterprise runs real-time analytics. A well-optimized database can speed up your query responses, have zero impact on its application functionality, reduce resource consumption, and improve operational efficiency.

Query performance is made faster because of indexes; however, it is cumbersome for DBAs to maintain indexes manually. Database performance tuning with traditional approaches can be tiresome—manually changing everything, needing deep technical knowledge, and never knowing when your optimizations are no longer working. Here's where Microsoft Copilot in Azure comes in. While features such as automatic tuning already exist in Azure SQL, Copilot in Azure simplifies and surfaces these capabilities through an AI-driven interface, making them more accessible and integrated into daily workflows. Much like a traffic navigation system with traffic information insights to offer optimized routes, Microsoft Copilot in Azure analyzes your database state and delivers AI-driven insights to optimize data processing.

Based on usage patterns, Microsoft Copilot in Azure can automatically create, remove, or reorganize indexes so queries can run faster, databases stay optimized, and there's no need for manual intervention. Copilot can monitor and resolve routine tasks like index maintenance, query performance tuning, and so on.

In this section, we'll learn how Microsoft Copilot in Azure facilitates businesses in optimizing database performance for Azure Database for MySQL and Azure SQL Database by using advanced AI-driven techniques. Copilot intelligently optimizes queries to tune database configuration, and with performance prediction, it tells you where the performance bottlenecks will show up and what to do about them.

The following areas for database optimization and tuning will be outlined:

- **AI-powered query optimization**: Enhancing database efficiency. Using Copilot, you can rewrite inefficient queries, simplify execution plans, and decrease the demand on the database by putting less strain on it and removing useless data.
- **Index optimization**: Enhancing data retrieval speed. By drawing from its real-time query patterns, Copilot dynamically adapts to the indexing strategies used to retrieve data as quickly and efficiently as possible.
- **Query execution plan optimization**: Streamlining performance. Copilot continuously analyzes the execution plans and suggests using the most efficient plans or freezes proven plans as soon as possible.
- **Predictive performance tuning**: AI-driven insights. Copilot leverages AI-driven insights into potential problems in the future with recommendations that predict slowdowns and help maintain databases operating efficiently.

Each of these areas is explored in the following sections.

AI-powered query optimization

The **query** is at the foundation of every database operation; this is the command that gets and manipulates data. Consequently, complex queries that are poorly written can have a performance impact on the databases, which causes delays in critical business operations. Microsoft Copilot for Azure provides AI-driven query optimization, allowing databases to deal with complex and large queries quickly and efficiently.

Microsoft Copilot for Azure can provide intelligent query rewrite suggestions. In the same way that a road traffic app can recommend optimal routes by checking the current road conditions, Copilot continuously reviews query execution plans and recommends rewriting inefficient queries, then suggests how the query might be suboptimal (for example, unnecessary joins or poorly designed filters) and where you can refactor the query.

Copilot can identify and eliminate redundant queries, potentially detecting unnecessary or repetitive queries that burden the system. By recommending query consolidation or caching strategies, Copilot ensures efficient resource utilization, preventing the database from repeatedly fetching identical information.

Next, consider an example where Azure SQL Database experiences slowdowns during high-traffic periods, especially when running product search queries.

Copilot identifies that many of these queries involve complex **joins** (a method to combine rows from two or more tables based on a related column between them) across multiple tables, which impact overall performance. It suggests rewriting these queries to streamline the joins (optimize the process of combining rows from multiple tables to improve query efficiency and performance) and filters, improving response times for search results. Consequently, customers receive faster search results, even during peak times such as Black Friday sales.

Now that you have understood *query optimization*, the next section looks at *index optimization*.

Index optimization

Indexes serve as the table of contents in a book—without them, locating specific information requires more time as the system must search through all available data. While indexing is essential for efficient data retrieval, manually managing indexes can be arduous. An excessive number of indexes or poorly designed ones can degrade performance instead of enhancing it. Microsoft Copilot in Azure mitigates these issues by consistently analyzing query patterns and dynamically optimizing indexes to align with the current workload.

While automatic tuning in Azure SQL is AI-based and works autonomously, Copilot in Azure complements it by offering a more transparent and conversational way to access performance tuning insights. This makes index optimization more accessible to a wider range of users, especially those without deep database expertise.

Microsoft Copilot in Azure uses **usage-based indexing**, which can provide dynamic index creation and removal. Like how a librarian updates a library's catalog to continually improve how books can be found by those requesting access, Copilot adjusts the indexes in a database. When a new query pattern becomes frequent, Copilot creates new indexes to support it, thereby speeding up data retrieval. Conversely, if certain indexes are no longer used or are impacting write operations, Copilot will suggest their removal.

An example could be a media streaming service utilizing Azure Database for MySQL to frequently expand its content catalog. As user behavior evolves and new content categories are introduced, Copilot detects shifts in query patterns, particularly as users start filtering content by genre, release year, and ratings. By dynamically generating new indexes to support these queries, Copilot ensures that users can efficiently locate and stream their desired content, even as the database continues to scale.

With index optimization explained in this section, you will explore optimization for an execution plan.

Query execution plan optimization

Efficient query execution is a crucial element in database performance. When a query is executed, the database engine generates an execution plan, which serves as a blueprint for retrieving the required data. However, execution plans can vary significantly in their effectiveness. The query's complexity, the data's structure, and the presence of indexes all influence the quality of the execution plan. A suboptimal execution plan can markedly diminish performance.

Microsoft Copilot in Azure assists your database, like a personal trainer or coach, continuously monitoring its performance under various workloads and providing recommendations to enhance execution plans.

Similar to how an athlete enhances performance through consistent training and adjustments in regime, Copilot methodically analyzes query execution plans and proposes adjustments to optimize performance. It identifies instances where the database may select suboptimal plans and automatically refines the execution strategy to reduce resource consumption and enhance speed.

Copilot may suggest utilizing **parallel execution plans** to optimize available CPU cores. This approach enables large queries to be divided into smaller tasks that can be executed simultaneously, enhancing overall query performance.

In situations where a specific execution plan has been identified as optimal for a frequently run query, it is possible to recommend freezing that plan to maintain consistent performance. However, if there are changes in database structure or workload, adjustments can be made to unfreeze and modify plans as necessary.

Consider the following real-world use case: A global logistics company using Azure SQL Database performs complex queries to track shipments, predict delivery times, and optimize routes. These queries include large datasets with multiple joins and filters.

Microsoft Copilot in Azure reviews the execution plans for these queries and suggests adjustments, such as enabling parallel query execution to use available CPU resources more effectively. This leads to faster reporting times and more efficient decision-making, particularly during peak seasons when shipment volumes are highest.

In this section, you learned about query execution plan optimization, which you will now follow by exploring predictive performance tuning.

Predictive performance tuning

Microsoft Copilot in Azure includes a feature that can predict potential performance issues before they occur. Instead of waiting for a database to slow down or fail, Copilot uses machine learning models to analyze historical performance data and identify when and where problems might arise, identifying bottlenecks before they happen.

Copilot can provide **workload forecasting**, which uses AI to predict when workloads will spike based on previous activity patterns, helping DBAs prepare for resource-intensive periods by tuning queries or adjusting settings beforehand.

Similar to how weather applications utilize historical and real-time data to anticipate imminent weather conditions, Copilot evaluates workload trends and database metrics to predict potential bottlenecks. Copilot will notify DBAs and recommend proactive optimizations if a query requires more time than anticipated due to increased data volume or complex logic.

Consider the following real-world use case: A global retail chain utilizing Azure Database for MySQL anticipates substantial database traffic during the holiday season. Instead of addressing slowdowns after they occur, Microsoft Copilot in Azure leverages historical holiday traffic data to forecast potential bottlenecks. It provides recommendations for optimizing frequently executed queries and adjusting index strategies to manage the increase in activity. Consequently, the company maintains smooth performance during peak shopping days, avoiding the necessity for emergency interventions.

In this section, you went through how Microsoft Copilot in Azure optimizes database performance for Azure Database for MySQL and Azure SQL Database using AI-driven insights, dynamic tuning, and predictive tuning. These AI-driven capabilities allow organizations to guarantee database performance, even as workloads change or data volumes, velocity, and variety grow.

In summary, the key takeaways from this section include the following:

- **AI-powered query optimization**: Copilot assists in rewriting suboptimal queries, streamlining execution plans, and reducing database load by eliminating redundancy and optimizing resource utilization.

- **Index optimization**: Copilot adjusts indexing strategies in real-time based on query patterns to ensure quick and efficient data retrieval.

- **Execution plan optimization**: By regularly analyzing execution plans, Copilot identifies the most efficient options. It suggests parallel execution or maintains stable plans when appropriate.

- **Predictive performance tuning**: Copilot uses AI to foresee performance issues and offers preemptive recommendations, helping businesses maintain optimal database performance.

In the next section, you will see practical use cases where Microsoft Copilot in Azure can simplify the management and optimization of Azure Database for MySQL and Azure SQL Database. You'll learn how Copilot's AI-driven insights and automation help optimize database performance and simplify complex tasks using real-world scenarios.

Practical examples of data management and optimization

With deep integration with Azure, Microsoft Copilot allows database management to be automated by completing routine tasks in real time and providing proactive suggestions on performance, security, and cost optimization. With the help of machine learning and AI, Copilot frees DBAs and DevOps teams from spending their time on low-level operations, which are both time-consuming and prone to human error, enabling them to ideate and strategize at a larger scale.

In this section, you will explore how Microsoft Copilot in Azure can assist with database management processes for Azure Database for MySQL and Azure SQL Database. These examples demonstrate that Copilot can quickly and reliably perform complex and mundane tasks using AI-driven prompts, enabling more efficient and consistent operations.

The following management process areas will be covered:

- Backup and recovery
- Patch management and version upgrades
- Data archiving and retention
- Data integrity checks
- Performance optimization
- Index and statistics management
- Security and compliance

> Make sure to make these prompts your own by replacing them with the actual values from your environment, or experiment and tailor the prompts in a way to meet your needs.

Now, let's move on to the prompting examples for Microsoft Copilot in Azure for data management.

Backup and recovery

In this section, you will see how Microsoft Copilot in Azure can assist in backup and recovery processes for Azure Database for MySQL and Azure SQL Database, resulting in more robust and efficient database management.

Prompt example 1

In this prompt example, the user asks Copilot to review their Azure SQL Database backup schedule and can recommend how recovery objectives could be improved:

- **Copilot prompt:** Can you review my current backup schedule for Azure SQL Database and suggest optimizations for better RPO and RTO?
- **Copilot output:** Analyzing current backup frequency and retention policies, dependent on your resources deployment, Copilot may make recommendations for improvement—such as increasing backup frequency or moving backups to geo-redundant storage for disaster recovery—based on workload patterns and will adjust backup frequency to lower **recovery point objective (RPO)** and lower **recovery time objective (RTO)**.

The following illustration provides an example output based on the Azure SQL resources deployed in this demo environment; your output may differ:

Can you review my current backup schedule for Azure SQL Database and suggest optimizations for better RPO and RTO?

Copilot AI generated content may be incorrect

To optimize your backup schedule for better Recovery Point Objective (RPO) and Recovery Time Objective (RTO) in Azure SQL Database, consider the following points:
Backup Scheduling

- **Initial Full Backup**: The first full backup is scheduled immediately after a new database is created or restored. This backup usually finishes within 30 minutes but can take longer for larger databases.
- **Subsequent Backups**: After the initial full backup, all further backups are scheduled and managed automatically. The exact timing of all database backups is determined by the SQL Database service as it balances the overall system workload. You cannot change the schedule of backup jobs or disable them.

Short-term Retention

- **Point-in-Time Restore (PITR)**: Azure SQL Database retains sufficient backups to allow PITR within the last 7 days by default. You can change the backup retention period for each active database in the range of 1 to 35 days, except for Basic databases, which are configurable from 1 to 7 days.
- **Differential Backups**: Differential backups can be configured to occur either once in 12 hours or once in 24 hours. A 24-hour differential backup frequency might increase the time required to restore the database compared to the 12-hour frequency. In the vCore model, the default frequency for differential backups is once in 12 hours. In the DTU model, the default frequency is once in 24 hours.

Long-term Retention

- **LTR Backups**: You can configure full long-term retention (LTR) backups for up to 10 years in Azure Blob Storage. After the LTR policy is configured, full backups are automatically copied to a different storage container weekly. You can select different retention periods for weekly, monthly, and/or yearly full backups.

Optimizations for Better RPO and RTO

- **Increase Differential Backup Frequency**: If you are using the DTU model, consider switching to the vCore model to benefit from a more frequent differential backup schedule (every 12 hours).
- **Enable Zone Redundancy**: Enable zone redundancy for the database or elastic pool to ensure resiliency for zonal failures.
- **Use Failover Groups**: Enable failover groups for a group of databases to ensure continuous data synchronization and automatic failover in case of a regional outage.
- **Active Geo-Replication**: Alternatively, enable active geo-replication to have a readable secondary database in a different Azure region.
- **Monitor Replication Lag**: Use the replication_lag_sec column of the sys.dm_geo_replication_link_status dynamic management view (DMV) on the primary database to monitor lag with respect to RPO.
- **Geo-Redundant Backup Storage**: If failover groups or active geo-replication are not possible, consider setting the backup storage redundancy option to geo-redundant backup storage to use geo-restore.

Additional Tips

- **Reduce Backup Retention Period**: Reduce the backup retention period to the minimum for your needs to save on backup storage costs.
- **Clustered Columnstore Indexes**: For large data load operations, consider using clustered columnstore indexes and following related best practices.
- **Use tempdb**: Use tempdb instead of permanent tables in your application logic for storing temporary results or transient data.
- **Locally Redundant Backup Storage**: Use locally redundant backup storage whenever possible (for example, dev/test environments).

References

- Automated Backups Overview
- Change Short-term Retention Policy
- Long-term Retention Overview
- High Availability and Disaster Recovery Checklist

By implementing these optimizations, you can achieve better RPO and RTO for your Azure SQL Database.

Figure 7.1 – Backup prompt example

🔍 **Quick tip:** Need to see a high-resolution version of this image? Open this book in the next-gen Packt Reader or view it in the PDF/ePub copy.

📖 **The next-gen Packt Reader** is included for free with the purchase of this book. Scan the QR code OR go to `packtpub.com/unlock`, then use the search bar to find this book by name. Double-check the edition shown to make sure you get the right one.

Prompt example 2

In this prompt example, the user asks Copilot to assist with a point-in-time restore:

- **Copilot prompt:** `I want an az cli command to initiate point-in-time restore and explain what are other options to initiate it.`

- **Copilot output:** Copilot provides a CLI command to perform the restore.

    The following illustration provides a generic example; your output based on the resources deployed in your environment may differ:

I want an az cli command to initiate point-in-time restore and explain what other options to initiate it.

🤖 **Copilot** AI-generated content may be incorrect

To initiate a point-in-time restore for an Azure SQL Database using Azure CLI, you can use the following command:

```Bash
az sql db restore --resource-group <resourceGroupName> --server <serverName> --name <databaseName> --dest-
name <newDatabaseName> --time <restorePointTime>
```

Replace the placeholders with your specific values:

- `<resourceGroupName>`: The name of the resource group.
- `<serverName>`: The name of the SQL server.
- `<databaseName>`: The name of the existing database you want to restore.
- `<newDatabaseName>`: The name for the new database that will be created as a result of the restore.
- `<restorePointTime>`: The point in time to which you want to restore the database, in ISO 8601 format (e.g., 2023-10-01T12:00:00Z).

Other Options to Initiate Point-in-Time Restore

1. **Azure Portal**: You can initiate a point-in-time restore directly from the Azure Portal by navigating to the SQL Database resource, selecting "Restore" from the menu, and specifying the desired restore point.
2. **Azure PowerShell**: Use the Restore-AzSqlDatabase cmdlet to perform a point-in-time restore via PowerShell.
3. **REST API**: You can use the Azure REST API to initiate a point-in-time restore by making a POST request to the appropriate endpoint with the necessary parameters.

These options provide flexibility depending on your preferred method of interaction with Azure services.

Figure 7.2 – Restore prompt example

In conclusion, this illustrates how Copilot can assist with your backup and restore strategies and, where applicable, provide customized recommendations that improve RPO and RTO. By leveraging these capabilities, you can create a more resilient data environment, optimize backup schedules, and strengthen disaster recovery plans.

As you continue exploring the potential of Copilot, remember that these proactive insights streamline operations and significantly enhance your databases' overall security and reliability. Embracing such automation will enable you to focus on strategic initiatives while ensuring robust data protection measures are in place.

The following section will look at patch management and version upgrades.

Patch management and version upgrades

In this section, you will see how Microsoft Copilot can assist with patch management and upgrade Azure Database for MySQL and Azure SQL Database so administrators can run and maintain databases with the least amount of administration effort.

Prompt example 1

In this prompt example, the user asks Copilot to recommend the best practices to deploy patches that won't cause Azure SQL Database workload disruption:

- **Copilot prompt**: `Recommend best practices to apply patches to my Databases without disrupting workloads.`

- **Copilot output**: Copilot provides an output of a list of best practices you can adopt.

  The following illustration provides an example of output based on the Azure SQL resources deployed in this demo environment; your output may differ:

Recommend best practices to apply patches to my Databases without disrupting workloads.

Copilot AI-generated content may be incorrect

To apply patches to your Azure SQL Databases without disrupting workloads, consider the following best practices:
Best Practices for Applying Patches

1. **Schedule Maintenance Windows**:
   - Plan and schedule maintenance windows during off-peak hours to minimize the impact on your users.
   - Communicate the maintenance schedule to all stakeholders in advance.
2. **Use Active Geo-Replication**:
   - Enable active geo-replication to create readable secondary databases in different regions.
   - During patching, failover to the secondary database to ensure continuous availability.
3. **Leverage Failover Groups**:
   - Configure failover groups for automatic failover of a group of databases in case of a regional outage.
   - This ensures high availability and minimal disruption during patching.
4. **Implement Rolling Updates**:
   - Apply patches in a rolling manner across different database instances to ensure that not all instances are down simultaneously.
   - This approach helps maintain availability and reduces downtime.
5. **Monitor and Test**:
   - Monitor the performance and health of your databases before, during, and after patching.
   - Test patches in a staging environment before applying them to production databases to identify potential issues.
6. **Use Azure Automation**:
   - Automate the patching process using Azure Automation to ensure consistency and reduce manual errors.
   - Schedule automation runbooks to apply patches during the maintenance window.
7. **Backup Databases**:
   - Take full backups of your databases before applying patches to ensure you can restore them in case of any issues.
   - Verify the integrity of backups to ensure they are usable.
8. **Optimize Connection Pooling**:
   - Configure connection pooling settings to minimize the overhead of creating new connections during patching.
   - Implement retry logic to handle transient connectivity failures gracefully.

Additional Resources

- **Batch Queries**: Use batch queries to reduce the number of data access operations and improve performance. Batch Queries
- **Cross-Database Sharding**: Consider sharding techniques to spread database operations over multiple databases. Cross-Database Sharding
- **Functional Partitioning**: Split different functions of an application into different databases to scale independently. Functional Partitioning

By following these best practices, you can apply patches to your Azure SQL Databases with minimal disruption to your workloads.
References

- Performance Tuning Guidance for Applications and Databases
- Monitor Azure SQL Database
- Azure Automation

Figure 7.3 – Patch management prompt example

Prompt example 2

In this prompt example, you ask Copilot to evaluate what would happen if you changed your Azure SQL instance to the latest version and whether you need to do anything in preparation:

- **Copilot prompt:** What impacts should I be aware of when upgrading to the latest version of Azure SQL

- **Copilot output:** Copilot evaluates the impact and preparation required for a version upgrade.

The following illustration provides an example of output based on the Azure SQL resources deployed in this demo environment; your output may differ:

What impacts should I be aware of when upgrading to the latest version of Azure SQL

Copilot   AI-generated content may be incorrect

When upgrading to the latest version of Azure SQL, there are several impacts you should be aware of:
Compatibility Issues

- **Transact-SQL Differences**: There may be differences in Transact-SQL syntax and functionality between SQL Server and Azure SQL Database. Review the Transact-SQL differences to identify any potential issues.
- **Discontinued Features**: Some features available in older versions of SQL Server may be discontinued in Azure SQL Database. Check the discontinued database engine functionality to ensure your applications are not relying on deprecated features.
- **Compatibility Levels**: Ensure that your database compatibility level is set appropriately. Some features are only available at certain compatibility levels. Learn more about database compatibility levels.

Performance Considerations

- **Log Generation Rate**: The log generation rate and latency on your database log file can impact migration speed. For example, Azure SQL Database Business Critical Gen5 8 vCore provides a maximum log generation rate of 96 MB/s, while the Hyperscale service tier provides a log rate of 100 MB/s. Review the Hyperscale service tier for more details.
- **Network Bandwidth**: Ensure your network bandwidth can accommodate the maximum log ingestion rate. Typically, Azure ExpressRoute is used for high bandwidth connectivity.

Migration Best Practices

- **Service Tier and Compute Size**: Choose the highest service tier and compute size that your budget allows to maximize transfer performance. You can scale down after migration to save costs.
- **BACPAC Files**: Minimize the distance between your BACPAC file and the destination data center to improve performance.
- **Statistics and Indexes**: Disable auto update and auto create statistics during migration, partition tables and indexes, and drop indexed views to be recreated post-migration.
- **Historical Data**: Remove rarely queried historical data to another database and migrate this data separately. Use elastic queries to query historical data.

Post-Migration Tasks

- **Update Statistics**: Perform a full scan to update statistics after migration.
- **Remediate Applications**: Ensure all applications consuming the source database start consuming the target database, which may require changes to the applications.
- **Testing**: Develop validation tests, set up a test environment, run validation and performance tests, and analyze results.

Advanced Features

- **High Availability**: Utilize built-in high availability features.
- **Threat Detection**: Enable threat detection to secure your database.
- **Monitoring and Tuning**: Use monitoring and tuning tools to optimize your workload.

References

- Transact-SQL differences between SQL Server and Azure SQL Database
- Discontinued Database Engine functionality in SQL Server
- Database compatibility level
- Hyperscale service tier
- Azure ExpressRoute
- Elastic queries

By considering these impacts and following best practices, you can ensure a smooth upgrade to the latest version of Azure SQL.

Figure 7.4 – Version upgrade prompt example

In this section, we saw that Microsoft Copilot in Azure can help speed up patch management and upgrade versions of Azure Database for MySQL and Azure SQL Database. With the help of AI-driven insights, administrators can remove the complexity and the burden that these tasks would ordinarily entail.

The examples given for the prompts show that Copilot reviews the consequences of version upgrades to ensure a smooth transition that preserves workloads.

It is worth mentioning that all suggestions that Copilot provided as responses could be returned to Copilot with other prompts, so it provides practical `az cli` commands that can actually do something, in contrast to just advising.

With the growing importance of database environments to business operations, Copilot is positioned to free DBAs from performing mundane but vital tasks, enabling them to concentrate on more strategic projects that drive database management efficiency overall.

The following section will look at data archiving and retention.

Data archiving and retention

This section will show how Microsoft Copilot in Azure can streamline data archiving and retention for Azure Database for MySQL and Azure SQL Database. With AI-driven prompts, Copilot provides smart recommendations for coordinating data lifecycle management.

Prompt example 1

This is one example of a user asking Copilot to find old or unused data that it should archive or purge to improve the performance of Azure SQL Database:

- **Copilot prompt:** `I want to identify old or unused data in my Azure SQL Database that I can archive or purge to improve performance.`
- **Copilot output:** Copilot provides queries that can be used to search for data that hasn't been accessed recently or modified in a long time.

The following illustration provides an example of output based on the Azure resources deployed in this demo environment; your output may differ:

I want to identify old or unused data in my Azure SQL Database that I can archive or purge to improve performance.

Copilot AI-generated content may be incorrect

Identifying Old or Unused Data in Azure SQL Database

To identify old or unused data in your Azure SQL Database that you can archive or purge to improve performance, you can use several tools and techniques provided by Azure SQL Database:

1. **Query Performance Insight**

- **Query Performance Insight** allows you to see a history of the top resource-consuming queries and long-running queries for a specific database. This can help you identify queries that are accessing old or infrequently used data.
- You can quickly identify top queries by resource utilization, duration, and frequency of execution. This feature requires **Query Store** to be enabled and active for the database.

2. **Dynamic Management Views (DMVs)**

- You can query the sys.dm_db_resource_stats dynamic management view to return resource consumption statistics history from the last hour.
- The sys.resource_stats system catalog view returns history for the last 14 days. These views can help you understand CPU, IO, and memory consumption, which can indicate which data is being accessed frequently and which is not.

3. **Azure Portal Monitoring**

- The Azure portal shows a database's utilization by selecting the database and viewing the chart in the Overview pane. You can modify the chart to show multiple metrics, including CPU percentage, DTU percentage, Data IO percentage, Sessions percentage, and Database size percentage.
- From this chart, you can also configure alerts by resource. These alerts allow you to respond to resource conditions with an email, write to an HTTPS/HTTP endpoint, or perform an action.

4. **Database Watcher**

- **Database Watcher** collects in-depth workload monitoring data to give you a detailed view of database performance, configuration, and health. Dashboards in the Azure portal provide a single-pane-of-glass view of your Azure SQL estate and a detailed view of each monitored resource.
- Data is collected into a central data store in your Azure subscription. You can query, analyze, export, visualize collected data, and integrate it with downstream systems.

5. **SQL Database Advisor**

- **SQL Database Advisor** provides tailored recommendations for your database workload to keep your applications running at an optimal level. It can automatically implement index recommendations based on your workload, which evolves as your application workload changes.

Steps to Archive or Purge Data

1. **Identify Old Data**: Use the tools mentioned above to identify tables or records that are rarely accessed or have not been modified for a long time.
2. **Archive Data**: Move old data to a separate archive database or storage solution. This can be done using BACPAC files or other data export methods.
3. **Purge Data**: Delete old or unused data that is no longer needed. Ensure you have backups before performing any deletions.
4. **Monitor Performance**: Continuously monitor the performance of your database to ensure that the archiving and purging processes have the desired effect.

References

- Query Performance Insight
- sys.dm_db_resource_stats
- sys.resource_stats
- Database Watcher Overview
- SQL Database Advisor

By following these steps and utilizing the available tools, you can effectively identify and manage old or unused data in your Azure SQL Database to improve performance.

Figure 7.5 – Data archival prompt example

Prompt example 2

In this example, a user asks Copilot to advise on a cost-effective data retention policy for Azure SQL Database:

- **Copilot prompt:** Can you help me configure a cost-effective long-term retention for my database backups?

- **Copilot output:** Copilot recommends cost-effective recommendations and options.

   The following illustration provides an example of output based on the Azure resources deployed in this demo environment; your output may differ:

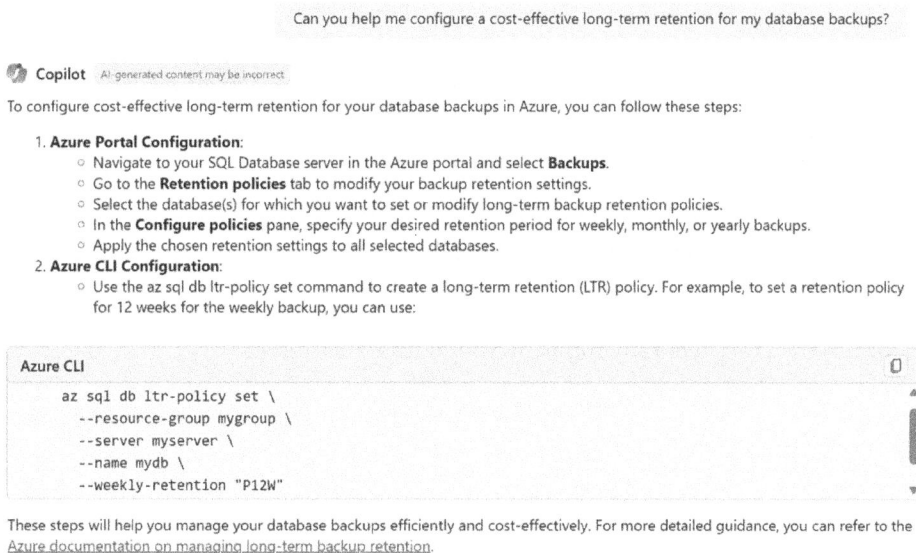

Can you help me configure a cost-effective long-term retention for my database backups?

Copilot AI-generated content may be incorrect

To configure cost-effective long-term retention for your database backups in Azure, you can follow these steps:

1. **Azure Portal Configuration:**
   - Navigate to your SQL Database server in the Azure portal and select **Backups**.
   - Go to the **Retention policies** tab to modify your backup retention settings.
   - Select the database(s) for which you want to set or modify long-term backup retention policies.
   - In the **Configure policies** pane, specify your desired retention period for weekly, monthly, or yearly backups.
   - Apply the chosen retention settings to all selected databases.
2. **Azure CLI Configuration:**
   - Use the az sql db ltr-policy set command to create a long-term retention (LTR) policy. For example, to set a retention policy for 12 weeks for the weekly backup, you can use:

```
Azure CLI

az sql db ltr-policy set \
    --resource-group mygroup \
    --server myserver \
    --name mydb \
    --weekly-retention "P12W"
```

These steps will help you manage your database backups efficiently and cost-effectively. For more detailed guidance, you can refer to the Azure documentation on managing long-term backup retention.

Figure 7.6 – Data retention prompt example

In this section, you saw how Microsoft Copilot for Azure, using AI-driven prompts, can be used to identify obsolete data and create cost-effective retention policies. As a result, organizations can minimize storage costs, preserve their data's integrity, and ensure compliance while cutting back on the manual work often required for data archiving and retention.

The following section will look at data integrity checks.

Data integrity checks

This section will show how Microsoft Copilot can support data integrity checks for Azure Database for MySQL and Azure SQL Database. AI-driven prompts help you find, analyze, and fix data problems more easily and ensure that your data remains consistent, reliable, and ready for critical apps.

Prompt example 1

For this prompt example, the user asks Copilot to schedule integrity checks for Azure SQL Database in low-traffic periods:

- **Copilot prompt:** I want to schedule integrity checks for my Azure SQL Database during low-traffic periods.

- **Copilot output:** Copilot schedules DBCC CHECKDB integrity checks at times of low database activity, lets them run in the background without breaking peak performance, and notifies you when corruption or issues have been detected.

  The following illustration provides an example output based on the Azure SQL resources deployed in this demo environment; your output may differ:

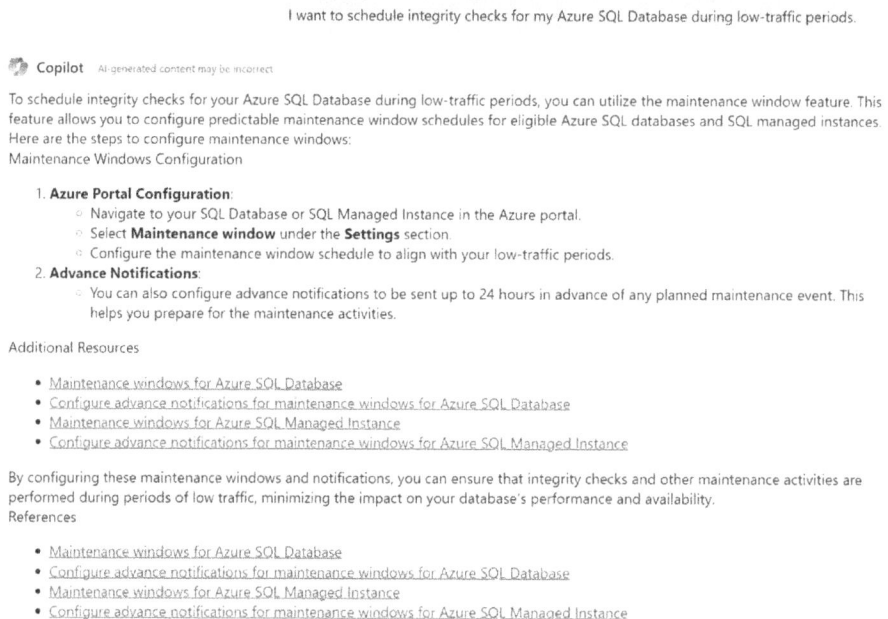

I want to schedule integrity checks for my Azure SQL Database during low-traffic periods.

Copilot AI-generated content may be incorrect

To schedule integrity checks for your Azure SQL Database during low-traffic periods, you can utilize the maintenance window feature. This feature allows you to configure predictable maintenance window schedules for eligible Azure SQL databases and SQL managed instances. Here are the steps to configure maintenance windows:
Maintenance Windows Configuration

1. **Azure Portal Configuration:**
   - Navigate to your SQL Database or SQL Managed Instance in the Azure portal.
   - Select **Maintenance window** under the **Settings** section.
   - Configure the maintenance window schedule to align with your low-traffic periods.
2. **Advance Notifications:**
   - You can also configure advance notifications to be sent up to 24 hours in advance of any planned maintenance event. This helps you prepare for the maintenance activities.

Additional Resources

- Maintenance windows for Azure SQL Database
- Configure advance notifications for maintenance windows for Azure SQL Database
- Maintenance windows for Azure SQL Managed Instance
- Configure advance notifications for maintenance windows for Azure SQL Managed Instance

By configuring these maintenance windows and notifications, you can ensure that integrity checks and other maintenance activities are performed during periods of low traffic, minimizing the impact on your database's performance and availability.
References

- Maintenance windows for Azure SQL Database
- Configure advance notifications for maintenance windows for Azure SQL Database
- Maintenance windows for Azure SQL Managed Instance
- Configure advance notifications for maintenance windows for Azure SQL Managed Instance

Figure 7.7 – Data integrity prompt example

Prompt example 2

With this prompt example, the user requests Copilot to judge the correct frequency for running checks on the integrity of their database, taking into account their current workload:

- **Copilot prompt:** How often should I run integrity checks on my database based on my current workload?

- **Copilot output:** Copilot analyzes workload trends, and the most appropriate frequency is suggested, aiming for a compromise between the urgency of checking integrity frequently and introducing performance overhead.

The following illustration provides an example output based on the Azure SQL resources deployed in this demo environment; your output may differ:

How often should I run integrity checks on my database based on my current workload?

Copilot AI-generated content may be incorrect

The frequency of running database integrity checks depends on your specific workload and the criticality of your data. Here are some general guidelines to help you determine the appropriate frequency:
General Guidelines for Running Integrity Checks

1. **High Transaction Workloads:**
   - If your database handles a high volume of transactions, it is advisable to run integrity checks more frequently, such as daily or weekly. This ensures that any data corruption issues are detected and addressed promptly.
2. **Moderate Transaction Workloads:**
   - For databases with moderate transaction volumes, running integrity checks weekly or bi-weekly may be sufficient. This balances the need for data integrity with the overhead of running checks.
3. **Low Transaction Workloads:**
   - Databases with low transaction volumes can typically run integrity checks less frequently, such as monthly. This reduces the performance impact while still maintaining data integrity.

Scheduling Integrity Checks
To minimize the impact on your database performance, schedule integrity checks during low-traffic periods. You can use Azure Automation or SQL Server Agent to automate the scheduling of these checks.
Example Code for Running Integrity Checks
Here are examples of running database integrity checks using Visual C# and PowerShell:
Visual C#

```C#
using Microsoft.SqlServer.Management.Common;
using Microsoft.SqlServer.Management.Smo;
using System;
```

PowerShell

```PowerShell
# Set the path context to the local, default instance of SQL Server and get a reference to
AdventureWorks2022
CD \sql\localhost\default\databases
$db = get-item AdventureWorks2022
```

References

- Running Database Integrity Checks in Visual C#
- Running Database Integrity Checks in PowerShell

By following these guidelines and scheduling integrity checks appropriately, you can ensure the integrity of your database while minimizing the impact on performance.

Figure 7.8 – Data integrity prompt example

It can be seen that Microsoft Copilot in Azure provides invaluable support to keep your data up to date and reliable. AI-driven prompts make it easy to schedule and tune integrity checks specifically for your database workload while ensuring your critical applications always have access to accurate and trusted data. The examples shown here show how Copilot makes operations more efficient and counteracts some of the inherent risks of data corruption, ensuring the integrity of your databases and controlled operations.

The following section will look at performance optimization.

Performance optimization

In this section, you will see how Microsoft Copilot can assist in performance optimization for Azure Database for MySQL and Azure SQL Database. Using Copilot's AI-driven insights, you can discover how to manage database operations better, uncover performance bottlenecks, and apply optimization techniques efficiently.

Prompt example 1

In this prompt example, the user asks Copilot to find the top five slowest queries in Azure SQL Database and offer optimizations:

- **Copilot prompt:** Identify the top 5 slowest queries in my Azure SQL Database and suggest optimizations.
- **Copilot output:** Using logs and query stores, Copilot analyzes query performance, selects the top five slow-performing queries, and, if possible, suggests changes such as creating indexes, rewriting queries, or changing query plans to improve query performance.

The following illustration provides an example output based on the Azure SQL resources deployed in this demo environment; your output may differ:

Identify the top 5 slowest queries in my Azure SQL Database and suggest optimizations.

Copilot AI-generated content may be incorrect

Identifying and Optimizing the Top 5 Slowest Queries in Azure SQL Database
To identify the top 5 slowest queries in your Azure SQL Database and suggest optimizations, you can use the Query Performance Insight tool available in the Azure portal. This tool provides detailed insights into your database's resource consumption, including CPU, duration, and execution count for queries. Here are the steps to identify and optimize the slowest queries:
Steps to Identify Slow Queries

1. **Open Query Performance Insight**:
   - Navigate to your Azure SQL Database in the Azure portal.
   - From the left-side menu, select **Intelligent Performance** > **Query Performance Insight**.
2. **Review Top Resource-Consuming Queries**:
   - On the first tab, review the list of top resource-consuming queries by CPU, duration, and execution count.
   - Select an individual query to view its details, including the query text and history of resource utilization.
3. **Customize Metrics**:
   - Open the **Custom** tab in Query Performance Insight.
   - Change the metrics to **duration** to identify long-running queries.
   - Select the number of queries and the observation interval.
   - Use aggregation functions like **Sum**, **Max**, or **Avg** to analyze the execution time.
4. **View Performance Recommendations**:
   - Open **Intelligent Performance** > **Performance recommendations** to check if any performance recommendations are available from Azure SQL Database Advisor.

Example Query to Identify Top Queries by CPU Usage
You can use the following query to identify the top queries by CPU usage:

```SQL
WITH AggregatedCPU AS (
    SELECT q.query_hash,
           SUM(rs.total_cpu_time_ms) AS total_cpu_ms,
           AVG(rs.avg_cpu_time_ms) AS avg_cpu_ms,
           MAX(rs.max_cpu_time_ms) AS max_cpu_ms
```

Optimizing Identified Queries
Once you identify the problematic queries, you can tune them to reduce CPU utilization. Here are some optimization techniques:

1. **Index Optimization**:
   - Ensure that appropriate indexes are created and maintained for the columns used in the queries.
2. **Query Rewriting**:
   - Rewrite queries to be more efficient, such as using joins instead of subqueries, and avoiding unnecessary computations.
3. **Parameter Sniffing**:
   - Use query hints to optimize for specific parameter values if parameter sniffing is causing suboptimal query plans.
4. **Resource Scaling**:
   - Consider increasing the compute size of the database or elastic pool to handle the workload more efficiently.

References

- [Diagnose and troubleshoot high CPU on Azure SQL Database](https://learn.microsoft.com/azure/azure-sql/database

Figure 7.9 – Performance optimization prompt example

Prompt example 2

The user asks Copilot to recommend a database scaling option for a predicted period in this prompt example:

- **Copilot prompt:** Can you recommend a scaling option for my database to handle the increased traffic expected over the next month?

- **Copilot output:** Copilot can suggest scaling strategies such as an increase in vCores, moving to a higher service tier, or using elastic pools that would accommodate increased traffic.

  The following illustration provides an example output based on the Azure SQL resources deployed in this demo environment; your output may differ:

Can you recommend a scaling option for my database to handle the increased traffic expected over the next month?

Copilot AI-generated content may be incorrect

Scaling Options for Increased Traffic
To handle the increased traffic expected over the next month, you can consider the following scaling options for your Azure SQL database:
1. **DTU-Based Purchasing Model**

- **Service Tiers**: Basic, Standard, and Premium.
- **Use Case**: Suitable for lightweight to heavyweight database workloads.
- **Resources**: Offers a blend of compute, memory, and I/O resources.

2. **vCore-Based Purchasing Model**

- **Service Tiers**: General Purpose, Business Critical, and Hyperscale.
- **Use Case**: Allows you to choose the number of vCores, the amount of memory, and the amount and speed of storage.
- **Resources**: Provides more flexibility in resource allocation.

3. **Serverless Compute Tier**

- **Use Case**: Automatically scales compute resources based on workload activity.
- **Resources**: Ideal for databases with intermittent, unpredictable usage patterns.

4. **Elastic Pools**

- **Use Case**: Optimized for multiple databases with varying resource demands.
- **Resources**: Allows you to define maximum resource limits per group of databases in the pool.

5. **Azure SQL Managed Instance**

- **Use Case**: Suitable for scenarios requiring high compatibility with SQL Server.
- **Resources**: Uses vCores to define maximum CPU cores and storage allocated to the instance.

Key Considerations

- **Dynamic Scaling**: You can change the service tier, compute tier, and resource limits for a database, elastic pool, or managed instance at any time.
- **Impact of Scaling**: Scaling operations may restart the database engine process, causing a brief connection break.

Additional Resources
For more detailed information, you can refer to the following documentation:

- vCore-Based Purchasing Model
- Serverless Compute Tier
- Azure Pricing Calculator

Figure 7.10 – Performance optimization prompt example

In this section, you explored how Microsoft Copilot in Azure can easily and timely improve your Azure Database for MySQL and Azure SQL Database performance optimization.

Adopting Microsoft Copilot means using these tools to manage your databases more easily and make informed, data-driven decisions that improve your database's performance beyond expectations.

The following section will look at index and statistics management.

Index and statistics management

This section will show how Microsoft Copilot can provide index and statistics management for Azure Database for MySQL and Azure SQL Database. Efficient index and statistics management is important as it guarantees query performance and retrieves data as efficiently as possible. Using AI-powered prompts, Copilot surfaces insights and automates these tasks to make the database admin's job easier, allowing query performance to be optimized with the least amount of manual intervention.

Prompt example 1

In this prompt example, the user asks Copilot to identify and suggest which unused or redundant indexes to drop in Azure SQL Database:

- **Copilot prompt:** Can you identify unused or redundant indexes in my Azure SQL Database and suggest which ones to drop?

- **Copilot output:** Copilot uses index usage to analyze whether indexes are redundant or unused, and it recommends removing redundant or unused indexes to reduce storage consumption and drive performance improvements.

    The following illustration provides an example output based on the Azure SQL resources deployed in this demo environment; your output may differ:

Can you identify unused or redundant indexes in my Azure SQL Database and suggest which ones to drop?

Copilot   AI-generated content may be incorrect

Identifying Unused or Redundant Indexes in Azure SQL Database

Azure SQL Database provides built-in intelligence to help identify and manage indexes that may be unused or redundant. Here are the key points regarding the identification and recommendation process for dropping indexes:

Drop Index Recommendations

1. **Detection of Unused Indexes**:
   - Azure SQL Database continuously analyzes the performance of existing indexes.
   - An index is recommended for dropping if it is a duplicate of another index (same indexed and included column, partition schema, and filters).
   - An index is also recommended for dropping if it hasn't been used for a prolonged period (more than 90 days).
2. **Verification Process**:
   - After a drop index recommendation is applied, Azure SQL Database monitors the performance of the queries.
   - If performance improves, the impact report is available.
   - If performance degrades, the recommendation is reverted.
3. **Automatic Index Management**:
   - Azure SQL Database can automatically apply identified recommendations.
   - When a DROP INDEX recommendation is applied, it automatically monitors the performance of the queries affected by the index.
   - If the performance of the affected queries improves, the index is retained. If not, the index is re-created.

Manual Index Management

If you prefer manual management, you can query the sys.dm_db_index_usage_stats view to find indexes that have not been used recently. Here is an example query to identify potentially unused indexes:

```SQL
SELECT
    OBJECT_NAME(i.object_id) AS TableName,
    i.name AS IndexName,
    i.index_id,
    u.user_seeks,
```

This query lists non-clustered indexes that have not been used for seeks, scans, or lookups, which may indicate they are unused.

Next Steps

- **Automatic Tuning**: Consider enabling automatic tuning to let Azure SQL Database manage index recommendations for you.
- **Manual Review**: Use the provided query to manually review and identify unused indexes.

For more detailed information, you can refer to the following documentation:

- Azure SQL Database automatic tuning
- Find index recommendations in Azure portal

These resources will help you understand the process and make informed decisions about index management in your Azure SQL Database. All dates and times mentioned are in UTC timezone.

Figure 7.11 – Indexing prompt example

Prompt example 2

In this prompt example, the user asks Copilot about the optimal timing for updating database statistics and whether this can be automated:

- **Copilot prompt:** When should I update statistics for my database, and can you automate this for me?

- **Copilot output:** Copilot suggests the most frequent updating of statistics based on workload patterns and updates the statistics automatically to use them for accurate query optimizer-based execution plans.

The following illustration provides an example output based on the Azure SQL resources deployed in this demo environment; your output may differ:

When should I update statistics for my database, and can you automate this for me?

Copilot AI-generated content may be incorrect

When to Update Statistics

Updating statistics is crucial for maintaining optimal query performance. Here are the key scenarios when you should consider updating statistics:

1. **Query Execution Times are Slow**:
   - If query response times are slow or unpredictable, ensure that queries have up-to-date statistics before performing additional troubleshooting steps.
2. **Insert Operations on Ascending or Descending Key Columns**:
   - Statistics on ascending or descending key columns, such as IDENTITY or real-time timestamp columns, might require more frequent updates. Insert operations append new values to these columns, and the number of rows added might be too small to trigger an automatic update. This can result in inaccurate cardinality estimates and slow query performance.
3. **After Maintenance Operations**:
   - Consider updating statistics after performing maintenance procedures that change the distribution of data, such as truncating a table or performing a bulk insert of a large percentage of the rows. This can avoid future delays in query processing while queries wait for automatic statistics updates.

Automating Statistics Updates

You can automate the process of updating statistics using the following methods:

1. **AUTO_UPDATE_STATISTICS Option**:
   - Ensure that the AUTO_UPDATE_STATISTICS option is set to ON. This allows the Query Optimizer to routinely update statistics as needed.
2. **Adaptive Index Defrag**:
   - Use solutions such as Adaptive Index Defrag to automatically manage index defragmentation and statistics updates for one or more databases. This procedure automatically chooses whether to rebuild or reorganize an index according to its fragmentation level and updates statistics with a linear threshold.

Manual Update of Statistics

If you prefer to manually update statistics, you can use the following methods:

1. **Using SQL Server Management Studio (SSMS)**:
   - Navigate to the database, expand the **Tables** folder, select the table, expand the **Statistics** folder, right-click the statistics object, and select **Properties**. Then, select the **Update statistics for these columns** check box and click **OK**.
2. **Using Transact-SQL**:
   - Update a specific statistics object:

```SQL
USE AdventureWorks2022;
GO
UPDATE STATISTICS Sales.SalesOrderDetail AK_SalesOrderDetail_rowguid;
GO
```

- Update all statistics in a table:

```SQL
USE AdventureWorks2022;
GO
UPDATE STATISTICS Sales.SalesOrderDetail;
GO
```

- Update all statistics in a database:

```SQL
USE AdventureWorks2022;
GO
EXEC sp_updatestats;
```

References

- UPDATE STATISTICS (Transact-SQL)
- sp_updatestats (Transact-SQL)
- AUTO_UPDATE_STATISTICS Option
- Adaptive Index Defrag

These resources will help you understand when and how to update statistics for your database, and how to automate the process effectively. All dates and times mentioned are in UTC timezone.

Figure 7.12 – Statistics prompt example

In conclusion, you looked at examples that highlight how maintaining database efficiency and query performance is essential, and this is achieved through index and statistics management. Using Microsoft Copilot in Azure, DBAs can greatly simplify managing indexes and statistics while reducing complexity and time spent. The examples of the AI-driven prompts in this section show how Copilot can automatically identify and update redundant or unused indexes and promote good performance with little manual work. These tools simplify database management and help you make data-driven decisions to optimize performance and increase overall database system reliability.

The following section will look at security and compliance.

Security and compliance

In this section, you will see how Microsoft Copilot for Azure can support database management by streamlining security and compliance for Azure Database for MySQL and Azure SQL Database. These examples demonstrate how Microsoft Copilot for Azure can help proactively harden your database's security position, maintaining data integrity, regulatory alignment, and peace of mind while dealing with critical data assets.

Prompt example 1

In this prompt example, the user asks Copilot to assess the security of Azure SQL Database and recommend actions to improve compliance with GDPR:

- **Copilot prompt**: Assess the security of my Azure SQL Database and recommend actions to improve compliance with GDPR.

- **Copilot output**: Copilot checks the security of your storage through encryption at rest checks, rules that control access to data, and the setup of audit logs. After running the check, Copilot recommends enhancements, including using **transparent data encryption (TDE)**, changing firewall rules, and implementing a data retention policy to ensure GDPR compliance.

The following illustration provides an example of output based on the Azure SQL resources deployed in this demo environment; your output may differ:

Assess the security of my Azure SQL Database and recommend actions to improve compliance with GDPR

Copilot AI-generated content may be incorrect

Security Assessment for Azure SQL Database
To assess the security of your Azure SQL Database and recommend actions to improve compliance with GDPR, we need to focus on several key areas including vulnerability management, data protection, and access control. Here are the relevant policies and actions you can take:

1. **Vulnerability Management**

- **Enable Vulnerability Assessment**: Ensure that vulnerability assessment is enabled on your SQL servers and SQL Managed Instances. This helps in identifying and remediating vulnerabilities.
  - Vulnerability assessment should be enabled on your SQL servers
  - Vulnerability assessment should be enabled on SQL Managed Instance
- **Resolve Vulnerability Findings**: Regularly review and resolve any vulnerability findings in your SQL databases.
  - SQL databases should have vulnerability findings resolved

2. **Data Protection**

- **Enable Transparent Data Encryption (TDE)**: Ensure that Transparent Data Encryption is enabled on your SQL databases to protect data at rest.
  - Transparent Data Encryption on SQL databases should be enabled
- **Use Customer-Managed Keys**: Use customer-managed keys to encrypt data at rest for SQL managed instances and SQL servers.
  - SQL managed instances should use customer-managed keys to encrypt data at rest
  - SQL servers should use customer-managed keys to encrypt data at rest

3. **Access Control**

- **Disable Public Network Access**: Ensure that public network access is disabled for Azure SQL Database to protect communications at external boundaries.
  - Public network access on Azure SQL Database should be disabled

4. **Monitoring and Compliance**

- **Enable Azure Defender for SQL**: Enable Azure Defender for SQL to provide advanced security capabilities, including vulnerability assessments and threat protection.
  - Azure Defender for SQL should be enabled for unprotected Azure SQL servers
  - Azure Defender for SQL should be enabled for unprotected SQL Managed Instances

References

- Azure SQL Database Security Controls Policy

These actions will help improve the security posture of your Azure SQL Database and ensure compliance with GDPR requirements. All dates and times mentioned are in UTC timezone.

Figure 7.13 – Security prompt example

Prompt example 2

In this prompt example, the user asks Copilot to check Azure SQL Database and Azure Database for MySQL for any recent suspicious activity and recommend steps to reduce risk:

- **Copilot prompt:** What are the best practices for securing Azure Database for MySQL?

- **Copilot output:** Copilot provides a detailed list of recommended best practices for securing Azure Database for MySQL. This includes guidance on using Azure Key Vault for encryption key management, restricting network access with private endpoints, enabling Microsoft Entra ID authentication, applying the principle of least privilege, monitoring threats with Microsoft Defender for Cloud, and enforcing security policies with Azure Policy to maintain compliance.

  The following illustration provides an example output; your output may differ:

  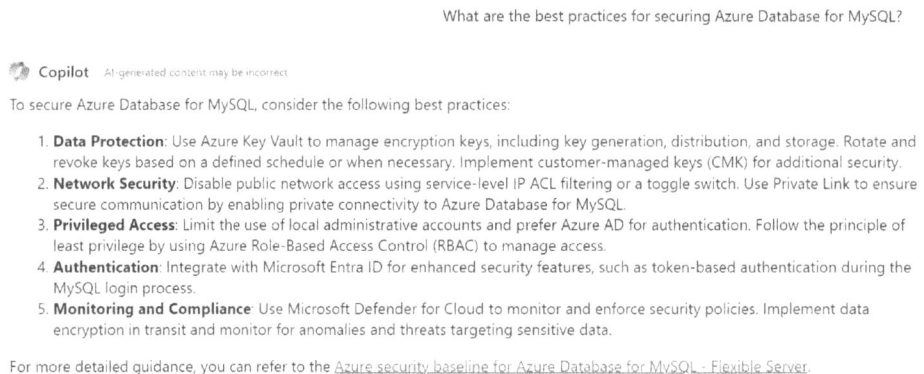

  What are the best practices for securing Azure Database for MySQL?

  Copilot AI-generated content may be incorrect.

  To secure Azure Database for MySQL, consider the following best practices:

  1. **Data Protection**: Use Azure Key Vault to manage encryption keys, including key generation, distribution, and storage. Rotate and revoke keys based on a defined schedule or when necessary. Implement customer-managed keys (CMK) for additional security.
  2. **Network Security**: Disable public network access using service-level IP ACL filtering or a toggle switch. Use Private Link to ensure secure communication by enabling private connectivity to Azure Database for MySQL.
  3. **Privileged Access**: Limit the use of local administrative accounts and prefer Azure AD for authentication. Follow the principle of least privilege by using Azure Role-Based Access Control (RBAC) to manage access.
  4. **Authentication**: Integrate with Microsoft Entra ID for enhanced security features, such as token-based authentication during the MySQL login process.
  5. **Monitoring and Compliance**: Use Microsoft Defender for Cloud to monitor and enforce security policies. Implement data encryption in transit and monitor for anomalies and threats targeting sensitive data.

  For more detailed guidance, you can refer to the Azure security baseline for Azure Database for MySQL - Flexible Server.

Figure 7.14 – Security best practices prompt example

You saw an example of security and compliance prompting in this Copilot prompt.

In this section, you saw how Microsoft Copilot in Azure extends security and compliance management offerings for Azure Database for MySQL and Azure SQL Database. With AI-driven insights, Copilot isn't only helping you diagnose security risks in your datasets, and helping your databases stay compliant with crucial privacy standards such as GDPR. Copilot also helps simplify the complexities of regulatory compliance by allowing you to monitor data integrity proactively and receive actionable recommendations without losing sight of your ability to uphold data integrity and manage access confidently. You'll continue to add these security insights and use Copilot's automation features to build a secure, compliant, and resilient data environment.

This subsection concludes the section on practical examples of data management and optimization using Microsoft Copilot in Azure and concludes the content of this chapter. Next, you will recap the skills learned in this chapter.

Summary

In this chapter, you explored the capabilities of Microsoft Copilot for Azure in the area of data management and optimization.

Starting with database performance and optimization, you saw how Copilot provides actionable insights and automates routine tasks to ensure your databases run efficiently. You then examined the role of Copilot in maintaining data quality, highlighting its ability to swiftly identify and resolve data inconsistencies and anomalies.

The discussion moved to the critical aspect of security and compliance. You saw how Copilot helps proactively harden database security, ensure data integrity, and align with regulatory standards such as GDPR.

You delved into practical examples that showcased how Microsoft Copilot for Azure can enhance various facets of database management across Azure Database for MySQL and Azure SQL Database.

Moving forward, the knowledge and skills gained in this chapter will be a foundation for leveraging Microsoft Copilot in Azure to its fullest potential, enabling you to enhance your Azure databases' efficiency, security, and compliance.

The next chapter will explore how to use Microsoft Copilot in Azure for real-time monitoring and diagnostics. You'll learn how to leverage AI-driven insights for proactive monitoring, troubleshooting, and optimizing cloud operations, enhancing performance, and ensuring system stability. This knowledge will help you manage cloud complexities, reduce downtime, and maintain a robust infrastructure.

8

Exploring Real-Time Monitoring and Troubleshooting

Microsoft Copilot in Azure provides a powerful toolset for real-time monitoring and diagnostics. It uses **Artificial Intelligence (AI)**-driven insights to help administrators and engineers stay ahead of problems, optimize resources, and keep them stable and secure.

This chapter will explore using Microsoft Copilot in Azure for real-time monitoring and diagnostics. It details troubleshooting techniques and emphasizes how AI-driven recommendations can enhance Azure operations and quick issue resolution in cloud environments. You will learn how to leverage Copilot in Azure to monitor Azure resources continuously, learn troubleshooting techniques using it in Azure, and implement Copilot in Azure recommendations to manage and optimize cloud infrastructure performance proactively.

Using Microsoft Copilot in Azure for real-time monitoring, troubleshooting, and AI-driven recommendations helps teams manage cloud infrastructure efficiently. By learning these techniques, you can address issues before they escalate, streamline operations, and make data-driven adjustments to improve system stability. As cloud environments become more critical and complex, these skills will help minimize downtime, enhance productivity, and maintain a stable infrastructure, making them valuable business assets. This chapter aligns with the operational excellence and performance efficiency pillars of the Microsoft **Well-Architected Framework (WAF)**.

In this chapter, you will cover the following main topics:

- Configuring permissions and access
- Using Copilot in Azure for real-time monitoring
- Using Copilot in Azure for troubleshooting techniques
- Using Copilot in Azure recommendations to ensure high availability and reliability

Technical requirements

It is recommended to have access to an active Azure subscription to follow the examples provided in this chapter.

It is also recommended to have first completed *Chapter 1, Understanding Microsoft Copilot in Azure,* to set a baseline knowledge of some concepts for working with Microsoft Copilot in Azure, as well as completing *Chapter 2, Getting Started with Microsoft Copilot in Azure,* so that you are aware of how to use the Azure portal to access Microsoft Copilot in Azure.

When prompting, the guidance is to be very specific with the phrases and words used to articulate the desired output. The more specific and concise you can be in the prompt, the better results you will get in the response. As of the time of writing, Copilot in Azure has a *500-character limit* per prompt; therefore, you need to be thoughtful about how you write your prompts to maximize value and achieve the desired output.

Ensure you have the appropriate *Azure role assignments* for any resources you are investigating as Copilot can only operate within the scope of your existing permissions and cannot grant access to data or services you are not already authorized to use. Additionally, some services must be explicitly enabled to provide data or surface relevant insights to Copilot; for example, for Copilot to use **Azure Monitor Investigator**, this does not need to be *enabled manually*; it is built into Azure Monitor and becomes available automatically when your resources are sending telemetry data such as logs and metrics. However, Azure Monitor-monitored resources must have diagnostic settings configured to send telemetry (such as logs and metrics) to a **Log Analytics workspace** for Investigator to surface relevant insights.

> You will still always need to manually review the code generated by AI and potentially modify the output to be able to complete the task or operation on the resource type.
>
> Outputs or code generated by AI may not be fully accurate or functional.

Configuring permissions and access

Before you can begin using Copilot in Azure for real-time monitoring and troubleshooting, it's essential to ensure that the right permissions are in place. Copilot operates within the boundaries of Azure's **Role-Based Access Control (RBAC)**, meaning it can only interact with resources and data that the current user is authorized to access. Proper role assignment is critical not only for enabling Copilot to retrieve monitoring data and perform actions but also for maintaining security and compliance in your environment.

The following section outlines the key Azure monitoring roles and their responsibilities to help you assign the appropriate level of access based on each user's tasks and responsibilities.

Assigning monitoring roles

To ensure proper access control and functionality, assign the appropriate Azure monitoring roles to users based on what they need to do. Azure offers several built-in roles for monitoring:

- **Monitoring Reader**: Grants read-only access to monitoring data such as metrics, alerts, diagnostic settings, and activity logs. This role is best for users who only need to *view* monitoring information without making changes.

- **Monitoring Contributor**: Includes all permissions of the Monitoring Reader role, plus the ability to *create, modify, and delete* monitoring settings such as alert rules, diagnostic settings, and action groups. Use this role for users responsible for *configuring and managing* monitoring.

- **Log Analytics Reader**: Provides read-only access to log data within Log Analytics workspaces and the ability to run queries. It is appropriate for users such as *auditors or analysts* who need to explore logs but not change workspace settings or saved queries.

- **Log Analytics Contributor**: Allows users to read, edit, and create queries, dashboards, and other content in Log Analytics. This role is suitable for those responsible for *developing and maintaining* custom dashboards, visualizations, and insights.

To apply access control effectively, it's important to understand the distinction between the Reader and Contributor roles. When to use the **Reader** versus the **Contributor** role is detailed as follows:

- Assign **Reader roles** when the user's task is to *review or analyze* existing monitoring data without the need to alter any settings.

- Assign **Contributor roles** when the user needs to *create, update, or configure* monitoring tools, alerts, dashboards, or log queries.

Using these roles appropriately ensures secure and efficient management of monitoring operations in Azure while maintaining the principle of least privilege.

With monitoring roles assigned, the next step is to understand how Copilot in Azure accesses data within those permission boundaries. The following section explores how access control works behind the scenes to ensure Copilot operates securely and in compliance with Azure governance models.

Access control for Copilot data

In addition to assigning monitoring roles, it is important to manage who can use Microsoft Copilot in Azure. Azure allows you to enable or disable Copilot access for individual users or groups through the **Manage access to Microsoft Copilot in Azure** settings in the portal.

This allows organizations to do the following:

- Enable or restrict Copilot access for specific users or Microsoft Entra ID (formerly Azure Active Directory) groups
- Control who can interact with Copilot-generated monitoring insights
- Meet security and compliance requirements by limiting access to sensitive operational data

Assigning a monitoring-related role, such as Monitoring Reader or Contributor, does not automatically grant access to Copilot. Users must also be explicitly allowed to use Copilot through the access management settings; examples are as follows:

- A user with Monitoring Reader access will not be able to use Copilot unless Copilot has also been enabled for them.
- A user with Copilot access but without the appropriate monitoring role will not be able to view or query monitoring data, as Copilot enforces RBAC permissions.

By combining traditional RBAC with Copilot-specific permissions, you ensure that only authorized users can interact with sensitive data through Copilot in Azure. This layered approach reinforces security, minimizes risk, and supports compliance across your environment.

With access now properly configured, the next step is to define which resources you want Copilot to monitor—laying the foundation for targeted insights and meaningful diagnostics. The following section explores how to identify and scope these resources effectively.

Defining resources to monitor

Once permissions are in place, the next step is to select which resources Copilot should monitor. This involves doing the following:

- **Choosing resource types**: Copilot can monitor various resources, including **Virtual Machines (VMs)**, databases, apps, networks, and storage. Identify the critical resources within your architecture that require close monitoring.

- **Creating resource groups**: Grouping resources by type, function, or department can streamline monitoring. For example, resources that support a certain project, environment, function, or workload can be grouped separately to ensure governance and policy compliance. In addition, resource tags can be used as a strategy for resource governance.

Grouping and targeting resources strategically ensures that critical resources have the focus while reducing the chance of overwhelming users with too much data.

With the foundational setup complete, you can now use Copilot to query and observe resources in real time. The next section explores using the native Azure live metrics and dashboards available to Copilot to retrieve data and insights.

Using Copilot in Azure for real-time monitoring

Microsoft Copilot in Azure integrates AI capabilities within the Azure ecosystem, providing teams with deep insights into their cloud resources' data, performance, health, and efficiency. Copilot empowers users to manage resources proactively, allowing teams to detect and resolve potential issues before they impact users.

Microsoft Copilot in Azure offers robust capabilities to streamline and strengthen real-time monitoring and insights for Azure resources. By leveraging these features, teams can respond swiftly to issues, gain visibility into system health performance, and identify alerts and issues with minimal manual effort.

This section will explore how *natural language* can be used in Copilot in Azure to retrieve real-time monitoring data from collected metrics and provide the ability to drill down into diagnostics data for targeted insights.

The practical examples covered in this section illustrate how by using Copilot to query the native real-time monitoring solution in Azure, organizations can achieve operational efficiencies.

Core real-time monitoring capabilities

Microsoft Copilot in Azure enhances real-time monitoring by surfacing key insights and helping teams stay on top of system health. It has several built-in capabilities designed to detect issues early and keep stakeholders informed. These include the following:

- **Live metrics monitoring**
- **Anomaly detection**
- **Alerts and notifications**

Let us take a closer look at how each of these features works.

Live metrics monitoring

Azure Monitor is a comprehensive solution for collecting, analyzing, and acting on telemetry data from Azure and on-premises environments. It supports two core types of data: **metrics** and **logs**, each serving distinct purposes in monitoring resource performance and health.

Metrics are *numerical values* collected at regular intervals, offering near-real-time visibility into the performance of Azure resources. Common examples are **CPU utilization**, **memory usage**, **disk I/O**, and **network latency**. These metrics are lightweight and ideal for visualizing current system states through live dashboards.

Live metrics monitoring in Azure displays this data in real time across various resources, helping teams quickly detect performance bottlenecks or abnormal behavior. By surfacing the most relevant metrics per resource or environment, Azure enables fast, informed responses to developing issues.

Logs provide a more detailed view of *activity* across Azure resources. Unlike metrics, logs are *event-based* and capture historical data such as **user actions**, **system events**, **diagnostic information**, and **application errors**. This makes them essential for investigating issues, tracking usage patterns, and auditing activity.

Azure Monitor integrates with **Log Analytics** to manage and query log data from multiple sources. Log Analytics uses the **Kusto Query Language (KQL)**, allowing teams to build powerful custom queries to filter, correlate, and analyze log events based on time ranges, specific conditions, or service behavior.

Logs can be further visualized through **Azure Monitor workbooks**, which provide interactive dashboards to help identify trends, detect recurring issues, and gain operational insights.

By combining real-time metrics with in-depth log analysis, Azure Monitor gives teams a complete, end-to-end view of system health and performance. This enables proactive monitoring, faster root cause analysis, and improved reliability of services running in Azure.

Anomaly detection

Azure Monitor offers advanced monitoring features that utilize machine learning to detect anomalies and provide predictive insights. By analyzing historical data, it establishes performance baselines and identifies deviations that may indicate potential issues, such as unexpected spikes in resource utilization.

To enhance this capability, Azure Monitor includes the following:

- **Insights**: Resource-specific monitoring solutions (e.g., for VMs, containers, databases, and applications) that offer tailored metrics, visualizations, and alerting templates, facilitating a deeper understanding of resource health and performance.

- **Azure Monitor issues and investigations (in preview at the time of writing)**: An AI-powered feature that automates the analysis of alerts, correlates data across various sources, and presents findings to expedite root cause identification and resolution. Currently, this feature supports alerts from Application Insights resources in select regions.

By leveraging these tools, teams can proactively address anomalies, predict potential issues, and maintain optimal system reliability.

Resource alerts and notifications

This feature assists with providing information on Azure resource alerts. Users can query various metrics, such as CPU usage, storage I/O, or application latency and response times, allowing for targeted alerts to be identified at machine speed.

Alerts are only effective if they reach the right people in time. Automated responses allow specific actions to trigger automatically when an alert is issued. When paired with automated responses, these alerts and notifications create a responsive environment where resources can adjust based on demand and issue severity.

The next section will provide practical examples of using Azure monitoring tools. You'll learn how to use real-time metrics, anomaly detection, and automated notifications to manage resources efficiently and maintain operational excellence.

Practical examples of monitoring

By mastering the features of live metrics monitoring, anomaly detection, and automated alerts and notifications, teams can ensure high availability, reduce response times for critical events, and optimize resource use, all of which are essential for a robust cloud environment. This section will explore some practical examples of prompts that can be used with Microsoft Copilot for Azure.

The following areas will be covered:

- Resource monitoring
- Real-time metrics
- Alerts
- Notifications
- Anomaly detection

Make sure to make the prompts discussed in this chapter your own by using the actual values from your environment, or experiment and tailor them in a way that meet your needs.

Let's move on to the prompting examples for Microsoft Copilot in Azure for monitoring and diagnostics.

Resource monitoring and real-time metrics

In this section, you'll explore how Microsoft Copilot in Azure enhances resource monitoring through intuitive prompts and real-time metrics. Copilot can quickly deliver actionable insights by simply requesting performance data, such as CPU and memory utilization for your VMs. You'll be able to view real-time graphs, spot resource usage trends, and, if needed, dive deeper into **Metrics Explorer** to make informed scaling and optimization decisions.

Prompt example

The following prompt allows you to view the current performance of VMs, helping to identify any resources that are over- or under-utilized:

- **Copilot prompt:**

  ```
  Which of my virtual machines are currently under high CPU or memory load?
  Show live usage metrics.
  ```

- **Copilot output:**

    Copilot analyzes real-time performance metrics across all VMs and displays a visual chart highlighting VMs with elevated CPU or memory usage. VMs exceeding defined thresholds (e.g., over 80% utilization) are flagged for attention. The output includes a sortable list of affected VMs with current usage values, and a "click-through" option to open each in Metrics Explorer for deeper analysis or to set up alerts.

You saw an example of resource monitoring and real-time metrics prompting in this Copilot prompt. Monitoring resources and real-time metrics are crucial for efficient Azure resource use. These prompts identify over- or under-utilized resources, enabling teams to resolve performance issues, optimize allocation, or plan scaling activities quickly. This improves decision-making and ensures a responsive, high-performance cloud environment.

Alerts

In this section, you'll see how Microsoft Copilot in Azure can assist in monitoring critical alerts for your resources in real time. With simple, targeted prompts, Copilot enables you to quickly access a comprehensive list of recent alerts—asking in *natural language* for severity, affected resources, and timestamps. This functionality helps you stay on top of urgent issues, allowing faster responses and improved resource reliability and availability in your Azure environment.

Prompt example

This prompt lets you quickly identify critical alerts for your VMs over the past six hours, helping you monitor urgent issues in real time:

- **Copilot prompt:**

    ```
    Show me all critical alerts during the last 6 hours for my virtual machines
    ```

- **Copilot output:**

    Copilot will retrieve and display a list of all critical alerts from the last six hours, specifically for your VMs. This output will provide details such as alert names, affected resources, severity levels, and timestamps, giving you immediate insights into pressing issues that require attention.

You saw an example of alert prompting in this Copilot prompt. Alerts provide real-time insights, allowing for fast responses and improved resource reliability. Prompts like that shown in the example help monitor urgent issues with details on severity, affected resources, and timestamps. Use this to manage critical issues and keep a stable Azure environment.

Notifications

In this section, you will see how Microsoft Copilot in Azure can guide you in implementing automated resource alert notifications to keep your team informed and responsive. Using simple prompts, Copilot can provide step-by-step guidance from the Microsoft documentation to set up automated alerts—such as notifying a Microsoft Teams channel when available disk space on a database server falls below a critical threshold. This feature helps ensure you can quickly act on issues that could disrupt operations, improving response times and minimizing downtime.

Prompt example

This prompt provides information from the Microsoft documentation to automate notifications to a specific communication channel (such as Microsoft Teams), helping you act quickly on critical issues such as low disk space that could disrupt operations. You can refine the prompt by providing the context of a specific Teams channel:

- **Copilot prompt:**

  ```
  Notify via Teams if available disk space on any database server drops below
  20%
  ```

- **Copilot output:**

  Copilot will comb through the Microsoft documentation, identify the general approach, and provide further reference articles you should follow that contain the steps to configure the required automated notifications.

You saw an example of notifications prompting in this Copilot prompt. Notifications allow you to set up automated alerts to keep your team informed. Prompts like that shown in the example guide you through configuring important notifications, ensuring timely action to prevent disruptions. This feature can be used to potentially improve response times, reduce downtime, and maintain operations in an Azure environment.

Anomaly detection

In this section, you will see how Microsoft Copilot in Azure can assist in identifying anomalies in your resource metrics and setting up automated notifications for potential issues. By leveraging Copilot's anomaly detection capabilities, you can quickly spot unusual patterns in your storage accounts, such as unexpected usage spikes or security risks. Copilot provides step-by-step guidance on configuring alerts, ensuring you are automatically notified whenever these anomalies occur, allowing you to take immediate action and maintain smooth operations.

Prompt example

This prompt leverages Copilot's anomaly detection capabilities to help you identify outliers in storage metrics, which may indicate abnormal usage patterns or potential security concerns. It also provides guidance on how to set up automated notifications for any detected anomalies in your storage accounts:

- **Copilot prompt:**

  ```
  How can I detect anomalies in my Azure resource metrics, such as storage
  accounts or virtual machines? What are the best practices for setting up
  anomaly detection and alerts in Azure Monitor?
  ```

- **Copilot output:**

  Copilot explains that anomaly detection in Azure Monitor can be done by creating alert rules with dynamic thresholds. These thresholds use historical data to learn normal behavior and automatically detect unusual changes in metrics such as CPU usage, latency, or failure rates. It guides you through selecting a resource and metric, enabling dynamic conditions, and setting up notifications through action groups. Copilot also recommends using Azure Monitor workbooks to visualize trends and identify patterns, and provides links to best practices and setup documentation.

You saw an example of anomaly detection prompting in this Copilot prompt. Anomaly detection allows for the identification of unusual patterns in resource metrics, including unexpected usage spikes or potential security risks. The prompt example offers valuable insights into these irregularities and assists in configuring automated alerts for future anomalies. This functionality enables immediate action to mitigate risks, sustain operational efficiency, and enhance system security.

Application and service health checks

In this section, you will see how Microsoft Copilot in Azure can assist in quickly identifying any active Azure service issues or outages affecting your resources. By leveraging Copilot's real-time monitoring capabilities, you can immediately see any service disruptions that might impact resource performance, availability, or connectivity.

Prompt example

This prompt checks for any active service disruptions, performance degradation, or outages in Microsoft Azure that could affect the user's cloud resources; this utilizes the underlying Azure Service Health platform. Microsoft Azure periodically experiences issues or service outages that can impact the performance or availability of its services. These issues might affect VMs, databases, storage accounts, or any other Azure services a customer relies on:

- **Copilot prompt:**

  ```
  Are there any Azure service issues or outages impacting my resources?
  ```

- **Copilot output:**

  Copilot will scan for relevant Azure service status updates and cross-reference them with your active resources. This enables you to determine whether an outage or performance issue in a specific Azure region or service might affect your resources; you can then decide on the next actions.

You saw an example of application and service health checks prompting in this Copilot prompt. Application and service health checks allow you to identify any Azure service issues or outages affecting your resources. Prompt responses provide real-time insights into disruptions, enabling you to assess their impact and plan appropriate responses. This feature helps you stay informed, reduce downtime, and maintain the performance and availability of your cloud services.

This section provided an in-depth look at using Microsoft Copilot in Azure for real-time monitoring. You can now create a proactive monitoring environment that enhances your Azure infrastructure through live metrics, AI-driven insights, alert systems, and notifications. In the next section, you will explore troubleshooting techniques to resolve issues efficiently, further building on the foundation laid in this chapter.

Using Copilot in Azure for troubleshooting techniques

Effective troubleshooting is essential for maintaining system performance, operational health, and availability in a cloud environment. Using logs and other diagnostics for troubleshooting is standard practice for gaining insight into the operational health of platforms and services, regardless of whether they are traditional on-premises environments, modernized hybrid estates, or fully cloud native.

The following are key capabilities of Microsoft Copilot in Azure for troubleshooting:

- **Proactive issue detection:** Copilot can assist in monitoring Azure resources and alert users to potential issues before they become critical, such as security vulnerabilities or performance bottlenecks.

- **Guided remediation steps:** For many issues, Copilot offers step-by-step guidance on resolving problems, referencing the Microsoft documentation where applicable, allowing even less-experienced administrators to handle complex troubleshooting tasks.

- **Root cause analysis:** Copilot uses machine learning models to analyze log and diagnostics data, metrics, and system events, helping to identify the root causes of issues with precision. Copilot drills down into logs to pinpoint the exact source of an issue. For instance, a database performance drop might be traced to high I/O wait times or an unexpected query.

- **Intelligent recommendations:** Based on historical data and best practices, Copilot suggests configuration changes or optimizations to prevent similar issues from recurring.

Adopting these capabilities can significantly reduce troubleshooting time, especially with the techniques and best practices outlined next.

A typical troubleshooting workflow with Copilot might look like the following:

1. **Identify the issue:** Receive an alert from Azure Monitor and review initial insights provided by Copilot.

2. **Analyze root cause:** Use Copilot's diagnostic tools to analyze logs, metrics, and configurations to determine the root cause.

3. **Review remediation steps:** Follow Copilot's suggested steps, implement changes gradually, and document progress.

4. **Optimize:** Implement any optimization recommendations to prevent recurrence.

5. **Document and automate:** Update the documentation, knowledge base, and playbooks with insights from this incident and consider automating repetitive resolutions.

Microsoft Copilot in Azure uses AI to aid in diagnosing and resolving issues efficiently. The following subsections discuss Copilot's capabilities, the best practices for troubleshooting with Copilot, and the troubleshooting workflow, focusing on techniques that can enhance accuracy, minimize downtime, and improve the overall reliability of an Azure environment.

Here is a summary of the best practices for troubleshooting with Microsoft Copilot in Azure that we will look at:

- Set up alerting and monitoring baselines
- Leverage AI-powered insights for root cause analysis
- Follow Copilot's guided remediation steps
- Optimize resource usage with Copilot's recommendations
- Use sandbox environments for testing solutions

Let's now look at each of these in more detail.

Set up alerting and monitoring baselines

Effective troubleshooting starts with clear visibility into your system's health and performance. Azure offers several monitoring tools that work together to provide this visibility.

Azure Log Analytics is a central component of Azure Monitor that collects and analyzes log and performance data from various sources, such as VMs, applications, and platform services. It allows you to run powerful queries across your data using KQL, helping you detect patterns, troubleshoot issues, and identify anomalies across your environment.

Application Insights is designed specifically for monitoring the performance and usage of your applications. It automatically collects telemetry data such as request rates, response times, exceptions, and dependencies, giving you deep insights into how your application is performing and where improvements are needed.

By enabling these services, you can establish monitoring baselines, set up custom alerts, and detect anomalies more effectively. With Copilot, you can query logs and metrics using natural language, surface specific events, and receive proactive recommendations based on trends in your data.

Together, these tools form a robust foundation for proactive monitoring, helping you respond to issues faster and maintain system reliability.

Leverage AI-powered insights for root cause analysis

Identifying the root cause of issues in a complex cloud environment can be difficult. Copilot's AI capabilities help streamline this process by analyzing data from logs, metrics, and resource configurations.

Copilot can run diagnostic queries across your logs, helping you locate issues quickly. For example, Copilot might suggest examining HTTP response times or dependency call latencies if a web application is slow.

By correlating events across services, Copilot identifies patterns that may indicate the cause of an issue. For example, Copilot could show that high memory usage on a VM correlates with spikes in inbound traffic.

Follow Copilot's guided remediation steps

For many common issues, Copilot provides guided remediation steps. These steps help solve the immediate problem and provide valuable learning for future troubleshooting.

While following Copilot's recommendations, it is a best practice to document the steps taken to resolve issues; this could also mean adding to a knowledge base. This documentation can be referenced for future incidents and help your team build organizational knowledge.

If Copilot suggests a series of configuration changes, then it is best to implement them one at a time to verify their impact. This can help you avoid cascading failures and identify which changes have the most significant impact on performance.

Optimize resource usage with Copilot's recommendations

Many issues in Azure environments stem from resource misallocation, such as under- or over-provisioned VMs or other resources. Copilot's recommendations often include optimization suggestions that can help prevent performance issues from recurring.

If Copilot detects that certain VMs or resources are consistently underutilized or overtaxed, consider resizing them to match workload demands better. This can improve both performance and cost efficiency.

Configure autoscaling policies following Copilot's suggestions for applications with varying demand patterns. This allows resources to automatically adjust according to workload changes, minimizing the likelihood of service interruptions.

Use sandbox environments for testing solutions

Before implementing significant changes suggested by Copilot, consider testing them in a sandbox environment to avoid unintended consequences. This approach is especially useful when Copilot suggests changes to resource configurations, security settings, or network policies.

You can use Azure solutions such as Azure DevTest Labs or a dedicated dev or test environment to evaluate the impact of changes before deploying them in production. This can help prevent disruptions to live services. It is always important to monitor testing results. This allows you to track the changes in the sandbox environment to determine whether they achieve the desired effect. If successful, apply the tested changes to production with confidence.

Testing changes in sandbox environments ensures Copilot's adjustments are safe before applying them to production. After testing, use Copilot to troubleshoot Azure issues. The next section covers using targeted prompts to detect problems, perform root cause analysis, and address risks early.

Practical examples of troubleshooting techniques

Azure can assist in proactively identifying and resolving issues across your cloud environment, leveraging advanced AI and machine learning capabilities to enhance troubleshooting effectiveness. Using targeted prompts, Copilot enables you to monitor resources, detect early warning signs, and gain actionable insights to maintain system reliability and optimize performance.

The following examples showcase how you can use Copilot for troubleshooting, from identifying potential security vulnerabilities to addressing performance bottlenecks before they escalate into larger issues.

The following areas will be covered:

- Proactive issue detection
- Root cause analysis
- Resource optimization recommendations

Let's move on to prompting examples for Microsoft Copilot in Azure.

Proactive issue detection

Let's start by exploring how Microsoft Copilot in Azure can proactively identify and flag potential issues in your cloud environment. Proactive issue detection is vital for keeping high availability and reducing downtime in dynamic applications. Copilot's AI-driven insights help monitor resources, detect anomalies, and send actionable alerts before minor issues become major incidents.

Prompt example

This prompt helps analyze your app and detect and alert you to pre-failure indicators and potential issues that can affect the availability and performance of your web app within your Azure resources:

- **Copilot prompt:**

  Track the health of my App Services and alert me to any pre-failure indicators, such as memory leaks or unhandled exceptions, that could impact availability

- **Copilot output:**

  Copilot will utilize the web app **Risks Assessments** troubleshooting category within the Azure portal, which can be found under the web app **Diagnose and solve problems** blade. It provides any identified potential issues directly back in the prompt dialog box, with a "click-through" link to the web app's **Risks Assessments** troubleshooting category so that more details can be provided on resolving any issues.

You saw an example of proactive issue detection prompting in this Copilot prompt.

Analyze root cause

Microsoft Copilot in Azure can use diagnostic tools to analyze logs, metrics, and configurations to determine the root cause of application performance issues. This demonstrates how Copilot can provide a detailed, real-time analysis of your application's performance. By tracking metrics such as response times, memory usage, CPU usage, and interactions with databases or external services, Copilot identifies the primary causes of slowdowns or downtime. This diagnostic data enables targeted troubleshooting to enhance application performance.

Prompt example

This prompt will initiate a request to collect a profiling trace to allow an in-depth, real-time analysis of your web application as it runs. This trace will track how various components of your application perform, measuring things such as response times, memory usage, CPU usage, and interactions with databases or external services.

Using this diagnostic data, Copilot will identify the primary causes of any slowdowns or downtime, enabling efficient troubleshooting and improved application performance:

- **Copilot prompt:**

  ```
  What are the top performance bottlenecks in my web application?
  ```

- **Copilot output:**

  Copilot will collect a profiling trace to identify the root cause of your app's downtime and slowness.

You saw an example of diagnostic data for troubleshooting prompting in this Copilot prompt. Root cause analysis with Microsoft Copilot is instrumental in identifying and resolving underlying issues, such as resource constraints or inefficient database queries, thereby reducing troubleshooting time and enhancing reliability.

This feature proves valuable during system slowdowns and unexpected downtimes, and when proactively optimizing performance to prevent potential issues. Additionally, it is beneficial for post-incident analysis to avert future problems.

Resource optimization recommendations

Let us see how Microsoft Copilot in Azure can assist in optimizing resource usage. This demonstrates how Copilot can assess your environment with low utilization and suggest actionable steps, such as downgrading instance types or shutting down unnecessary resources. By leveraging Azure Resource Graph and relevant monitoring metrics, Copilot provides specific recommendations that help ensure your resources are efficiently allocated and cost-effective.

Prompt example

This prompt allows you to identify underutilized VMs in your environment and receive tailored recommendations from Copilot for actions such as downgrading or shutting down unnecessary VMs:

- **Copilot prompt:**

  ```
  Show me underutilized VMs and suggest downgrades or shutdown options
  ```

- **Copilot output:**

  Copilot will query your Azure subscription using Azure Resource Graph to provide a list of these VMs and specific recommendations based on returned monitoring metrics.

You saw an example of resource optimization recommendations prompting in this Copilot prompt. Microsoft Copilot in Azure assists in optimizing resource usage by identifying underutilized resources and offering actionable recommendations, such as downgrading instance types or shutting down unnecessary VMs. This feature ensures efficient resource allocation and cost-effectiveness. Utilize this functionality to minimize waste, manage costs, and maintain an optimized environment, particularly during regular audits or when scaling operations.

In conclusion, troubleshooting with Microsoft Copilot in Azure can greatly enhance your ability to detect, diagnose, and resolve issues efficiently. By following these best practices, you can harness Copilot's capabilities to minimize downtime, maintain high performance, and keep your Azure environment resilient and responsive to evolving demands.

In the next section, you will explore Microsoft Copilot in Azure recommendations for high availability and reliability.

Using Copilot in Azure recommendations to ensure high availability and reliability

In today's digital world, high availability and reliability are non-negotiable for modern applications, especially for enterprises that rely on the cloud to run mission-critical workloads. Downtime and performance issues can lead to significant business impact, making proactive maintenance and strategic optimization essential. Microsoft Copilot in Azure offers AI-powered recommendations that help you meet these demands by enhancing availability, improving resilience, and reducing the risk of unexpected issues.

In this section, you will explore how Copilot's recommendations can boost your Azure environment's reliability. We have provided practical steps with prompt examples to leverage these insights.

First, let us understand Azure's high availability and reliability.

Understanding high availability and reliability in Azure

High availability ensures that your resource application is operational for the maximum time possible, while **reliability** focuses on consistently meeting performance expectations without unexpected errors or downtime. The Azure ecosystem achieves these goals through redundancy, failover solutions, load balancing, and automated protection and recovery processes.

Microsoft Copilot in Azure enhances these practices by offering real-time, intelligent recommendations on infrastructure health, performance optimizations, protections, and preventive maintenance. By leveraging machine learning and deep insights from Azure's robust monitoring tools, Copilot can help detect issues before they impact users and provide actionable recommendations to improve reliability and availability.

Practical examples of high availability and reliability

To ensure that your Azure environment remains resilient, Microsoft Copilot in Azure offers practical, guided, hands-on support for configuring high availability and reliability. These essential principles focus on maintaining operational continuity, preventing downtime, and providing a strong foundation for disaster recovery and service health.

We will be covering the following areas in this section:

- Disaster recovery in Azure
- Application and service health checks

Now, let's move on to the prompting examples for Microsoft Copilot in Azure for high availability and reliability.

Disaster recovery in Azure

Replicating VMs across regions is a common practice for achieving high availability, disaster recovery, and resilience against regional outages. Setting up VM replication ensures critical workloads can quickly recover in a different region if the primary region becomes unavailable.

With this prompt, Copilot will guide you through configuring **Azure Site Recovery**, the service used for VM replication, and provide recommendations on replication settings, failover options, and resource planning to help with achieving reliable, seamless disaster recovery.

Prompt example

Here's an example of how you might engage Copilot to set up VM replication for disaster recovery:

- **Copilot prompt:**

    ```
    Can you help me set up VM replication to another region?
    ```

- **Copilot output:**

  Copilot will provide a streamlined setup process for VM replication using Azure Site Recovery. Copilot will check your VM's compatibility, ensure permissions, and guide you in selecting the target region. It will then help configure Site Recovery by setting up replication policies and network mapping for seamless failover. Copilot will provide instructions on testing the replication to validate that failover works as expected, ensuring readiness without impacting production. Finally, Copilot will offer guidance on monitoring replication health and optimizing costs, completing a resilient disaster recovery setup for your VM.

You saw an example of disaster recovery in Azure in this Copilot prompt. Microsoft Copilot in Azure facilitates disaster recovery setup by assisting users through the replication of VMs to another region using Azure Site Recovery. It provides well-informed recommendations on replication settings, failover options, and resource planning to ensure high availability and resilience against outages. This capability is crucial for maintaining business continuity, particularly when preparing for potential regional failures or ensuring that critical workloads can recover seamlessly.

Next, we will look at application and service health checks.

Application and service health checks

Microsoft Copilot in Azure can assist in quickly identifying any active Azure service issues or outages affecting your resources. By leveraging Copilot's real-time monitoring capabilities, you can immediately see any service disruptions that might impact resource performance, availability, or connectivity.

Prompt example

The following example shows how you might ask Copilot to check for active service issues that could affect your resources:

- **Copilot prompt:**

  ```
  Are there any Azure service issues or outages impacting my resources?
  ```

- **Copilot output:**

  Copilot will scan for relevant Azure service status updates and cross-reference them with your active resources. This enables you to determine whether an outage or performance issue in a specific Azure region or service might affect your resources; you can then decide on the next actions.

You saw an example of application and service health checks in this Copilot prompt. Microsoft Copilot in Azure assists in identifying active Azure service issues or outages that might affect resource performance, availability, or connectivity. By offering real-time insights and cross-referencing service status with your resources, it facilitates quicker decision-making and aims to minimize disruption during incidents or while troubleshooting performance issues.

In conclusion, ensuring high availability and reliability in Azure is continuous, but Microsoft Copilot makes it manageable and efficient. You can maintain a resilient, reliable infrastructure that meets modern availability standards by proactively monitoring, analyzing, and optimizing your environment based on Copilot's intelligent recommendations.

By following Copilot's guidance on VM replication, you will have a robust disaster recovery configuration that ensures continuity of service if a regional failure occurs. This setup allows for faster recovery times, reduced data loss, and peace of mind knowing your applications and data are protected.

Copilot provides insights and tools to keep your Azure resources protected, available, and responsive. Embrace these recommendations as part of your operations strategy to build a robust, high-performing cloud ecosystem that users can rely on.

Summary

In this chapter, you explored the capabilities of Microsoft Copilot for Azure in the area of real-time monitoring and troubleshooting.

Here are the key skills and insights you have gained:

- You learned how Copilot can query monitoring and diagnostics to proactively collect insights from Azure resources, alerting you to potential issues such as performance bottlenecks or resource shortages before they develop into critical problems.

- You explored how Copilot's AI models can analyze diagnostics and telemetry data, logs, and metrics to swiftly identify the root causes of complex incidents, thereby accelerating the resolution process.

- You discovered how to adopt troubleshooting techniques and best practices utilizing Microsoft Copilot in Azure prompts to speed up the identification and resolution process.

- Lastly, you saw how Copilot can assess and provide high availability and reliability recommendations. These suggestions ensure optimal operations.

The main takeaway from this chapter is the understanding that maintaining high availability and reliability in Azure is a continuous and manageable process with Microsoft Copilot. Integrating proactive monitoring, detailed analysis, and intelligent optimization strategies ensures your cloud infrastructure runs with operational effectiveness, resilience, and responsiveness.

Utilizing Copilot's insights and tools enables you to monitor and manage resources effectively and efficiently and respond to incidents promptly. Adopt these recommendations as part of your operational strategy to build a robust and high-performing cloud ecosystem that meets the demands of modern availability standards.

In the next chapter, *Chapter 9, Scaling and Optimizing Cloud Operations*, you will learn how to build and maintain a scalable, efficient, and cost-effective cloud infrastructure that adapts to evolving business needs. This chapter will guide you through using Microsoft Copilot in Azure to automate scaling processes, optimize resource utilization, and implement strategies for handling fluctuating workloads. By examining AI-driven insights and real-world scenarios, you will gain practical knowledge on making decisions that ensure performance, cost-efficiency, and resilience. Additionally, you will understand how these techniques align with the key principles of the Microsoft Well-Architected Framework, emphasizing operational excellence and performance efficiency.

Unlock this book's exclusive benefits now

UNLOCK NOW

Scan this QR code or go to https://packtpub.com/unlock, then search for this book by name.

Note: *Keep your purchase invoice ready before you start.*

9

Scaling and Optimizing Cloud Operations

This chapter gives you the skills to maintain a scalable, optimized cloud infrastructure prepared for growth. It highlights the ability to manage evolving business demands, utilizing Microsoft Copilot in Azure as a strategic asset. Understanding scaling and optimizing cloud operations is fundamental. Scaling adjusts resources to meet demand, ensuring performance and cost-efficiency. Optimization fine-tunes resources to avoid waste and maximize utilization. Using Copilot in Azure, businesses can automate these processes with AI-driven insights, creating a dynamic cloud environment to handle fluctuating workloads and demands.

By reading this chapter, you will acquire practical knowledge on utilizing Copilot in Azure for scalable cloud infrastructure. Through real-world scenarios, you will learn how to automate and scale resources to meet changing demand. You will also explore integrating AI-driven recommendations from Copilot and applying data-backed insights to manage scaling processes proactively. This includes understanding Copilot's AI-driven analytics and how to make strategic decisions based on Copilot's suggestions.

As businesses evolve, cloud infrastructure must scale efficiently. Proactive strategies handle fluctuating workloads and unexpected spikes. Auto-scaling adjusts resources in real time, maintaining performance and controlling costs. Resource optimization ensures efficient cloud usage, avoiding over-provisioning and underutilization. Ongoing monitoring and optimization are vital.

Tools such as Azure Monitor and Application Insights provide real-time insights and recommendations for a well-tuned environment. Also, security and compliance become crucial as operations scale. Strong security measures and adherence to standards mitigate risks. Automation reduces manual tasks, improving efficiency and minimizing errors. Organizations can ensure agile, efficient, and resilient cloud operations by following these strategies.

Regarding the Azure **Well-Architected Framework (WAF)**, this chapter maps to the *operational excellence* and *performance efficiency* pillars.

In this chapter, we will cover the following main topics:

- Case study: Scaling cloud operations for peak demand with Copilot in Azure
- Strategy for adopting scaling cloud infrastructure using Copilot in Azure
- Scaling cloud infrastructure using Copilot in Azure
- Resource management techniques using Copilot in Azure

Let's have a look at the technical requirements to get you started.

Technical requirements

It is recommended to have access to an active Azure subscription to follow the examples provided in this chapter.

It is recommended to have first completed *Chapter 1, Understanding Microsoft Copilot in Azure,* to set a baseline knowledge of some concepts for working with Microsoft Copilot in Azure, as well as completing *Chapter 2, Getting Started with Microsoft Copilot in Azure*, so that you are aware of how to use the Azure portal to access Microsoft Copilot in Azure.

When prompting, the guidance is to be very specific with the phrases and words used to articulate the desired output. The more specific and concise you can be in the prompt, the better results you will get in the response. As of the time of publishing, Copilot in Azure has a *500-character limit* per prompt; therefore, you need to be thoughtful about how you write your prompts to maximize value and achieve the desired output.

Ensure you have the appropriate *Azure role assignments* for any resources you are investigating, as Copilot can only operate within the scope of your existing permissions and cannot grant access to data or services you are not already authorized to use. Additionally, some services must be explicitly enabled to provide data or surface relevant insights to Copilot. For example, for use of **Azure Monitor Investigator** by Copilot, this does not need to be *enabled manually*; it is built into Azure Monitor and becomes available automatically when your resources are sending telemetry data such as logs and metrics.

However, Azure Monitor monitored resources must have diagnostic settings configured to send telemetry (such as logs and metrics) to a **Log Analytics workspace** for Investigator to surface relevant insights.

> You will still always need to manually review the code generated by AI and potentially modify the output to be able to complete the task or operation on the resource type.
>
> Outputs or code generated by AI may not be fully accurate or functional.

With the foundational setup and knowledge complete, administrators can now use Copilot to assist with scaling cloud infrastructure. The next section explores a real-world case study for some of the concepts to be covered in this chapter.

Case study: Scaling cloud operations for peak demand with Copilot in Azure

This case study examines scaling cloud operations for a retail business during the holiday season. The background is that a global e-commerce company faced challenges in managing sudden spikes in traffic during holiday sales. Their static infrastructure often led to performance bottlenecks, increased downtime, and inefficient resource usage, resulting in revenue loss and customer dissatisfaction.

Utilizing Microsoft Copilot in Azure, the company implemented auto-scaling to dynamically adjust resources based on real-time demand. Copilot identified patterns in historical traffic data and recommended optimal scaling thresholds for their virtual machines and databases. Additionally, Copilot's AI-driven insights guided them in optimizing storage usage and shutting down underutilized resources, reducing costs by approximately 25% without compromising performance. Key implementation highlights included the following:

- **Auto-scaling**: Copilot recommended scaling policies to handle fluctuating workloads, ensuring smooth shopping experiences during peak times.

- **Resource optimization**: Copilot identified and recommended resizing over-provisioned instances, leading to efficient resource utilization.

- **Proactive monitoring**: With Azure Monitor and Application Insights, Copilot provided continuous health checks and performance insights, aiding the team in predicting and preventing potential outages.

As a result, the company successfully managed traffic surges, reducing downtime by around 40% and saving operational costs. This scalable and optimized setup allowed them to focus on maintaining a resilient cloud infrastructure while delivering a consistent customer experience.

This case study demonstrates the practical application of scaling strategies, resource optimization, and AI-driven insights discussed in this chapter. It shows how monitoring, auto-scaling, and automation can ensure operational efficiency and performance, aligning with the principles of the Azure WAF.

The following section outlines a strategy for using Copilot in Azure to assist with scaling cloud operations and optimizing infrastructure.

Strategy for adopting scaling cloud infrastructure using Copilot in Azure

Scaling cloud infrastructure requires a strategic approach. Microsoft Copilot in Azure offers AI tools to streamline this process with insights and automation.

This section covers strategies for using Copilot to create a scalable, efficient cloud setup. You'll learn how to evaluate your current system, set requirements, implement automation, and optimize performance and costs. With Copilot's smart recommendations and Azure's scaling features, you can foresee needs, automate scaling, and optimize resources while ensuring high availability and reliability.

To adopt scaling cloud infrastructure using Copilot in Azure, you can follow these strategic steps:

- **Assess current infrastructure**: Evaluate current infrastructure and identify scaling needs. This should be carried out at the start or during performance issues. Used to identify bottlenecks and scaling needs.

- **Optimize resource allocation**: Balance performance and cost. This should be carried out after assessment or during high-demand periods. Used to balance performance and cost.

- **Define scaling requirements**: Define specific requirements for scaling based on workload patterns. This should be carried out before implementing scaling solutions. Used to tailor scaling to workload patterns.

- **Implement load balancing**: Distribute traffic to ensure availability. This should be carried out before deployment or with uneven traffic. Used to ensure availability and reliability.

- **Leverage auto-scaling features**: Automatically adjust resources based on demand. This should be carried out during deployment to handle demand fluctuations. Used to automate resource adjustment, reducing manual effort.

- **Automate scaling policies**: Set automated scaling policies for resources. This should be carried out after setting scaling thresholds. Used to enable timely and consistent scaling actions.

- **Set up monitoring and alerts**: Use Azure Monitor to track issues or constraints and set alerts. This should be carried out immediately after deployment. Used to detect and resolve issues proactively.

- **Regularly review and adjust**: Review and adjust scaling policies to meet changing requirements. This should be carried out periodically or after workload changes. Used to ensure scaling policies stay effective over time.

By following these steps and including these sections in your strategy, you can effectively adopt scaling cloud infrastructure using Copilot in Azure. You will learn more about some of these in the following sections of this chapter, with some examples of prompts.

A real-world example of how Copilot can be utilized could be for a retail application that experiences high traffic during sales events, requiring additional computing resources to handle the spike. With Copilot, you can do the following:

- **Define scaling triggers**: Set up triggers in Azure Monitor for metrics such as CPU utilization or request count per minute. Copilot can suggest optimal thresholds, allowing you to implement responsive and precise scaling rules.

- **Automate scaling actions**: Copilot can recommend enabling the automatic addition or removal of **virtual machines (VMs)** within a specified range. For example, Copilot might suggest scaling the VM count from 2 to 10 during peak times based on past activity.

- **Review and adjust in real-time**: Use Copilot to review the scaling effectiveness and modify the rules dynamically, ensuring the infrastructure can scale up and down seamlessly to match demand.

This automation reduces manual intervention, allowing the infrastructure to scale fluidly in response to fluctuating workloads, optimizing performance and cost.

In this section, you learned about a comprehensive strategy for adopting scalable cloud infrastructure using Microsoft Copilot in Azure. By assessing your current setup, defining scaling requirements, and implementing Azure platform scaling features, you can adjust your cloud resources dynamically to meet business demands. Automating scaling policies and setting up robust monitoring further optimize performance and cost efficiency. With Copilot's AI-driven recommendations, organizations can proactively manage infrastructure, ensuring high availability, responsiveness, and operational efficiency as workloads evolve.

The next section will dive deeper into how to implement and refine these strategies for continuous optimization.

Scaling cloud infrastructure using Copilot in Azure

This section guides you through understanding and implementing scalable solutions using Microsoft Copilot in Azure. You will discover methods to expand infrastructure capacity efficiently, understanding how to dynamically adjust resources to align with workload demands while maintaining performance and minimizing costs.

In cloud infrastructure, **scaling** refers to adjusting computing resources allocated to an application or service to meet changing demands. The two primary scaling approaches to be aware of are as follows:

- **Vertical scaling (scaling up/down)**: Enhancing the capacity of an existing resource, such as increasing CPU, memory, or storage in a VM
- **Horizontal scaling (scaling out/in)**: Adding or removing resource instances, such as multiple VMs or containers, to handle increased or reduced workloads more effectively

To implement scaling effectively, however, it's important to understand the broader landscape of auto-scaling strategies commonly supported across cloud platforms:

- **Metric-based scaling**: Automatically adjusts resources in response to real-time performance indicators such as CPU utilization, memory usage, or custom metrics
- **Scheduled scaling**: Performs predefined scaling actions at specific times, aligned with known usage patterns such as business hours or planned events
- **Predictive scaling**: Uses historical usage data and machine learning to forecast future demand and proactively adjust resources in advance

While these auto-scaling strategies are broadly supported across cloud platforms, it's important to understand which are specifically available within Azure. The following subsection outlines Azure's auto-scaling capabilities.

Auto-scaling in Azure

While these auto-scaling strategies are broadly available across cloud platforms, Azure supports a comprehensive range of scaling capabilities that go beyond metric-based and scheduled rules.

Specifically, Azure enables both of the following:

- **Horizontal scaling**: Automatically or manually adding/removing instances (e.g., Azure VMs, containers, or App Service instances) to distribute the load and meet performance targets.

- **Vertical scaling**: Manually increasing the size or capacity of an individual resource, such as scaling an Azure VM to a higher SKU. In some cases, this can be done through automation or scripting.

For automated, rule-based adjustments, Azure supports two main autoscaling strategies:

- **Metric-based scaling**: Azure Monitor allows you to configure rules that automatically scale resources in or out based on real-time performance metrics, such as CPU usage, memory consumption, or custom telemetry from Application Insights.

- **Scheduled scaling**: Azure Autoscale profiles enable you to define scaling actions that trigger at specific times or on recurring schedules, ideal for predictable workload changes such as business hours or marketing campaigns.

> Predictive scaling is not a native feature of Azure Autoscale. However, similar functionality can be achieved using custom solutions or third-party tools that combine forecasting with automation.

Microsoft Copilot in Azure enhances these scaling capabilities by providing intelligent recommendations tailored to your infrastructure. Copilot helps identify optimal metric thresholds, suggest schedule patterns, and guide you through implementing or refining auto-scaling rules based on historical usage and performance data.

By combining Azure's support for horizontal and vertical scaling with automated auto-scaling capabilities and layering in Copilot's AI-driven insights, organizations can build a responsive, cost-efficient infrastructure that adapts to workload demands in real time.

In the following subsections, you will learn how to deliver the strategy steps for adopting scaling cloud infrastructure using Copilot in Azure.

Infrastructure assessment

In this strategy step, you evaluate your current cloud infrastructure to identify areas needing scaling by analyzing resource use, performance metrics, and bottlenecks.

The infrastructure assessment should include the following aspects:

- Inventory of resources
- Performance analysis
- Bottleneck identification

Each of these will be examined in the following sections, along with examples of prompts that you can change to suit your particular scenarios and needs.

By leveraging these prompts, you'll be able to streamline your scaling approach, which is both effective and efficient.

> Make sure to make the prompts discussed in this chapter your own by using actual values from your environment, or experiment and tailor these prompts in a way that meet your needs.

Inventory of resources

This aspect recommends that you catalog all existing Azure resources, including VMs, databases, storage accounts, and applications.

The following are some example prompts that can be used with Microsoft Copilot in Azure for this aspect of the strategy:

- Can you provide an inventory of all my Azure resources, including VMs, databases, and storage accounts?
- Show me a summary of all resources in my Azure subscription.
- List all my Azure VMs, databases, and storage accounts.

Cataloging your Azure resources is a foundational step in managing scalability with Microsoft Copilot. Organizing resources such as VMs, databases, and storage accounts gives you a clear overview of your cloud environment, making implementing and refining scaling strategies easier.

Performance analysis

This aspect recommends that you evaluate current performance metrics to identify underutilized or overburdened resources.

The following are some example prompts that can be used with Microsoft Copilot in Azure for this aspect of the strategy:

- `Help me analyze the current performance metrics for my Azure resources.`
- `Provide a detailed performance analysis of my Azure SQL databases.`
- `Analyze the CPU and memory usage trends for my Azure VMs over the past month.`

Evaluating performance metrics helps identify underutilized or overburdened resources in Azure, enabling efficient resource allocation and optimization.

Bottleneck identification

This aspect recommends pinpointing any performance bottlenecks or resource constraints impacting scaling.

The following are some example prompts that can be used with Microsoft Copilot in Azure for this aspect of the strategy:

- `Identify any performance bottlenecks in my current Azure infrastructure.`
- `Identify any network bottlenecks in my current Azure setup.`
- `Detect performance issues in my Azure App Service and suggest improvements.`

Identifying performance bottlenecks and resource constraints is essential for effective scalability. Microsoft Copilot can assist in identifying these issues.

Scaling requirements

This strategy step determines the scaling requirements based on your workload patterns. Identify peak usage periods, anticipated growth, and performance objectives.

The infrastructure assessment should include the following aspects:

- Workload patterns
- Performance goals
- Capacity planning

Each of these will be examined in the following subsections, along with example prompts that you can change to suit your particular scenarios and needs.

Workload patterns

This aspect recommends that you analyze historical usage data to understand peak and off-peak periods.

The following are some example prompts that can be used with Microsoft Copilot in Azure for this aspect of the strategy:

- What are the peak usage times for Azure App Service over the last year?
- Analyze historical usage data to understand peak and off-peak periods for my resources.
- Analyze the historical workload patterns of Azure Functions.

Analyzing historical usage data is crucial for identifying peak and off-peak periods, allowing you to optimize scaling decisions based on trends. Microsoft Copilot can assist with this by providing detailed insights into past resource usage.

Performance goals

This aspect recommends that you define performance targets such as acceptable response times and throughput rates.

The following are some example prompts that can be used with Microsoft Copilot in Azure for this aspect of the strategy:

- Help me define performance targets for response times and throughput rates.
- What throughput rate should I aim for based on current usage patterns?
- Recommend performance benchmarks for my Azure VMs.

Defining clear performance targets, such as acceptable response times and throughput rates, is essential for setting a benchmark that ensures optimal user experience and resource efficiency. Microsoft Copilot can assist you by setting and monitoring these performance goals.

Capacity planning

This aspect recommends that you estimate future resource needs based on expected growth and usage trends.

The following are some example prompts that can be used with Microsoft Copilot in Azure for this aspect of the strategy:

- Estimate future resource needs based on expected growth and usage trends.
- What resources will be needed if usage increases by 20% over the next quarter?
- Estimate future capacity requirements for my Azure storage accounts.

Estimating future resource needs based on anticipated growth and usage trends is key to proactive scaling and efficient resource planning. Microsoft Copilot can provide insights and projections to help you stay ahead of demand.

Load balancing

This strategy phase uses Azure Load Balancer or Traffic Manager to ensure high availability by distributing traffic across multiple instances.

The infrastructure assessment should include the following aspects:

- Azure Load Balancer
- Traffic Manager
- Health probes

Each of these will be examined in the following sections, along with example prompts that you can change to suit your particular scenarios and needs.

Azure Load Balancer

This aspect recommends implementing Azure Load Balancer to distribute incoming traffic across multiple VMs or instances.

The following are some example prompts that can be used with Microsoft Copilot in Azure for this aspect of the strategy:

- Assist me in configuring Azure Load Balancer to distribute traffic across my VMs.
- What load balancing options are recommended for my current workload?
- Set up a load balancing rule to manage incoming traffic across instances.

Utilizing Azure Load Balancer facilitates the even distribution of incoming traffic across multiple virtual machines or instances, enhancing performance and reliability. Microsoft Copilot can assist with the setup and optimization of load balancing.

Traffic Manager

This aspect recommends that you use Azure Traffic Manager for global load balancing, ensuring high availability and performance across regions.

The following are some example prompts that can be used with Microsoft Copilot in Azure for this aspect of the strategy:

- Help me configure Azure Traffic Manager for global load balancing across regions.
- What Traffic Manager settings are recommended to ensure high availability?
- Set up Traffic Manager to optimize performance based on user location.

Utilizing Azure Traffic Manager for global load balancing is essential to maintain high availability and achieve optimal performance across multiple regions. This helps distribute user traffic efficiently, enhancing the user experience worldwide. Microsoft Copilot can assist in setting up and fine-tuning Traffic Manager configurations.

Health probes

This aspect recommends that you configure health probes to monitor the availability and performance of your applications and services.

The following are some example prompts that can be used with Microsoft Copilot in Azure for this aspect of the strategy:

- Help me configure health probes to monitor the availability of my applications.
- Configure health probes to monitor the availability of my services.
- What health probe configurations should I use to monitor my Azure resources effectively?

Setting up health probes is essential for monitoring the availability and performance of applications and services, thereby ensuring that Microsoft Copilot can assist in setting up and managing these probes.

Auto-scaling configuration

In this strategy, you leverage Azure's auto-scaling capabilities to adjust resources dynamically according to demand. Copilot can assist in configuring these settings to align with your specific requirements.

The infrastructure assessment should include the following aspects:

- **Azure Autoscale**: Enables metric-based or scheduled scaling for services such as App Service and **Azure Kubernetes Service (AKS)**

- **AKS**: Supports Pod-level and node-level auto-scaling for containerized workloads

- **Application Insights**: Provides telemetry that can inform auto-scaling decisions based on application performance

Each of these will be examined in the following subsections, along with example prompts that you can take and adapt to suit your scenarios and needs.

> **Virtual Machine Scale Sets (VMSS)** is an Azure service for automatically scaling VM instances horizontally. While VMSS is important for VM-based workloads, it is a much broader topic to be understood than can be covered here, and so the focus is on services where Copilot provides more direct, integrated autoscaling support.

Azure Autoscale

This aspect recommends utilizing Azure Autoscale to adjust resources automatically based on demand. Configure scaling rules for different resource types.

The following are some example prompts that can be used with Microsoft Copilot in Azure for this aspect of the strategy:

- Assist me in setting up Azure Autoscale to adjust resources automatically based on demand.
- What scaling rules should I configure for different resource types to optimize performance?
- Can you help me define auto-scaling thresholds for my VMs and databases?

Utilizing Azure Autoscale enables your resources to adjust automatically based on demand, helping maintain performance while controlling costs. By configuring scaling rules for different resource types, you can ensure your infrastructure responds to varying workloads.

AKS

This aspect recommends using the auto-scaling features of AKS for containerized applications to manage Pod and node scaling.

The following are some example prompts that can be used with Microsoft Copilot in Azure for this aspect of the strategy:

- What auto-scaling settings should I use for my AKS cluster to manage varying workloads?
- Help me set up auto-scaling for my AKS cluster to manage Pod and node scaling.
- How can I configure AKS auto-scaling rules to optimize resource usage and performance for containerized applications?

For containerized applications, using the auto-scaling features of AKS assists in managing Pod and node scaling dynamically, ensuring efficient resource use and application performance. Microsoft Copilot provides guidance on configuring AKS auto-scaling.

Application Insights

This aspect recommends integrating with Application Insights to monitor application performance and trigger scaling actions based on telemetry data.

The following are some example prompts that can be used with Microsoft Copilot in Azure for this aspect of the strategy:

- How do I integrate Application Insights to monitor performance and trigger scaling actions?
- Set up Application Insights to track key metrics and initiate scaling as needed.
- What telemetry data should I monitor in Application Insights to optimize scaling decisions?

Integrating with Application Insights allows you to monitor application performance in real time and trigger scaling actions based on telemetry data, ensuring responsive and efficient scaling. Microsoft Copilot can assist in configuring this integration to ensure effective monitoring and automated responses.

Automated scaling policies

In this strategy step, you utilize Copilot to automate scaling policies for your resources. This encompasses scaling VMs, Azure App Service, Azure Functions, and other resources based on predefined criteria such as CPU utilization, memory consumption, or request rates.

The infrastructure assessment should include the following aspects:

- Defining scaling triggers
- Creating auto-scaling rules
- Policy testing

Each of these will be examined in the following subsections, along with example prompts that you can change to suit your particular scenarios and needs.

Defining scaling triggers

This aspect recommends establishing the criteria for scaling actions, such as CPU or memory thresholds, request rates, or custom metrics.

The following are some example prompts that can be used with Microsoft Copilot in Azure for this aspect of the strategy:

- `What request rate should trigger auto-scaling in my environment?`
- `What do I need to do to establish criteria for scaling actions based on CPU or memory thresholds?`
- `How do I set up auto-scaling for my VMs based on CPU usage exceeding 75%?`

Establishing clear criteria for scaling actions, such as CPU or memory thresholds, request rates, or custom metrics, is essential for responsive and efficient scaling. With Microsoft Copilot, you can set up precise rules to trigger scaling based on these metrics.

Creating auto-scaling rules

This aspect recommends that you use Copilot to help define auto-scaling rules for different resources based on the identified triggers.

The following are some example prompts that can be used with Microsoft Copilot in Azure for this aspect of the strategy:

- `Help me define auto-scaling rules for my VMs based on identified triggers.`
- `Assist me in setting up auto-scaling rules for my VMs based on CPU usage triggers.`
- `Help create auto-scaling policies for my AKS cluster to handle varying workloads.`

Using Microsoft Copilot to define auto-scaling rules tailored to different resources and identified triggers ensures that scaling actions are responsive to actual needs. This approach helps maintain performance and resource efficiency across your Azure environment.

Policy testing

This aspect recommends that you test the scaling policies in a controlled environment to ensure they work as expected.

The following are some example prompts that can be used with Microsoft Copilot in Azure for this aspect of the strategy:

- `I need to test the scaling policies in a controlled environment; how do I do this?`
- `How can I simulate high CPU usage to test my auto-scaling rules?`
- `Assist me in setting up a test environment to validate my scaling policies.`

Testing scaling policies in a controlled environment ensures that they function as intended before deploying them in production. This helps identify and resolve any issues in scaling triggers or thresholds. Microsoft Copilot can guide you through testing and validating these policies.

This section provided a comprehensive guide to using Microsoft Copilot in Azure for scaling cloud infrastructure. You learned about strategies to assess existing resources, define scaling requirements, and implement automated scaling policies, helping organizations dynamically adjust resources to match workload demands effectively. Scaling in the cloud involves adapting resource levels to meet fluctuating application demands, whether by adding or enhancing existing instances. Key concepts discussed included Azure's scaling rules, which trigger resource adjustments based on metrics such as CPU usage and memory consumption, and Copilot's ability to recommend and optimize these rules for efficient and cost-effective scaling.

Additionally, real-world applications, such as scaling resources during high-traffic events, illustrated Copilot's practical uses. With example prompts for assessing infrastructure, managing autoscale rules, and configuring load balancers, you gained actionable insights into optimizing Azure environments for high availability and performance. Integrating tools such as Azure Load Balancer, Traffic Manager, and Application Insights with Copilot further enhances resource management, allowing for continuous scaling improvements and supporting business objectives by meeting performance demands seamlessly.

In the next section, you will dive into resource management techniques, focusing on using Microsoft Copilot to optimize cloud resource allocation and reduce costs. You will explore strategies for resource optimization and continuous review, enabling you to maintain efficient, high-performance cloud operations that adapt to changing demands.

Resource management techniques

In this section, you will examine advanced resource management techniques that align with the steps you learned in the *Strategy for adopting scaling cloud infrastructure using Copilot in Azure* section to enhance cloud efficiency and control costs.

Effective resource management is critical for ensuring that your cloud environment remains resilient and economical. Microsoft Copilot plays a key role in supporting these goals by providing intelligent recommendations for cost-effectively allocating resources and adjusting usage based on real-time data.

In this section, you will explore the strategy of resource optimization, where Copilot can help analyze usage patterns, enabling you to optimize resource distribution and reduce unnecessary expenses while maintaining performance. Using Copilot's insights, you can fine-tune resource allocations over time to support an agile and cost-efficient cloud environment.

Resource optimization

When looking at resource optimization, you use Copilot in Azure to analyze usage patterns and optimize resource distribution, minimizing costs while maintaining performance.

The resource optimization step of the strategy you looked at in the beginning of this chapter should include the following aspects:

- Right-sizing resources
- Cost management
- Optimization insights

Each of these will be examined in the following subsections, along with example prompts that you can change to suit your particular scenarios and needs.

By leveraging these prompts, you'll be able to streamline resource management and ensure your scaling approach is both effective and efficient.

Right-sizing resources

This aspect requires you to ensure that my resources are appropriately sized based on current usage.

The following are some example prompts that can be used with Microsoft Copilot in Azure for this aspect of the strategy:

- Can you help me ensure my resources are appropriately sized based on current usage?
- Identify underutilized VMs and recommend resizing options.
- Can you suggest optimal configurations for my Azure SQL databases?

Right-sizing resources helps optimize cloud efficiency by aligning resource allocation with actual usage. Using Copilot's insights, you can ensure that resources are neither over-provisioned nor underutilized, achieving cost-effectiveness and maintaining performance.

Cost management

This aspect recommends identifying cost savings opportunities by resizing or deallocating underutilized resources.

The following are some example prompts that can be used with Microsoft Copilot in Azure for this aspect of the strategy:

- How can I identify opportunities for cost savings by resizing or deallocating underutilized resources?
- Can you help me analyze my Azure cost reports and identify cost-saving opportunities?
- Can you provide recommendations to reduce costs by optimizing resource usage?

Managing costs effectively is important for maintaining a cost-efficient cloud environment. Using Copilot to identify and adjust underutilized resources allows you to implement strategies to optimize costs while maintaining performance.

Optimization insights

This aspect recommends that you provide insights into optimization opportunities for Azure resources.

The following are some example prompts that can be used with Microsoft Copilot in Azure for this aspect of the strategy:

- Can you provide insights into optimization opportunities for my Azure resources?

- Suggest performance improvements based on current usage patterns.
- Identify services with potential performance or cost inefficiencies and provide optimization suggestions.

Utilizing optimization insights through Copilot enables continuous improvement in resource allocation. By identifying areas where resources can be optimized, you can enhance efficiency, reduce costs, and ensure that your Azure environment remains effective and streamlined.

This concludes this section and the content of this chapter.

In wrapping up, we have delved into various cost management and resource optimization strategies within your Azure environment. Utilizing the powerful capabilities of Microsoft Copilot, we explored practical approaches to identify underutilized resources and implement cost-saving measures. The example prompts demonstrated how Copilot can continually offer valuable insights and actionable recommendations to refine and enhance your cloud infrastructure.

As we conclude this chapter, it is evident that leveraging Copilot in Azure can lead to significant improvements in operational efficiency and financial sustainability. Proactively managing resources ensures that your cloud environment remains agile and effective, aligning with organizational goals. Achieving a cost-efficient, high-performing Azure setup is an ongoing process; the discussed tools and strategies will help you navigate this path successfully.

Summary

This chapter was a comprehensive guide to harnessing Copilot's capabilities to scale infrastructure intelligently and optimize resource management effectively, helping you meet your operational goals with precision and agility.

It discussed strategies for managing and reducing cloud costs through effective resource optimization. It emphasized maintaining a cost-efficient cloud environment, which is important for operational excellence and financial prudence. The chapter underscored the significance of proactive management and continuous improvement in cloud operations to ensure optimal resource use, controlled costs, and high performance.

The chapter introduced Microsoft Copilot in Azure as a tool for this purpose. Copilot assists in identifying underutilized resources and recommends cost-saving measures. Using Copilot's optimization insights, users can adjust their resource allocation to meet changing demands while avoiding unnecessary expenses. This tool automates routine tasks and provides real-time recommendations to enhance overall efficiency.

You have now gained practical knowledge and strategies for maintaining an effective Azure environment. You have learned how to implement and benefit from Copilot's features, ensuring your cloud infrastructure is agile and efficient. This approach to cloud cost management helps organizations achieve better operational efficiency and financial sustainability in a competitive landscape.

In the upcoming chapter, *Integrating AI-Driven Insights for Cost Management*, you will examine how AI can revolutionize the management and optimization of organizational cloud expenditures. The chapter will detail how Microsoft Copilot in Azure offers actionable insights by leveraging AI to simplify cost analysis, recommend optimizations, and automate resource management for maximum efficiency. Through both theoretical understanding and practical examples, this chapter will equip you with the ability to interpret cost metrics, apply AI-driven recommendations, and implement strategies that are consistent with the *cost optimization* pillar of the Azure WAF.

By the conclusion of this chapter, you will have acquired practical skills to manage cloud expenses effectively, enhance operational efficiency, and make data-driven decisions that support your organization's cloud strategy.

This exploration paves the way for comprehending how AI can transform cost management into a strategic advantage.

Unlock this book's exclusive benefits now

UNLOCK NOW

Scan this QR code or go to `https://packtpub.com/unlock`, then search for this book by name.

Note: Keep your purchase invoice ready before you start.

Part 3

Ensuring Comprehensive Security and Compliance

The final part of this book brings everything together by showing how Microsoft Copilot in Azure supports secure, compliant, and cost-conscious cloud operations. You'll explore how AI-driven insights can optimize spending, how Copilot can help enforce regulatory standards and security policies, and how to build a proactive governance model that keeps pace with evolving risks. This section also ties together the book's key lessons, offering tools, resources, and guidance for continuous learning so you can confidently expand your use of Copilot in Azure well beyond the basics.

This part of the book includes the following chapters:

- *Chapter 10, Integrating AI-Driven Insights for Cost Management*
- *Chapter 11, Implementing Security Measures with Microsoft Copilot in Azure*
- *Chapter 12, Putting It All Together*

10

Integrating AI-Driven Insights for Cost-Management

As organizations expand their infrastructure, they face challenges, including escalating cloud expenses, complex pricing structures, and managing resources efficiently while maintaining optimal performance and security standards. Microsoft Copilot in Azure provides an AI-driven solution to address these issues by offering users actionable insights and recommendations, suggesting how to implement intelligent automation designed for cost optimization.

This chapter introduces you to the capabilities of Microsoft Copilot in Azure for cost management, providing a blend of theoretical knowledge and hands-on examples to bring these concepts to life. By leveraging **Artificial Intelligence (AI)**-driven insights, Copilot enables organizations to gain deep visibility into their Azure environment's costs, interpret cost and performance metrics, and identify opportunities for operational savings.

By the end of this chapter, you will have a solid foundation in utilizing Microsoft Copilot's AI capabilities to support effective cost management. The practical, example-driven approach will enable you to apply what you learn immediately, making informed decisions that can lead to substantial cost savings and a more efficient cloud environment.

In this chapter, you will cover the following main topics:

- Leveraging metrics-based insights
- Examples of using AI-driven recommendations to optimize costs

Regarding the Microsoft **Well-Architected Framework (WAF)**, this chapter maps to the **Cost Optimization** pillar.

Now that you know what you'll be learning in this chapter, let's have a look at the technical requirements to get you started.

Technical requirements

It is recommended to have access to an active Azure subscription to follow the examples that will be provided in this chapter. It is also suggested that a user with Global Admin permission be utilized in the Azure subscription.

It is recommended to have first completed *Chapter 1, Understanding Microsoft Copilot in Azure*, to set a baseline knowledge of some concepts for working with Microsoft Copilot in Azure, as well as completing *Chapter 2, Getting Started with Microsoft Copilot in Azure*, and *Chapter 3, Managing Access to Microsoft Copilot in Azure*, so that you are aware of how to use the Azure portal to access Microsoft Copilot in Azure as well as understanding access management.

When prompting, the guidance is to be very specific with the phrases and words used to articulate the desired output. The more specific and concise you can be in the prompt, the better the results you will get in the response. As of the time of publishing, Copilot in Azure has a *500-character limit* per prompt; therefore, you need to be thoughtful about how you write your prompts to maximize value and achieve the desired output.

Ensure you have the appropriate *Azure role assignments* for any resources you are investigating, as Copilot can only operate within the scope of your existing permissions and cannot grant access to data or services you are not already authorized to use. Additionally, some services must be explicitly enabled to provide data or surface relevant insights to Copilot; for example, **Cost Management** must be enabled to access cost data. To use **Azure Monitor Investigator** by Copilot, this does not need to be *enabled manually*; it is built into Azure Monitor and becomes available automatically when your resources are sending telemetry data such as logs and metrics. However, Azure Monitor monitored resources must have diagnostic settings configured to send telemetry (such as logs and metrics) to a **Log Analytics workspace** in order for Investigator to surface relevant insights.

> You will still always need to manually review the code generated by AI and potentially modify the output to be able to complete the task or operation on the resource type. Outputs or code generated by AI may not be fully accurate or functional.

To start, let us look at how to deploy and manage infrastructure resources in Azure.

Leveraging metrics-based insights

This section looks into the strategic use of Copilot in Azure to manage and reduce Azure expenses, ensuring your cloud environment remains cost-efficient and effective.

Metrics-based insights are the cornerstone of effective cost management in Azure; simply put, the more you consume (*use*), the more you pay.

Microsoft Copilot in Azure lets you use **natural language prompting** to retrieve insights and actionable information from the built-in native Azure platform tools, providing insights capabilities that help you monitor and understand your resource usage patterns. With this data and insights, you can identify areas where costs can be optimized and resources can be utilized more efficiently.

In this section, the following aspects will be covered:

- Understanding usage patterns
- Anomalies and unexpected changes
- Analyzing cost trends
- Forecasting and budgeting
- Setting cost alerts

Understanding usage patterns

Effective management of cloud resources necessitates vigilant monitoring of resource utilization and comprehension of usage patterns. Microsoft Copilot in Azure facilitates this process by providing comprehensive insights into CPU, memory, storage consumption, and so on from the underlying Azure platform monitoring metrics data. These metrics enable users to monitor resource usage and identify areas of underutilization accurately.

Organizations can identify those operating below capacity by analyzing the utilization of virtual machines and app services. This allows teams to make informed decisions, such as changing the pricing tier, resizing, or deallocating these resources to optimize costs and efficiency. Reducing a virtual machine's size when it is not fully utilized can reduce expenses, often without affecting performance if the resource was already over-provisioned in capacity demand.

Copilot's ability to utilize continuous monitoring features supports resource management by providing real-time data. Regular assessment and adjustment of resource allocation help address issues such as over-provisioning or underutilization, which are common challenges in cloud management.

Copilot's ability to query real-time metrics enables organizations to refine their cloud strategies as usage patterns and business requirements change. This ongoing optimization helps maintain a flexible and efficient cloud infrastructure that can adapt to evolving demands.

Prompt examples

Here are some sample prompts you can use with Copilot to gather and analyze usage data for better resource management:

- Show me detailed metrics on CPU, memory, and storage consumption for my Azure VMs.
- Help me provide a daily report of resource usage metrics for my current Azure resources.
- Identify underutilized VMs and suggest optimizations based on current usage patterns.

> *Make sure to make the prompts discussed in this chapter your own by using actual values from your environment, or experiment and tailor these prompts in a way that meet your needs.*

By utilizing the insights provided by Copilot, organizations can improve their decision-making processes related to resource allocation and achieve more efficient operations. This method aims to reduce unnecessary expenses and optimize the performance and reliability of the cloud environment, thereby supporting the organization's overall strategic objectives.

Anomalies and unexpected changes

Encountering anomalies and unexpected cost changes can be a significant challenge in cloud environments. These fluctuations may arise from sudden increases in resource usage, changes in pricing models, or even configuration errors. Microsoft Copilot in Azure is an invaluable tool for identifying and addressing these anomalies, ensuring your cloud environment remains cost-efficient and effective.

One of the primary causes of cost anomalies is unexpected spikes in resource consumption. For instance, a surge in user traffic might require additional virtual machines to scale out to handle this demand, leading to higher costs. Additionally, changes in application behavior, such as the deployment of inefficient code, can cause increased compute usage. Configuration errors, such as forgetting to *deallocate* or not *scaling in* resources that are no longer needed, can also contribute to the continuance of these unexpected expenses even after the demand has ceased.

Copilot in Azure addresses these challenges by utilizing advanced monitoring capabilities native to the Azure platform.

Upon identifying an anomaly, conducting a thorough root cause analysis is crucial. Copilot facilitates this by offering detailed insights into the specific resources or services contributing to unexpected costs. For instance, if a particular virtual machine exhibits a sudden increase in CPU usage, Copilot can help trace this back to recent changes in the application running on that VM, determining whether new code, features, or updates are responsible. Furthermore, by reviewing logs and usage patterns, Copilot assists in identifying inefficient processes or misconfigurations.

Addressing anomalies requires a multifaceted approach. Immediate actions might include scaling down, scaling in, deallocating, pausing underutilized resources, optimizing code, and correcting misconfigurations. Copilot can also assist you in understanding how to automate some of these responses, dynamically managing resource allocation to prevent similar issues from recurring. Additionally, more granular cost alerts and thresholds can be set up with the assistance of Copilot to ensure that future anomalies are detected even earlier, minimizing their financial impact.

Organizations can leverage Copilot's AI-driven recommendations for cloud governance to manage costs proactively and prevent anomalies. Regular reviews and updates of resource usage policies, conducting cost-optimization audits, and ensuring all stakeholders are aware of best practices can significantly reduce the risk of unexpected expenses. Copilot's advanced insights further enhance this proactive stance by suggesting potential cost-saving measures and resource optimizations.

Prompt examples

Here are some example prompts you can use with Copilot to detect, analyze, and respond to cost anomalies in your Azure environment:

- Identify patterns in my monthly Azure spending and provide recommendations for optimization.
- How can I set up alerts for cost spikes in Azure?
- Suggest proactive strategies to optimize Azure resource allocation and prevent future unexpected cost anomalies.

Anomalies and unexpected changes in cloud costs are inevitable, but with Microsoft Copilot in Azure, they can be managed effectively. Through robust monitoring, detailed root cause analysis, and proactive cost management strategies, Copilot ensures a stable and predictable financial outlook for cloud operations. This comprehensive approach mitigates the impact of anomalies and optimizes overall cloud expenditure, aligning it with the organization's strategic goals.

Forecasting and budgeting

Forecasting and budgeting are essential for managing cloud costs. Using historical data and metrics from Microsoft Copilot in Azure makes it possible to predict future expenses and allocate budgets effectively. This ensures funds are available for periods of high demand while avoiding unnecessary expenditure during quieter times.

By leveraging historical data, Copilot analyzes past usage and spending trends to provide insights into cost evolution. Recognizing these trends helps plan for predictable spikes in costs. Accurate predictions are generated based on historical data, considering factors such as usage trends and expected growth, which allows for proactive budget planning.

Create flexible budgets informed by real-time data, allowing responsive financial planning. Adjust budgets as needed based on Copilot's predictions. Regularly monitor expenses with Copilot's real-time updates, making timely adjustments to budgets and resource allocations, preventing overspending.

Prompt examples

Here are some sample prompts you can use with Copilot to forecast expenses, plan budgets, and stay ahead of potential cost overruns:

- How can I forecast my Azure spending for the next quarter based on historical data?
- Help me create a budget plan for my Azure resources for the upcoming year using past spending trends.
- How do I set up an alert to warn me if my storage costs exceed $300 monthly?

By leveraging Microsoft Copilot in Azure's forecasting and budgeting capabilities, you achieve greater financial control and optimize cloud costs, ensuring a cost-effective and efficient Azure environment.

Setting cost alerts

Setting cost alerts is a useful practice for managing cloud expenses. With Microsoft Copilot in Azure, users can set alerts to notify them when spending exceeds predefined thresholds, offering a method for financial management. These alerts serve as an early warning system and help prevent unexpected expenses from impacting budgets.

By configuring these alerts, users receive immediate insights into their spending patterns. This real-time awareness enables immediate monitoring of the budget and spotting unusual cost increases. Prompt actions can be taken, such as reallocating resources, adjusting service levels, or investigating overspending causes.

Cost alerts also promote financial discipline within an organization. Timely notifications help ensure that spending remains within the allocated budget, avoiding end-of-month surprises that could impact financial planning and operations. This proactive expense management enhances informed budget adjustments and resource allocation decisions.

Additionally, cost alerts facilitate better forecasting and planning. Analyzing alerts over time can identify trends and patterns in spending. This historical data is invaluable for predicting future expenses and planning accordingly. For example, if certain periods consistently show higher costs, plans can be made in advance to allocate adequate budgets to cover these expenses without compromising other areas.

Prompt examples

Here are some example prompts you can give Copilot to help configure cost alerts and stay on top of your Azure spending:

- ```
  Help me set up cost alerts to notify me when my Azure spending exceeds 80%
  of my monthly budget.
  ```
- ```
  How do I set up an alert to notify me when my daily Azure spending exceeds
  $500?
  ```

This proactive approach helps prevent unexpected costs and fosters a culture of financial accountability and efficiency, ensuring that your cloud operations remain within budget and optimized for performance.

In this section, you learned that effective cost management in the cloud is essential for organizations to maintain financial health while leveraging the full potential of Azure. Microsoft Copilot in Azure is a powerful tool that aids in optimizing costs by providing metrics-based insights and AI-driven recommendations. In the next section, you will look at examples of optimizing costs through AI-driven recommendations.

Examples of using AI-driven recommendations to optimize costs

Effective cost management in Azure goes beyond monitoring metrics for resources consumed; it involves using insights for strategic adjustments. Microsoft Copilot in Azure provides AI-driven recommendations to help businesses optimize costs and use resources efficiently.

By adopting a proactive approach, Copilot adapts to evolving usage patterns and aids in preventing overspending. It analyzes resource utilization to identify potential waste or inefficiency areas and provides tailored suggestions to meet an organization's needs.

These AI recommendations make it easier to manage costs automatically. For instance, Copilot might recommend resizing virtual machines, adjusting storage tiers, or freeing up underused resources, all in real time. This level of insight helps companies avoid unnecessary expenses and get the most out of their cloud investments. With Copilot, businesses can see their spending patterns more clearly and get specific advice on where to save, leading to a leaner, more flexible cloud setup.

Following Copilot's recommendations can also simplify budgeting, help plan for busy periods, and fine-tune resource allocation. By leveraging AI-driven cost optimization, organizations can stay on budget without compromising performance, creating a foundation for efficiency and sustainable growth.

In this section, you will explore various prompts that can be used to harness these AI-driven recommendations, accompanied by explanations of what each prompt does.

The following recommendation areas will be covered:

- Resource optimization
- Storage management
- Eliminating idle resources
- Optimizing licensing costs
- Using reserved instances
- Cost management by tagging
- Scaling resources based on demand

In the following sections, you will look at each of these with practical examples of natural language prompts that can be used.

Resource optimization

Microsoft Copilot in Azure makes it easier to keep cloud costs under control by adjusting resources based on actual usage.

If Copilot detects that a VM is underutilized, it may suggest switching to a smaller, cheaper instance. For VMs idle during non-peak hours, Copilot could recommend temporary shutdowns to save costs. This ensures you only pay for what you need.

Copilot's utilization of real-time optimization assistance makes your cloud environment more cost-effective and efficient by aligning resources with actual usage. This reduces waste and enhances overall performance in your Azure setup.

Prompt examples

Here are some sample prompts you can use with Copilot to identify underutilized resources and get recommendations for optimizing their usage:

- Can you help me identify underutilized virtual machines and recommend actions to optimize their usage?
- Analyze my current VM utilization and recommend optimizations to reduce costs.
- Suggest optimization actions for VMs that are idle during off-peak hours.

Using Copilot's recommendations, you can significantly lower your cloud expenses while ensuring that your resources are aligned with actual demand, leading to a more streamlined and financially sustainable operation.

Storage management

Managing storage effectively is key to keeping cloud costs in check, especially with large datasets that can get expensive quickly. Azure provides different storage tiers for its Blob Storage service, such as Standard, Cool, and Archive—each suited to specific usage patterns and budget needs.

The Standard (Hot) tier suits frequently accessed data needing low latency, such as live apps and real-time processing. The Cool tier fits infrequently accessed data such as backups, accessed less than once a month. The Archive tier, best for rarely accessed archival data, offers the lowest storage costs but higher retrieval costs and longer access times.

Microsoft in Azure helps lower storage costs by analyzing how often your data is accessed. It can assist you in identifying data that isn't used frequently and suggests moving it to cheaper storage options. Copilot may suggest moving it to the Cool or Archive tiers in Azure Blob Storage if you have infrequently accessed data that must be kept for compliance or archival.

The Cool tier is great for rarely accessed data that must be readily available. In contrast, the Archive tier is ideal for data that's accessed even less frequently and can handle some delay in retrieval. By using these lower-cost storage tiers for inactive data, Copilot helps you save on storage costs without sacrificing accessibility when you need it.

Prompt examples

Here are some sample prompts you can give Copilot to help analyze storage usage and recommend cost-saving tier adjustments:

- Review my current storage costs and identify which blobs could be moved to the Cool or Archive tier to reduce expenses.
- Identify opportunities to move rarely accessed data to lower-cost storage tiers.
- Provide cost recommendations for optimizing my storage account configurations.

Copilot's recommendations help you manage storage costs while maintaining data availability. By placing data in cost-effective storage tiers, you can achieve savings. Additionally, Copilot provides ongoing monitoring and suggestions to ensure your storage strategy adjusts with usage patterns and business requirements.

Eliminating idle resources

Idle resources in a cloud environment represent an unnecessary expense that can significantly inflate your Azure bill. Virtual machines or other resources running without significant workloads consume costs and contribute to inefficiencies in your cloud infrastructure. Microsoft Copilot in Azure excels at identifying these idle resources and providing actionable recommendations to address them.

Copilot utilizes data and insights from the native Azure platform tooling that continuously monitors the usage patterns of all your resources. When it detects resources, such as VMs, that are not being actively used or are running below capacity for extended periods, it flags them as idle. This detection is crucial because idle resources often go unnoticed, leading to ongoing, unnecessary expenses.

Copilot identifies idle resources and suggests shutting them down or reassigning them. For instance, an idle virtual machine during off-peak hours can be powered down or used for batch processing.

Prompt examples

Here are some sample prompts you can use with Copilot to detect idle resources and get guidance on decommissioning or repurposing them:

- Identify idle resources in my Azure environment and recommend decommissioning actions.
- Identify VMs that have been idle for the past month and recommend actions.
- Analyze my resource utilization and suggest ways to eliminate idle resources.

By eliminating or repurposing idle resources, Azure costs can be reduced overall. This method allows for paying only for resources used in operations, improving both cost-efficiency and performance.

Optimizing licensing costs

Microsoft Copilot in Azure provides insights and recommendations to help ensure the use of cost-effective licensing options for workloads. Copilot analyzes current usage patterns and the specific licenses in place. It examines how these licenses are utilized and identifies opportunities for optimization. For example, if certain licenses are underused or more cost-effective licensing models are available, Copilot will highlight these options. Suppose SQL Server licenses are used on multiple virtual machines. In that case, Copilot might identify that switching to a different licensing model, such as per-core licensing or leveraging Azure Hybrid Benefit, could result in savings. Similarly, Copilot might suggest moving to a subscription-based licensing model that aligns with usage patterns for Windows Server.

Prompt examples

Here are some sample prompts you can use with Copilot to review and optimize licensing choices for potential cost savings:

- Review my current licensing for SQL Server and recommend cost-saving alternatives.
- Analyze my current Windows Server licenses and suggest cost-saving alternatives.
- Review my server licensing and tell me if alternative licensing models can reduce costs.

Managing licensing costs is an important part of controlling cloud expenses. Licensing for software and services, such as SQL Server or Windows Server, can represent a significant portion of overall cloud costs.

Using reserved instances

Using reserved instances can help manage long-term predictable and static cloud costs. Azure reserved instances enable you to reserve virtual machine space at a lower rate than on-demand pricing, resulting in savings for consistently *always-on* utilized resources. This strategy suits workloads with predictable and static usage patterns where specific VM sizes are committed over one or three years.

Microsoft Copilot in Azure plays a crucial role in this optimization process by analyzing your historical usage patterns and identifying which resources would benefit most from reserved instances. Copilot examines your past consumption data, workload trends, and application requirements to recommend the most suitable reserved instances that align with your usage.

Using these insights, you can save costs by reserving instances for consistently used resources. This locks in lower rates and ensures predictable, reduced expenses over a given time period. Strategic allocation makes your resource provisioning cost-efficient and suited to long-term needs.

Prompt examples

Here are some sample prompts you can give Copilot to identify opportunities for savings by using reserved instances:

- ```Analyze my virtual machine usage and recommend reserved instance purchases.```
- ```Recommend reserved instance purchases based on my past three months of VM usage.```
- ```Identify which VMs would benefit from reserved instances for long-term savings.```

You maintain a cost-efficient Azure environment by adopting reserved instances based on Copilot's data-driven recommendations. This approach supports the financial sustainability of your cloud operations, ensuring that you get the best value for your investment and that your infrastructure is well-prepared to meet future demands.

Cost management by tagging

Tagging helps manage costs in Azure by organizing and tracking expenses. Assign tags to resources based on criteria such as departments, projects, or environments to improve visibility and control over cloud spending.

Microsoft Copilot in Azure can analyze your tagging structure and recommend enhancing strategies. For instance, Copilot might suggest tags that help you categorize resources according to their business units or cost centers, making allocating and monitoring budgets easier. This improved categorization allows for detailed cost reports and insights, helping you identify areas where you can optimize spending.

Prompt examples

"Here are some sample prompts you can use with Copilot to improve and refine your Azure resource tagging strategy for better cost management:

- Suggest a tagging strategy to improve cost management across my Azure resources.
- Suggest a tagging strategy for tracking costs across different departments.
- Help me review my current resource tags and recommend improvements for better cost tracking.

Effective tagging allows tracking resource usage and costs, providing insights into spending patterns and enabling informed decisions about resource allocation. This detailed cost management ensures accountability for usage and expenses within each part of an organization, promoting efficient and transparent financial management in the cloud.

Scaling resources based on demand

Adjusting resources based on demand is essential for cost savings and efficiency in the cloud. Automatic scaling modifies resources dynamically, increasing capacity during high demand and decreasing it during low demand.

Microsoft Copilot in Azure assists in setting up and configuring auto-scaling policies tailored to specific requirements. By analyzing usage patterns and traffic trends in detail, Copilot determines the optimal application scaling configurations. It recommends establishing thresholds for scaling operations and promptly adding or removing resources to meet demand without incurring unnecessary expenses.

With the guidance of Copilot, configuring effective auto-scaling becomes a streamlined and efficient process, facilitating a balanced and cost-effective utilization of Azure resources.

Prompt examples

Here are some sample prompts you can use with Copilot to configure and fine-tune auto-scaling policies based on demand:

- `Help me set up auto-scaling policies for my web applications on virtual machines to handle varying traffic.`
- `Analyze my workload patterns and recommend auto-scaling configurations for optimal performance.`
- `Show me how to set up auto-scaling policies for my application servers based on user traffic patterns.`

By adopting these auto-scaling policies, organizations can sustain high-performance levels during peak usage periods while realizing cost savings during off-peak times. This strategy ensures that cloud infrastructure remains adaptable and responsive, aligning with business requirements in real time and reducing the need for continual manual adjustments.

Summary

This chapter examined how Microsoft Copilot in Azure can assist with cloud cost management by incorporating AI-driven insights.

By utilizing Copilot's features, organizations can obtain important visibility into their Azure environments, identify areas for cost optimization, and make informed, data-based decisions. The ability to analyze resource usage patterns, set cost alerts, and apply AI recommendations supports the efficient use of cloud resources, reducing unnecessary expenses and enhancing performance.

By applying the examples and strategies discussed in this chapter, you can better manage your organization's Azure costs. Whether it involves forecasting future expenses, adjusting resource allocation, or monitoring cost trends, Microsoft Copilot provides organizations with tools to oversee their cloud spending while maintaining a flexible, efficient infrastructure.

As cloud environments continue to develop, the insights and tools offered by Copilot will be valuable for businesses aiming to balance performance with cost-effectiveness, supporting operational success and long-term growth.

Unlock this book's exclusive benefits now

UNLOCK NOW

Scan this QR code or go to `https://packtpub.com/unlock`, then search for this book by name.

Note: Keep your purchase invoice ready before you start.

11

Implementing Security Measures with Microsoft Copilot in Azure

As cloud adoption grows, so does the responsibility to secure infrastructure, enforce compliance, and implement governance at scale. Regulatory requirements, from PCI DSS to ISO 27001, demand that organizations demonstrate not just configuration intent but ongoing operational control. Historically, this has required specialized expertise, fragmented tools, and manual oversight. **Copilot in Azure** changes that.

This chapter explores how Copilot in Azure enables you to move from reactive to *intent-driven*, *policy-backed* security, all initiated through *natural language* interactions. Through a series of real-world scenarios, you will see how Copilot in Azure helps you *create*, *apply*, and *enforce* security policies across cloud resources with strategic alignment.

In this chapter, you are going to cover the following main topics:

- Maintaining compliance with organizational and regulatory standards
- Implementing security policies using Copilot in Azure

Technical requirements

It is recommended that you have access to an active Azure subscription to follow the examples provided in this chapter. It is also suggested that a user with Global Admin permission be used in the Azure subscription.

Additionally, it is recommended that you complete *Chapter 1, Understanding Microsoft Copilot in Azure*, to set a baseline knowledge of some concepts for working with Microsoft Copilot in Azure, as well as *Chapter 2, Getting Started with Microsoft Copilot in Azure*, and *Chapter 3, Managing Access to Microsoft Copilot in Azure*, so that you are aware of how to use the Azure portal to access Microsoft Copilot in Azure, as well as understand access management.

When prompting, the guidance is to be very specific regarding the phrases and words used to articulate the desired output. The more specific and concise you can be in the prompt, the better results you will get in the response. At the time of writing, Copilot in Azure has a *500-character limit* per prompt; therefore, you need to be thoughtful about how you write your prompts to maximize value and achieve the desired output.

Ensure you have the appropriate *Azure role assignments* for any resources you are investigating; Copilot can only operate within the scope of your existing permissions and cannot grant access to data or services you are not already authorized to use or that are not already enabled/configured in the subscriptions. Note that some services must be explicitly enabled/configured to provide data or surface relevant insights to Copilot.

> You will still always need to manually review the code generated by AI and potentially modify the output to be able to complete the task or operation on the resource type.
>
> Outputs or code generated by AI may not be fully accurate or functional.

Maintaining compliance with organizational and regulatory standards

Organizations must often adhere to regulatory standards such as the **International Organization for Standardization (ISO) 27001**, the **Health Insurance Portability and Accountability Act (HIPAA)**, and the **General Data Protection Regulation (GDPR)**, among others, and ensure their environments remain aligned with legal and organizational guidelines. Before diving into how Copilot in Azure can assist with compliance, it's important to understand two key concepts: **security baselines** and **security score**.

Security baselines are predefined sets of security controls and configuration settings recommended by Microsoft or industry standards for securing Azure environments. These baselines help organizations standardize security settings across resources, making it easier to maintain compliance and reduce risk.

Security score, provided by solutions such as **Microsoft Defender for Cloud**, is a numerical representation of your current security posture. It assesses your environment against established baselines and best practices, offers a recommendations engine, and identifies areas for improvement while quantifying the security of your configuration.

Understanding these concepts provides the necessary context for how Copilot in Azure can help monitor, manage, and recommend changes to security configurations to ensure compliance with organizational and regulatory standards.

While Azure policies can help implement controls to align with a specific framework, it can sometimes become overwhelming to manage Azure *policies* and *initiatives* (a group of Azure policies) at scale. Copilot in Azure can provide intelligent insights into these frameworks and reduce the complexity associated with compliance management. The essence here is to leverage Copilot in Azure's capabilities for potential recommendations, such as verifying whether the current network security groups meet the HIPAA standards.

Bear in mind that Copilot in Azure can access **Resource Graph**. Based on the current context, it can respond with the relevant Azure resources associated with the query, guide you through reviews of security controls, and suggest corrections or enhancements.

In the next section, you will explore how Copilot in Azure can assist in configuring and managing Azure policies to align with compliance frameworks.

Policy recommendations

Security and compliance frameworks such as **PCI DSS, ISO 27001**, and **HIPAA** are not merely technical checklists; they are *strategic imperatives*. These standards influence how organizations manage risk, build customer trust, demonstrate accountability, and maintain audit readiness. For cloud-first enterprises, compliance is no longer a point-in-time event but a continuous process that requires robust governance and adaptability.

Traditionally, the challenge has been translating high-level regulatory mandates into enforceable technical controls. This process is often fragmented, requiring interpretation by compliance teams and manual implementation by engineering teams, a cycle that can introduce delay, inconsistency, and human error.

Azure Policy provides an effective means to establish and enforce rules across cloud environments. However, choosing and applying the right policies requires substantial expertise and effort.

This is where **Copilot in Azure** begins to shift the paradigm. Instead of relying solely on documentation or security experts to determine which policies to apply, teams can now ask Copilot in Azure directly.

Using *natural language*, Copilot can surface relevant, context-aware policy recommendations aligned with your regulatory goals, whether you're securing an app service, hardening a storage account, or preparing for a formal audit.

By embedding AI-assisted policy selection into workflows, organizations can close the gap between a compliance strategy and day-to-day implementation. Let's look at our first scenario.

Scenario

A SaaS provider processes sensitive customer payment data and must demonstrate compliance with PCI DSS. This includes proving that all customer-facing services, such as their Azure App Services, follow secure transport protocols, encrypt sensitive data at rest, and apply access restrictions aligned with least-privilege principles.

The cloud engineering team knows that Azure policies are the mechanism to enforce these controls at scale. However, manually authoring, assigning, and verifying these policies is complex, time-consuming, and prone to gaps. They need a way to understand what policies apply to which services and how best to implement them without having to manually trawl through documentation or internal compliance matrices.

Instead of starting from nothing, they decide to engage **Copilot in Azure** as a *strategic assistant* to help them align their current App Services with PCI DSS.

> Make sure to make the prompts discussed in this chapter your own by using actual values from your environment, or experiment and tailor these prompts in a way that meet your needs.

Prompt

```
Which Azure policies can I apply to this App Service to align with PCI DSS?
```

Outcome

Copilot in Azure interprets the intent behind the prompt and begins by assessing the context of the App Service, including its current configuration and compliance posture. It returns a set of *recommendations*; not just raw scripts or policy names, but descriptions that connect the policy's technical enforcement with its relevance to PCI DSS.

For instance, Copilot recommends the following:

- A policy that enforces **HTTPS-only traffic**, ensuring no unsecured data transmission occurs
- Another policy that mandates a **minimum TLS version of 1.2 or higher**, safeguarding data in transit
- A policy that requires **encryption at rest** for any connected storage accounts
- Additional rules that limit **administrative access** and enforce secure authentication mechanisms

Each of these recommendations is positioned not as a mandate but as an option, allowing the team to evaluate and tailor them based on their specific risk appetite, workload sensitivity, and organizational policies.

Rather than passively reviewing compliance documentation or reacting to audit findings, the team now has a *proactive starting point* for building a secure cloud foundation.

Moreover, this is not just a one-off insight. Copilot can re-run the same query periodically, supporting continuous improvement and adaptive compliance as infrastructure and threat landscapes evolve.

As the team begins implementing these policy recommendations, they discover one already in place: a policy enforcing that App Services use the latest TLS version. However, upon inspection, they see that this policy is *not being met by all services*, including the one named Springtoyeshop.

Once the team has identified that certain resources are not compliant with the assigned TLS enforcement policy, the next logical step is to determine how to correct these discrepancies. In Azure, this process is known as **remediation**, the act of applying changes to existing resources so that they conform to defined policy standards.

Rather than manually inspecting and adjusting each *non-compliant service*, the team turns to Copilot in Azure to explore how remediation can be automated. Their goal is to understand what options are available for initiating a remediation task and to identify the most efficient method based on their operational workflow.

Identifying the right policies is a crucial first step, but selecting them is only part of the equation. Even with strong policies in place, real-world environments can drift out of compliance due to legacy configurations, misaligned deployments, or operational oversights. This gap between policy assignment and actual enforcement surfaces the need for targeted remediation. In the next section, you'll explore how Copilot in Azure helps teams move beyond identification and into automated, intelligent correction of non-compliant resources, turning insights into secure, compliant infrastructure at scale.

Non-compliant resources remediation

Policy compliance is no longer just a checkbox; it is a continuous discipline woven into platform operations. Yet the gap between policy definition and practical enforcement often leads to inconsistent remediation, reliance on specialized security roles, and delayed resolution. The following scenario illustrates how Copilot in Azure enables a more strategic approach. By interpreting policy non-compliance in real time and recommending remediation paths aligned with team workflows, via the Azure portal, PowerShell, or the Azure CLI, Copilot in Azure operationalizes compliance. It not only surfaces what actions to take, but why they matter, tying them directly to regulatory controls such as PCI DSS. This transforms remediation from an ad hoc reaction to a scalable, traceable, and automated process, empowering platform teams to take ownership of security and accelerating the path to continuous compliance.

Scenario

After using Copilot in Azure to identify and apply a set of recommended policies aligned with PCI DSS, the cloud platform team performs a compliance scan to verify enforcement. The scan reveals that while policies are correctly assigned, several existing resources—specifically, a subset of Azure App Services—are not yet compliant. One of these is `Springtoyseshop`, an application handling customer payment data, that still allows legacy TLS versions below 1.2.

This non-compliance poses both a technical risk and a regulatory liability. It undermines secure data transmission, violates PCI DSS requirements, and would likely trigger findings in an audit. The team recognizes that remediation is needed, not just for visibility, but to maintain a defensible compliance posture.

Rather than triaging these findings manually or writing remediation scripts from scratch, the team consults Copilot in Azure. Their goal is to understand the best way to align the non-compliant App Services quickly, repeatably, and in a way that scales across the environment.

Prompt

```
How can I create a remediation task for this policy?
```

Outcome

Copilot responds with a multi-path response. It outlines several ways the team could create a remediation task, depending on their operational model, whether they're using the Azure portal for visibility, Azure PowerShell for scriptable remediation, or the Azure CLI for integration into automated pipelines.

In each case, Copilot explains not just *how to remediate* non-compliance, but *why remediation* is necessary, linking the policy to the PCI DSS control and emphasizing the risk associated with non-compliance. For instance, maintaining legacy TLS versions introduces exposure to known vulnerabilities, weakening the integrity of encrypted sessions.

The remediation steps include identifying non-compliant resources within the assigned policy scope, scheduling the remediation operation, and verifying that the required configuration, TLS 1.2 or above, is enforced post-update.

The team selects the Azure CLI approach and uses the suggested command to create a remediation task. Within minutes, Springtoysehop is updated to meet the TLS policy requirements.

Practical impact

This interaction highlights Copilot in Azure's role not just as a task assistant but as an *enabler of a secure operational culture*. For technical leaders, this represents a step-change in how compliance is approached. Rather than being a once-a-year audit fire drill, compliance becomes a *living process*, powered by AI and embedded in the natural workflows of engineering teams.

Strategically, Copilot in Azure reduces the reliance on security experts to manually interpret regulatory requirements and codify them into enforceable policies. Instead, those requirements are *translated*, *contextualized*, and *operationalized* through dialogue. This *democratizes* (makes available to all) security governance, allowing platform teams to share responsibility and accelerate adoption.

From a tooling perspective, integrating Azure Policy, Copilot in Azure's documentation plugin, and remediation tasks into a unified experience means teams spend less time switching tools and more time executing. And because all interactions are query-driven, Copilot in Azure supports a *learning loop*; users become more fluent in both security best practices and the tools available to enforce them.

For organizations operating in regulated environments, this unlocks faster time to compliance, fewer audit surprises, and increased trust from regulators, partners, and customers alike.

With non-compliant resources identified and remediated using Copilot's guidance, the team has closed immediate gaps, but true cloud security maturity demands more than reactive corrections. The next step is to prevent these issues from occurring in the first place. This is where Copilot in Azure shifts from a remediation assistant to a proactive governance partner. By helping teams implement and enforce security policies at the time of deployment, Copilot in Azure ensures compliance is not an afterthought, but a built-in guardrail.

In the following section, you'll explore how Copilot in Azure streamlines the creation and assignment of Azure security policies, enabling teams to embed security best practices directly into their deployment workflows.

Implementing security policies using Copilot in Azure

Before we dive deep into how we can implement security policies using Copilot in Azure, we need to understand **security policies**. Think of an *Azure security policy* as a rule or condition applied to your environment to ensure that resources and operations adhere to the security standard of your organization. Security policies are typically utilized in **Microsoft Defender for Cloud** to help you improve your cloud security posture.

Consider the scenario where you need to ensure that all your newly created Azure storage accounts enforce *SSL encryption*. Copilot in Azure can suggest the right Azure security policy that is best aligned with your goal.

To illustrate this, we shall examine how Copilot in Azure can facilitate the creation and enforcement of security policies. By implementing appropriate policies, we can ensure that our cloud resources adhere to security best practices and compliance standards.

Security policy creation

To implement security best practices, it is essential to configure policies that ensure compliance across our cloud resources. Copilot in Azure can assist in identifying and recommending appropriate security policies based on our specific requirements, thereby ensuring that critical configurations, such as encryption and access control, are enforced consistently.

As organizations mature in their use of the cloud, their security needs become more sophisticated. They move beyond reactive configuration fixes and begin building proactive guardrails that ensure future deployments comply with internal and regulatory standards by default.

For technology leaders, this shift represents a crucial step toward establishing a *secure-by-design culture*, where security is embedded into platform engineering, rather than bolted on after deployment. A key tool in this journey is **Azure Policy**, which allows organizations to define and enforce governance rules across their environment.

But writing Azure Policy definitions can be an intimidating task. These policies are typically authored in *JSON*, with specific syntax, references to resource providers, and logic statements that define what is allowed or denied.

For many teams, this complexity can become a bottleneck, slowing down policy adoption or introducing errors that weaken enforcement.

This is where **Copilot in Azure** becomes a force multiplier. Instead of expecting teams to master the intricacies of policy language, Copilot interprets intent expressed in natural language and translates it into enforceable governance rules.

Implementing security recommendations from Microsoft Defender for Cloud

Microsoft Defender for Cloud is a comprehensive security monitoring solution designed to assess, protect, and strengthen your Azure resources. It provides intelligent threat detection and surfaces actionable security recommendations when vulnerabilities or misconfigurations are found. A common scenario includes alerts for App Services or other resources using outdated TLS versions, which can expose sensitive data to attackers.

TLS is the encryption protocol that secures communications between users and applications. Versions below **TLS 1.2** are considered insecure due to known vulnerabilities and should no longer be used in modern cloud environments. Ensuring that TLS 1.2 or higher is enforced is the best practice for both compliance and real-world security.

This section demonstrates how Copilot in Azure can streamline the process of resolving security alerts raised by Defender for Cloud using natural language prompts that generate remediation scripts instantly.

Scenario

An Azure App Service has been flagged by Defender for Cloud for using an outdated version of TLS. To comply with organizational policies and resolve the security issue, the DevOps team needs to upgrade the TLS version to 1.2 without introducing delays or manual intervention.

Prompt

```
Provide a CLI script to update the TLS version of this App Service.
```

Outcome

Copilot returns a pre-configured Azure CLI command that updates the TLS setting of the App Service to version 1.2. The command can be executed immediately in the Azure Cloud Shell or integrated into a CI/CD pipeline.

Practical impact

This saves time and reduces the risk of human error by automating remediation. The Defender alert is resolved, the App Service is now compliant, and sensitive data is better protected.

While remediating a single service is valuable, preventing misconfigurations during deployment is even more effective. Let's look at how Copilot can help enforce these requirements proactively.

Ensuring secure App Service deployments

Azure Policy is a service in Azure that allows you to create, assign, and manage rules that enforce standards across your Azure environment. These policies help ensure resources are deployed in a compliant and secure manner. One such use case is enforcing TLS 1.2 or higher on all new App Services to prevent weak configurations from being introduced. This scenario demonstrates how Copilot can help generate and assign a policy using a simple natural language prompt.

Scenario

Your organization requires all web applications to use secure transport protocols. Instead of manually verifying each deployment, you want to automatically block any App Service that does not meet TLS 1.2 requirements using Azure Policy.

Prompt

```
Create a CLI script that creates a security policy that ensures that all App
Services use TLS version 1.2.
```

Outcome

Copilot in Azure generates both a policy definition and an assignment script using the Azure CLI. The policy includes rules that deny deployments that do not comply with TLS 1.2 standards.

Practical impact

This shifts security left by catching misconfigurations before they are deployed. It reduces risk, speeds up audits, and ensures consistent policy enforcement across teams.

Now that App Services are protected at deployment time, let's look at how to secure storage accounts, another critical area for encryption enforcement.

Ensuring secure storage account deployments

Azure storage accounts store a wide range of data, including blobs, files, queues, and tables. These data stores are often accessed by multiple apps, users, and services. Ensuring encrypted data transfer via TLS 1.2 is essential to prevent data breaches and unauthorized access. Copilot can assist in applying these configurations quickly across multiple resources.

Scenario

Security scans reveal that some storage accounts allow TLS 1.0 or 1.1, which are no longer compliant with industry standards. Your team wants to update all affected storage accounts to enforce TLS 1.2 for all client connections.

Prompt

```
Suggest a CLI script to enforce TLS 1.2 for all clients accessing the storage
account.
```

Outcome

Copilot generates a CLI script that sets the `--min-tls-version` flag to `TLS1_2`, ensuring that only secure connections are accepted by the storage account.

Practical impact

Configuration is applied quickly and consistently across your environment without scripting expertise. This improves security posture and ensures regulatory compliance.

Beyond individual services, many organizations aim to apply encryption requirements across all network communications to protect data in transit.

Ensuring secure data in transit

Data in transit refers to any data actively moving between locations, whether across the internet or through a private network. Securing this data using TLS is vital to prevent *interception* and *tampering*. Azure allows you to enforce this through centralized policy management. With Copilot in Azure, even broad security initiatives like this can be implemented with a simple, intuitive prompt.

Scenario

You want to ensure that all data transferred within your cloud environment is encrypted using TLS 1.2 or higher. This includes traffic between services, storage, and APIs.

Prompt

```
Suggest an Azure Policy initiative to enforce TLS 1.2 or higher across all supported
services, including Storage Accounts, App Services, and Key Vaults.
```

Outcome

Copilot recommends creating an Azure Policy initiative that enforces TLS 1.2 or higher on all supported resources, including storage accounts, App Services, and Key Vaults.

Practical impact

Encryption is enforced uniformly across services, strengthening data privacy and supporting industry compliance standards such as HIPAA, PCI DSS, and ISO 27001.

With these configurations in place, your Azure environment is not only compliant but also more resilient to common attack vectors involving unencrypted traffic.

Summary

In this chapter, you explored how Copilot in Azure supports a more intelligent and scalable approach to cloud security. Through a series of practical scenarios, you saw how Copilot helps teams align with compliance frameworks, remediate misconfigured resources, and create enforceable policies using natural language prompts.

You began by identifying and applying Azure policies aligned with standards such as PCI DSS, then looked at how Copilot simplifies the process of remediating non-compliant services. From there, you explored how teams can define custom policies to prevent misconfigurations before they occur, and how Copilot assists in securing data in transit across both App Services and storage accounts.

This chapter concluded with an example of integrating Microsoft Defender for Cloud with Copilot to act on security recommendations and enforce TLS standards proactively.

Overall, Copilot in Azure empowers teams to move from manual, reactive security practices to proactive, policy-driven operations, helping organizations build secure, compliant, and resilient cloud environments by default.

In the next chapter, you will be provided with a summary of everything you have learned throughout this book.

Unlock this book's exclusive benefits now

UNLOCK NOW

Scan this QR code or go to `https://packtpub.com/unlock`, then search for this book by name.

Note: Keep your purchase invoice ready before you start.

12

Putting It All Together

We have approached the end of this book, and it's time to bring together all the learnings we have shared and absorbed about Copilot in Azure. This chapter will serve as a summary of Copilot in Azure and ensure that you know where to find ongoing knowledge and resources. It is meant to encourage you to continue learning and experimenting with Copilot in Azure. We will also share additional reading materials, tools, and online resources to improve your learning experience.

We will begin by recapping the key learning outcomes, focusing on the essential skills and take-aways from previous chapters. Following this, we will discuss future developments and potential enhancements in Copilot technology, providing an overview of upcoming changes. Next, we will stress the importance of continuous learning and exploration, highlighting the benefits of staying engaged and experimenting with Copilot in Azure to fully utilize its capabilities. To support your understanding, we have included a comprehensive glossary of terms for quick reference to important concepts. Finally, we will provide a list of useful tools to improve your productivity with Copilot in Azure and suggest creative ways to apply its features.

Here's a list of what we will cover in this chapter:

- Recap of key learning outcomes
- Future developments and potential enhancements
- Continuous learning and exploration of Copilot in Azure capabilities
- Glossary of terms
- Useful tools and promptbook
- Additional resources

Let's first revisit the main concepts of Copilot in Azure to consolidate and reflect on the skills you have acquired in terms of Copilot in Azure.

Recap of key learning outcomes

We started our journey in this book by reviewing how Copilot in Azure represents a significant advantage in designing, operating, optimizing, and troubleshooting cloud environments.

By the end of *Chapter 1*, you understood the role of Microsoft Copilot in Azure and its impact on modern cloud operations. You learned about its architecture, integration with Azure services, and key features, gaining insights into how it leverages AI to simplify tasks, unlock insights, and enhance cloud capabilities. This knowledge empowers you to effectively utilize Copilot to simplify complex tasks and unlock valuable insights, enhancing your efficiency in managing cloud environments.

In *Chapter 2*, we guided you through the initial steps of using Copilot in Azure via the Azure portal, providing a robust foundation for future development. This chapter ensured that your environment is properly configured and highlighted fundamental use cases where Copilot can deliver immediate benefits. By covering key adoption considerations, you were well equipped to leverage Copilot's features from the outset.

In *Chapter 3*, we explored how to effectively manage access to Copilot in Azure using the admin center. This chapter empowered you to configure access according to your organization's unique needs. Whether you want to roll out Copilot for all users or limit it to specific groups using **role-based access control** (**RBAC**), you have been armed with the tools to strike the right balance between accessibility and security.

In *Chapter 4*, simplifying infrastructure deployment was covered. Infrastructure management can be complex, but with Copilot in Azure, deploying resources such as storage accounts and virtual machines becomes much simpler. By providing practical examples of prompts, this chapter equipped you to quickly deploy and manage key infrastructure components. You learned how to save time and reduce manual intervention by letting Copilot handle repetitive deployment tasks.

In *Chapter 5*, building on deployment, we demonstrated how Copilot in Azure can streamline ongoing infrastructure management. From managing Kubernetes clusters to deploying App Services, this chapter helped you streamline operations and improve productivity. With clear prompts and step-by-step guidance, you've seen how Copilot can take the complexity out of managing autoscalers, running commands, and even enabling application monitoring with tools such as Application Insights.

In *Chapter 6*, we then introduced boosting development efficiency with AI Shell integration, which takes your development process to the next level. By leveraging AI-driven code suggestions, this chapter empowered you to write infrastructure as code more efficiently using Bicep and the Azure CLI. Whether you're deploying resources or improving code quality, this chapter showed how Copilot in Azure can enhance your productivity and reduce the time spent on repetitive coding tasks.

In *Chapter 7*, we looked at enhancing data management. Data management is critical in any cloud environment, and this chapter highlighted how Copilot in Azure can simplify tasks such as automated backups, index optimization, and performance tuning. You've gained insights into how to manage Azure SQL databases more efficiently and ensure your data resources are optimized without the need for manual intervention.

In *Chapter 8*, we looked at proactive monitoring and diagnostics. Real-time monitoring and diagnostics are essential for maintaining a stable cloud environment. This chapter showed how Copilot in Azure can proactively monitor resources, detect anomalies, and provide AI-driven insights for troubleshooting and optimization. By utilizing these capabilities, you can ensure that your cloud infrastructure is always performing at its best, with minimal downtime.

Then, in *Chapter 9*, we discussed strategies for scaling and optimizing your cloud infrastructure to handle growing and fluctuating business demands. As your organization grows, scaling cloud resources becomes crucial. This chapter focused on how Copilot in Azure can help you scale your infrastructure to meet business demands. You learned about practical strategies for managing resource growth efficiently, ensuring that your cloud environment remains both cost-effective and capable of handling fluctuations in demand.

In *Chapter 10*, we focused on using Copilot in Azure to manage and optimize costs. Cost management is a significant concern for cloud users. In this chapter, we explored how to use Copilot in Azure to track, forecast, and optimize costs. By leveraging AI-driven insights, you can better understand your cost metrics, set alerts, and ensure your cloud environment is optimized to avoid unnecessary expenses. Practical tips such as right-sizing resources and eliminating idle instances help you achieve more cost-effective cloud operations.

Lastly, in *Chapter 11*, we reviewed how you can utilize Copilot in Azure to effectively work with Azure Policy, one of the core services that will help you meet compliance requirements and adhere to regulatory standards in your organization. You learned how to use AI-driven recommendations to create and manage security policies that improve your organization's security posture. From authoring custom policies to assigning them across subscriptions, this chapter provided the guidance you need to ensure your cloud environment remains secure and compliant with industry standards.

Building upon the foundational knowledge of using Copilot for Azure Policy covered in *Chapter 11*, we will now shift our thinking to what the future holds for Copilot in Azure. In the following section, you will explore the evolution of Copilot, providing you with insights to maximize the benefits of these innovations.

Future developments and potential enhancements

The future of Copilot in Azure presents numerous opportunities. As the Microsoft Copilot ecosystem continues to advance, it is essential to remain informed about forthcoming enhancements and developments to fully leverage its potential as a strategic asset within your organization. Preparing your cloud environment for these ongoing improvements will be crucial and beneficial.

Here are some key areas of future development and potential enhancements:

- **Multimodal**: Future versions of Azure Copilot will support multimodal capabilities, integrating text, images, video, and other data types in AI applications. These advancements will enable more comprehensive and versatile AI solutions, tailored to diverse organizational needs.

- **Custom copilots**: Developers will have the ability to create their custom copilots using managed or custom stacks, providing tailored experiences and functionalities.

- **Real-time intelligence**: Advancements in real-time intelligence will allow for more efficient AI applications by qualifying, analyzing, and organizing data at the point of ingestion.

- **Storage capabilities**: Enhanced storage capabilities will facilitate the analysis of storage services metadata and logs, thereby streamlining tasks such as developing cloud solutions and resolving performance issues.

- **Lifecycle management**: Enhanced lifecycle management capabilities will automate processes such as tiering and deleting blobs that have not been accessed or modified for an extended period, thereby optimizing storage costs.

Keeping up with the latest features and updates in Copilot in Azure helps ensure that you are utilizing its full potential.

To take advantage of future enhancements, it's important to stay informed about updates with Copilot. Here are some key ways to stay informed:

- **Microsoft announcements**: Follow the Azure blog and Azure Updates page, and attend events such as Microsoft Build and Ignite for official updates

- **Microsoft Learn and documentation**: Regularly check Microsoft Learn and Copilot documentation for new tutorials and feature guides

- **Community forums**: Engage with the Microsoft Tech Community, Stack Overflow, and GitHub to exchange insights and stay updated
- **Features previews**: Set up your Azure subscriptions to track the Azure previews and test upcoming features early (`https://learn.microsoft.com/en-us/azure/azure-resource-manager/management/preview-features`)

By leveraging these resources, you can keep up with future Copilot advancements and apply them effectively in your cloud environment. Staying informed allows for continued optimization of your cloud environment, improved efficiency, and maintaining competitiveness in a constantly changing digital landscape.

Building on these anticipated advancements, it's also important to consider broader trends that could shape the next generation of Copilot capabilities. Two emerging areas worth exploring are agentic AI solutions and multicloud integration.

Expanding horizons: Agentic solutions and multicloud integration

As Copilot in Azure continues to evolve, two key areas to watch are the emergence of agentic solutions and multicloud integration.

Agentic solutions refer to AI agents capable of independently taking action to accomplish complex tasks with minimal human input. In future iterations, Copilot may leverage these capabilities to proactively manage cloud infrastructure, resolve incidents, or even execute optimization tasks autonomously based on policy-driven goals.

Simultaneously, the growing importance of **multicloud strategies**, where organizations leverage services across public cloud providers such as **AWS**, **Google Cloud**, and **Azure**, highlights the need for Copilot to support cross-platform visibility and interoperability. Future enhancements may enable Copilot to offer recommendations, manage resources, or monitor compliance across multiple cloud environments, helping enterprises maintain control, reduce risk, and optimize performance holistically. Addressing both these dimensions will be critical for organizations seeking resilient, scalable, and intelligent cloud operations.

As these advancements in agentic intelligence and multicloud capabilities begin to take shape, staying ahead will require more than technical readiness—it will demand a mindset of ongoing curiosity and adaptability. To fully capitalize on the evolving capabilities of Copilot in Azure, it's essential to foster a culture of *continuous learning and exploration* within your organization, which we will look at in the next section.

Continuous learning and exploration of Copilot in Azure capabilities

The rapid evolution of AI technology means that tools such as Copilot in Azure will continue to improve, offering more capabilities to streamline cloud operations, enhance productivity, and optimize costs. To make the most of future Copilot advancements, adopt a mindset that embraces continuous learning and adaptation.

Here's how to stay ready for what's next:

- **Maintain curiosity**: Continuously examine new Copilot prompts, features, and integrations to determine how emerging capabilities can enhance your workflows.

- **Promote continuous learning**: Cultivate a knowledge-sharing environment within your team. Organize internal sessions to discuss new Copilot updates and best practices.

- **Explore new applications**: Utilize Copilot in various scenarios to identify distinctive methods it can use to streamline processes, minimize expenses, or enhance security.

- **Align Copilot with business goals**: Continuously reassess how Copilot's evolving features can support your organization's strategic objectives, such as automation, cost optimization, and compliance.

- **Be open to feedback**: Encourage team members to share feedback on their experiences with Copilot, fostering a collaborative environment that drives continuous improvement.

By adopting these strategies, you'll be well prepared to adapt to future Copilot enhancements and drive innovation in your Azure environment.

To support your continued learning journey, it's helpful to have quick access to the foundational terms and concepts covered throughout this book. The following glossary serves as a convenient reference to reinforce your understanding and help you navigate Copilot in Azure and related technologies with confidence.

Glossary of terms

This section offers concise definitions of important terms and concepts that appear throughout the content. Use it as a reference to enhance your knowledge of Azure tools, AI technologies, and cloud operations:

- **Artificial intelligence (AI)**: This refers to the development of computer systems capable of performing tasks that typically require human intelligence, such as learning, reasoning, problem-solving, perception, and language understanding. It encompasses machine learning, natural language processing, robotics, and more.

- **Application programming interface (API):** This is a set of rules and protocols that allow different software applications to communicate and interact with each other, enabling data exchange and functionality sharing.

- **AI Shell**: This is a **command-line interface (CLI)** tool by Microsoft that integrates AI-powered assistance directly into the shell environment. It enables users to interact with AI agents, such as Azure OpenAI, for command suggestions, task automation, and contextual support in PowerShell or other terminal applications, streamlining workflows and enhancing productivity.

- **Azure Resource Manager (ARM)**: This is Microsoft's deployment and management service for Azure, enabling users to organize, deploy, and control cloud resources through templates and consistent management tools.

- **Automation**: This refers to the use of tools and scripts to automatically manage, deploy, and optimize cloud-based resources and services, reducing manual effort and improving efficiency in cloud operations.

- **Azure**: This is Microsoft's cloud platform offering a wide range of services, including computing, storage, networking, AI, and analytics, enabling organizations to build, deploy, and manage applications globally.

- **Azure CLI**: This is a CLI tool that enables users to manage Azure resources and services through text commands, allowing for efficient automation and streamlined workflows across different platforms.

- **Azure Database**: This is a cloud-based service provided by Microsoft that offers fully managed relational and non-relational databases, enabling scalable, secure, and high-performance data storage and management.

- **Azure Kubernetes Service (AKS)**: This is a fully managed service by Microsoft Azure that simplifies the deployment, management, and scaling of containerized applications using Kubernetes.

- **Azure AI API**: This provides developers with programmatic access to Azure's AI services, including natural language processing, computer vision, speech recognition, and machine learning models. It enables integration of advanced AI capabilities into applications, automating tasks such as text analysis, image processing, and conversational AI.

- **Azure App Service**: This is a fully managed platform for building, deploying, and scaling web apps, APIs, and mobile backends, supporting multiple programming languages and frameworks.

- **Azure Monitor**: This is a cloud-based service that provides comprehensive monitoring and analytics for Azure resources, collecting and analyzing data to ensure performance, availability, and security.

- **Azure OpenAI**: This is a managed service that provides access to OpenAI's advanced AI models, including GPT and DALL·E, enabling businesses to integrate powerful natural language processing, image generation, and AI-driven solutions into their applications.

- **Azure Policy**: This is a governance service that helps organizations enforce compliance by creating, managing, and applying rules and standards across Azure resources to ensure they meet security, operational, and regulatory requirements.

- **Azure portal**: This is a web-based interface that allows users to manage and monitor Azure services, resources, and subscriptions through a graphical dashboard, enabling configuration, deployment, and real-time insights.

- **Azure Resource Graph**: This is a service that enables users to explore, query, and analyze Azure resources across subscriptions quickly and efficiently, providing insights for resource management and governance.

- **Azure Service Health**: This is a personalized dashboard that provides real-time information on the health of Azure services, including planned maintenance and service issues, helping users manage and mitigate potential impacts on their resources.

- **Azure Well-Architected Framework**: This refers to a set of best practices and guidelines designed to help organizations build secure, reliable, scalable, and cost-effective solutions in Azure. It focuses on five key pillars: cost optimization, operational excellence, performance efficiency, reliability, and security.

- **Cloud Shell**: This is a browser-based command-line tool in Azure that provides a ready-to-use environment with pre-installed tools to manage Azure resources, supporting both Bash and PowerShell.

- **Cloud operations**: This refers to the practices and processes used to manage, monitor, and optimize cloud-based infrastructure, applications, and services, ensuring availability, performance, security, and cost-efficiency.

- **Conditional Access**: This is a security feature in Microsoft Entra that enforces access controls based on conditions such as user identity, device state, location, and application, ensuring that only trusted users and devices can access resources.

- **Copilot**: This is an AI-powered assistant integrated into Microsoft products, such as Azure, Microsoft 365, GitHub, and more, that helps users automate tasks, generate code, draft content, and improve productivity by providing context-aware suggestions.

- **Cost management:** This is an Azure service that helps users monitor, analyze, and optimize cloud spending by providing tools for budgeting, cost forecasting, and identifying opportunities to reduce expenses across Azure resources.

- **Data management:** This is the process of collecting, storing, organizing, and maintaining data securely and efficiently across cloud resources, ensuring accessibility, reliability, and compliance for both structured and unstructured data.

- **Entra ID:** Entra ID (formerly Azure Active Directory) is Microsoft's cloud-based identity and access management service that provides secure sign-in, user authentication, and role-based access control for applications, services, and resources.

- **Generative Pre-trained Transformer (GPT):** This is a type of AI model developed by OpenAI that processes and generates human-like text based on input. It uses deep learning techniques to understand language patterns, enabling tasks such as content creation, language translation, summarization, and conversational interactions.

- **Infrastructure:** This refers to the core cloud services and resources provided by Microsoft Azure to build, deploy, and manage IT environments. It includes virtual machines, networking, storage, databases, identity services, and security tools, enabling organizations to run scalable, secure, and highly available applications in the cloud.

- **Insights:** These are the tools and services that provide real-time monitoring, analytics, and actionable insights into the performance, health, and usage of applications and resources. Examples include Application Insights, Container Insights, and VM Insights, helping optimize performance and ensure operational excellence.

- **Interface:** This is a point of interaction between different systems, devices, or software components, enabling communication and data exchange. In Azure, interfaces can include APIs, portals, or command-line tools used to manage and interact with cloud resources.

- **Kubernetes:** This is an open source container orchestration platform that automates the deployment, scaling, and management of containerized applications across clusters of servers, ensuring high availability, scalability, and efficient resource utilization.

- **Kusto Query Language (KQL):** This is a powerful query language used in Azure services such as Azure Monitor, Log Analytics, and Azure Data Explorer to retrieve and analyze large volumes of structured, semi-structured, and unstructured data efficiently.

- **Large language model (LLM):** This is an advanced AI model trained on massive datasets to understand and generate human-like text. It powers tasks such as natural language processing, content creation, translation, summarization, and conversational AI, with examples such as OpenAI's GPT.

- **Natural language:** This refers to human languages, such as English or Spanish, used in everyday communication. In technology, **natural language processing (NLP)** enables computers to understand, interpret, and generate natural language, facilitating tasks such as text analysis, language translation, and conversational AI.

- **Orchestration:** This refers to the automated coordination and management of cloud services, resources, and workflows across different environments. It ensures that tasks such as provisioning, scaling, configuration, and application deployment are executed efficiently and consistently.

- **Plugins:** These are add-ons or extensions that enhance the functionality of software, applications, or platforms by integrating additional features or services. In Azure and AI tools, plugins can connect to third-party APIs or services, enabling tasks such as data retrieval, automation, or custom integrations.

- **Prompt:** This refers to the input provided to an AI model, typically in the form of text or instructions, that guides the model to generate a desired response or output. In AI systems, crafting effective prompts is essential for achieving accurate and relevant results.

- **Retrieval-augmented generation (RAG):** This is an AI framework that combines the retrieval of relevant information from external data sources with the generation of human-like responses by a language model. This approach improves accuracy and relevance by allowing the AI to reference up-to-date and domain-specific information during response generation.

- **Role-Based Access Control (RBAC):** This is a security mechanism that restricts access to resources based on a user's role within an organization. In Azure, RBAC allows administrators to manage permissions by assigning predefined or custom roles to users, groups, or applications, ensuring that users only have access to the resources they need.

- **Scaling:** This refers to the process of adjusting the capacity of cloud resources to meet changing demands. It can be vertical scaling (increasing resource capacity of a single instance) or horizontal scaling (adding or removing instances). In Azure, scaling ensures applications remain available and performant under varying workloads.

- **Security policies:** These are rules and configurations applied to protect cloud resources and data from unauthorized access and threats. In Azure, services such as Azure Policy and Microsoft Defender for Cloud enforce security policies to ensure compliance with best practices, regulatory requirements, and organizational security standards.

- **Token:** This refers to a unit of text (words, characters, or parts of words) that an AI model processes to understand and generate responses. In services such as Azure OpenAI, tokens are used to measure input and output usage, where 1,000 tokens roughly equal 750 words. The number of tokens impacts the performance, cost, and length of AI responses.

This glossary provides definitions of key terms and concepts related to Azure and Copilot. Familiarity with these terms is important for building a solid foundation in cloud operations and AI-driven solutions within Azure.

The next section will introduce useful tools and resources that can further support your Azure projects, offering practical guidance to enhance your efficiency and productivity.

Useful tools and promptbooks

This section will identify essential tools to assist with your projects:

- **Azure portal:** The Azure portal serves as the principal interface for engaging with Copilot in Azure. It grants access to essential services and enables users to issue prompts directly via the portal for infrastructure management and deployment. This tool facilitates the deployment, configuration, and management of resources by utilizing natural language prompts, while also providing real-time recommendations to enhance the efficiency of your infrastructure and applications.

- **Azure CLI:** The Azure CLI can be integrated with Copilot to facilitate the execution of commands and scripts, enhancing cloud management efficiency. Copilot generates accurate CLI commands based on natural language prompts, minimizing the need for manual scripting. This integration aids in automating tasks such as resource deployment, scaling infrastructure, and troubleshooting issues, helping users save time and reduce errors in their cloud operations.

- **Bicep language:** Bicep is a DSL designed for writing IaC in Azure. It offers a concise and user-friendly approach to managing cloud resources. Copilot enhances this experience by assisting in the generation of Bicep templates. Copilot aids in the creation of clean, reusable Bicep templates tailored to your resource deployment needs, thereby eliminating the complexity associated with manual coding. By leveraging Copilot's suggestions, you can streamline the process of managing IaC, reducing the time and effort required to maintain consistent and reliable cloud environments.

- **KQL**: KQL is a robust query language designed for extracting and analyzing data from various Azure services, including Azure Monitor, Log Analytics, Application Insights, and Azure Data Explorer. With the integration of Azure Copilot, users can enhance their experience by receiving assistance in writing, refining, and executing intricate queries through natural language prompts. This feature makes it easier for individuals with limited expertise in query languages to gain meaningful data insights.

Having looked at some useful tools to work with in your projects, now, let's turn our attention to promptbooks to increase your productivity and efficiency when working with Copilot within your Azure environments.

A **promptbook** is a collection of sample prompts and instructions intended to assist users in interacting with AI tools such as Azure Copilot. These prompts are organized to accomplish specific tasks, streamline processes, and enhance the efficiency of users who may not have extensive technical expertise.

Promptbooks serve as comprehensive guides or reference manuals designed to assist users interacting with Copilot, ensuring the delivery of accurate and actionable results. They offer pre-built queries, task commands, and suggestions intended to help users fully leverage Copilot's capabilities in cloud management, deployment, optimization, and troubleshooting.

Promptbooks serve as valuable productivity tools for both technical and non-technical users. By providing a comprehensive guide on interacting with Copilot, they enable users to efficiently utilize AI for managing Azure services, streamline cloud operations, and address complex challenges with minimal manual intervention.

Promptbooks simplify working with Copilot by providing ready-to-use prompts for common Azure tasks, such as the following:

- Deploying virtual machines or other resources
- Configuring security policies
- Managing costs and monitoring performance
- Automating infrastructure as code
- Troubleshooting cloud environments

For example, instead of figuring out the exact language to deploy a virtual machine, a user could refer to a promptbook and use a pre-built prompt such as the following:

- `Create a Linux virtual machine with 4 vCPUs and 16GB of RAM in the East US region.`
- `Help me create a high-availability virtual machine.`
- `Does this storage account follow security best practices?`

This allows users to interact with Copilot more confidently and efficiently without needing deep technical expertise.

Microsoft promptbook example prompts can be found at: `https://learn.microsoft.com/en-us/azure/copilot/example-prompts`.

A guide to write effective prompts can be found at: `https://learn.microsoft.com/en-us/azure/copilot/write-effective-prompts`.

The following are the benefits of using these pre-curated prompt examples:

- **Minimizes the learning curve**: Offers precise examples for users who are not acquainted with natural language commands in Copilot
- **Improves efficiency**: Allows users to complete tasks more quickly with pre-built, tested prompts
- **Enhances accuracy**: Minimizes errors by assisting users in formulating precise and effective prompts
- **Improves efficiency**: Enables users to concentrate on decision-making instead of dealing with technical specifics

Hopefully, with this comprehensive learning experience, you will better understand the wide range of use cases of Copilot in Azure and how to efficiently leverage this solution in your daily activities with Azure.

In this final section, we will share a few additional resources to help you with the next steps in your learning journey about Copilot in Azure.

Additional resources

The following list includes valuable resources you can reference for your journey of learning more about Copilot in Azure:

- Microsoft Copilot in Azure overview: `https://azure.microsoft.com/en-us/products/copilot`

- Microsoft Copilot in Azure | Microsoft Learn: `https://learn.microsoft.com/en-us/azure/copilot/`

- Responsible AI FAQ for Microsoft Copilot in Azure | Microsoft Learn: `https://learn.microsoft.com/en-us/azure/copilot/responsible-ai-faq`

- GitHub Copilot for Azure: `https://github.com/microsoft/GitHub-Copilot-for-Azure`

By following the strategies outlined in this chapter, you'll be well prepared to make the most of future developments in Copilot in Azure and stay ahead of the curve as AI-driven cloud management becomes increasingly essential.

‹packt›

Subscribe to our online digital library for full access to over 7,000 books and videos, as well as industry leading tools to help you plan your personal development and advance your career. For more information, please visit our website.

Why subscribe?

- Spend less time learning and more time coding with practical eBooks and Videos from over 4,000 industry professionals
- Improve your learning with Skill Plans built especially for you
- Get a free eBook or video every month
- Fully searchable for easy access to vital information
- Copy and paste, print, and bookmark content

At www.packtpub.com, you can also read a collection of free technical articles, sign up for a range of free newsletters, and receive exclusive discounts and offers on Packt books and eBooks.

Other Books You May Enjoy

If you enjoyed this book, you may be interested in these other books by Packt:

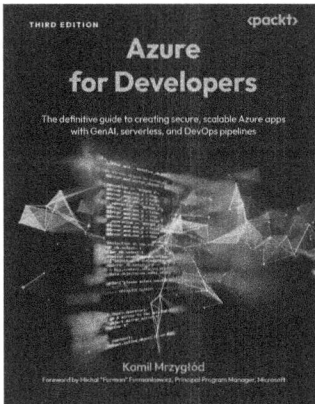

Azure for Developers - Third Edition

Kamil Mrzygłód

ISBN: 978-1-83620-351-3

- Integrate data solutions like Azure Storage and managed SQL databases into your applications
- Embed monitoring into your application using Application Insights SDK
- Develop serverless solutions with Azure Functions and Durable Functions
- Automate CI/CD workflows with GitHub Actions and Azure integration
- Build and manage containers using Azure Container Apps, Azure Container Registry (ACR), and App Service
- Design powerful workflows with both low-code and full-code approaches
- Enhance applications with AI and machine learning components

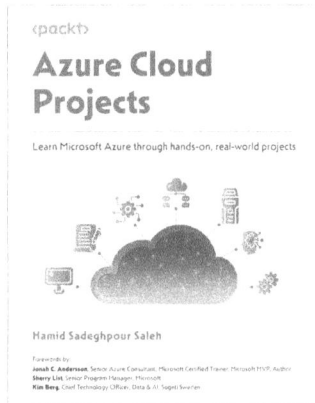

Azure Cloud Projects

Hamid Sadeghpour Saleh

ISBN: 978-1-83620-423-7

- Set up Azure and explore cloud fundamentals
- Implement Entra ID and hybrid identity solutions
- Build and secure storage with Azure Blob Storage
- Design virtual networks and configure VPN gateways
- Deploy your first web app using Azure App Service
- Automate workflows with Azure Functions
- Create CI/CD pipelines with Azure DevOps

Packt is searching for authors like you

If you're interested in becoming an author for Packt, please visit authors.packt.com and apply today. We have worked with thousands of developers and tech professionals, just like you, to help them share their insight with the global tech community. You can make a general application, apply for a specific hot topic that we are recruiting an author for, or submit your own idea.

Share your thoughts

Now you've finished *Microsoft Copilot in Azure*, we'd love to hear your thoughts! Scan the QR code below to go straight to the Amazon review page for this book and share your feedback or leave a review on the site that you purchased it from.

https://packt.link/r/1836200250

Your review is important to us and the tech community and will help us make sure we're delivering excellent quality content.

Index

www.ingramcontent.com/pod-product-compliance
Lightning Source LLC
Chambersburg PA
CBHW081100220326
41598CB00038B/7163